A Right
Royal Scandal

A Right Royal Scandal

Two Marriages That Changed History

Joanne Major

&

Sarah Murden

PEN & SWORD
HISTORY

First published in Great Britain in 2016 by
PEN & SWORD HISTORY
an imprint of
Pen & Sword Books Ltd
47 Church Street
Barnsley
South Yorkshire
S70 2AS

ISBN 978-1-47386-342-2

Typeset by Concept, Huddersfield HD4 5JL.
Printed and bound in England by CPI Group (UK) Ltd, Croydon CR0 4YY.

Pen & Sword Books Ltd incorporates the imprints of Pen & Sword Archaeology, Atlas,
Aviation, Battleground, Discovery, Family History, History, Maritime, Military, Naval,
Politics, Railways, Select, Social History, Transport, True Crime, and Claymore Press,
Frontline Books, Leo Cooper, Praetorian Press, Remember When, Seaforth Publishing
and Wharncliffe.

For a complete list of Pen & Sword titles please contact
PEN & SWORD BOOKS LIMITED
47 Church Street, Barnsley, South Yorkshire, S70 2AS, England
E-mail: enquiries@pen-and-sword.co.uk
Website: www.pen-and-sword.co.uk

Dedication

To Emma

Contents

List of Plates

Portrait of Princess Charlotte of Wales and Saxe-Coburg, *c.*1817, by George Daw.
(Gift of the New Zealand Academy of Fine Arts, 1936, Te Papa (1936-0012-92))

Prince Leopold, Queen Victoria's uncle, husband of Princess Charlotte, after Sir George Hayter, 1816.
(Yale Center for British Art, gift of Mr and Mrs Leon Korn)

Coronation procession of His Majesty King George IV, 19th July, 1821, by William Heath.
(Library of Congress)

Lord Charles Bentinck in his coronation dress as Treasurer of the Royal Household, depicted in The Coronation of His Most Sacred Majesty King George the Fourth solemnized in the Collegiate Church, the Treasurer of his Majesty's Household.
(SPL Rare Books)

Apsley House, Hyde Park Corner: the Residence of his Grace the Duke of Wellington, from Metropolitan Improvements … From original drawings by T.H. Shepherd, etc., 1830.

Bow Street Magistrates' Court, London by Thomas Rowlandson.
(The Microcosm of London, 1808–1810)

Belgian insurgents at the Parc de Bruxelles, portrait by Jean-Louis Van Hemelryck, 1830–31.
(Rijksmuseum)

Hôtel Bellevue on the Place Royale, Brussels after the battle in 1830, Jacques Sturm, 1830–31.
(Rijksmuseum)

An Extensive View of the Oxford Races, by Charles Turner, *c.*1820.
(Yale Center for British Art, Paul Mellon collection)

The Country Squire and the Gipsies, mezzotint by H. Quilley after C. Hancock, 1836.
(The Wellcome Library)

Panoramic view of Front Quadrangle, Merton College, Oxford University, with the main entrance to the college (left), the arcades of access to St Albans Quadrangle (centre) and the entrance to the College Hall (right).
(Photograph © Decan/Wikimedia Commons/CC BY-SA 3.0)

The coronation of Queen Victoria, engraving by Charles E. Wagstaff after Edmund Thomas Parris.
(Yale Center for British Art, Paul Mellon collection)

A View of St George's, Hanover Square in London.
(Rudolph Ackermann, Repository of Arts, Literature, Commerce, Manufactures, Fashions and Politics, November 1812)

Fashion plate from the Paris Élégant/Journal de Modes, object number RP-P-2009-1510.
(Rijksmuseum)

The marriage of Her Most Gracious Majesty Queen Victoria, engraving by Charles E. Wagstaff after Sir George Hayter, 1844.
(Yale Center for British Art, Paul Mellon collection)

Flitwick Manor, Bedfordshire, engraving from A Visitation of the Seats and Arms of the Noblemen and Gentlemen of Great Britain.
(John Bernard Burke Esq., Vol. I, 1852)

Charley's sister, Emily Bentinck.
(Sketch Book of Hyacinth Littleton, D1178/19/4, Staffordshire Record Office)

Hyacinthe, Lady Hatherton, when Mrs Littleton.
(Sketch Book of Hyacinth Littleton, D1178/19/4, Staffordshire Record Office)

Miniature of Reverend Henry Wellesley.
(Image reproduced by permission of Francis and Perry Farmar)

Foulislea, Ampthill, Bedfordshire.
(The Architectural Review, Vol. 1, July–December 1921)

The Duke of Wellington presenting a birthday casket to his godson Prince Arthur (later Duke of Connaught) in the presence of Queen Victoria and Prince Albert, by F.X. Winterhalter after Samuel Cousins, 1851.
(The Wellcome Library)

The christening of HRH Princess Elizabeth Alexandra Mary, 1926.
(George Grantham Bain collection, the Library of Congress via Flickr)

The Coronation of George VI and Queen Elizabeth.
(Authors' collection)

Acknowledgements

We would like to thank family and friends who have, once again, tolerated us spending hours in front of our computers and disappearing off to archives over the past few years, often to the exclusion of everything and everyone else; this book is the reason for it.

To the wonderful Cheryl Stonebridge who worked with us in the early stages of this research and went on countless 'gypsy hunting expeditions' with us. We always said someone should write a book about it – well here it is!

We would like to acknowledge our very great debt to the late Hugh Farmar. He was a descendant of the Wellesley family and had access to their letters when they were still held within the family and published his excellent book *A Regency Elopement* in 1969 (it is now sadly out of print). A very special thank you must go to his sons, Francis and Perry Farmar, for allowing us to quote freely from *A Regency Elopement* and to breathe new life into their father's research. Also for allowing us to use the miniature of the Reverend Henry Wellesley, reproduced in *A Regency Elopement* and owned by the Farmar family.

Many years ago now, we were in contact with the late Andrew Underwood, historian of Ampthill in Bedfordshire, who was kind enough to share his research into Sinetta Bentinck with us. We hope that he would be happy to finally see Sinnetta's story in print.

Also, our thanks to SPL Rare books who very kindly gave us permission to include the image of Lord Charles Bentinck in his coronation robes from *The Coronation of His Most Sacred Majesty King George the Fourth solemnized in the Collegiate Church*.

Once again, we extend our grateful thanks to our lovely and dedicated copy-editor Pamela and last, but not least, to the fantastic team at Pen & Sword Books for their continued patience with all our requests.

Joanne Major and Sarah Murden, 2016

Introduction

'Have you heard the story of the gypsy girl who married the queen's ancestor?' This was a question asked innocently enough almost a decade ago now, but one that started us on the path which ultimately led to this book. We are genealogists with a shared interest in English gypsy families and the story of Sinnetta Lambourne captivated us; we knew it had to be told.

In this book we document two marriages contracted by the well-connected Cavendish-Bentinck family, which were scandalous in their day, not in themselves but in society's attitude towards them, and they helped to shape the British royal family as we now know it. The Regency *haut ton* in London were shocked when the Duke of Wellington's niece eloped, just weeks after his victory at the Battle of Waterloo. The ensuing gossip and Criminal Conversation case set tongues wagging the length and breadth of the country and the subsequent hasty marriage did little more than gloss over the top of the scandal.

The second marriage was a true love match, only scandalous to the ducal Cavendish-Bentinck family because it broke society's rules and crossed class boundaries, the bride being the daughter of a Romany gypsy and a lowly Oxfordshire horse-dealer. It was a marriage that was kept secret for many years for fear of the family's and society's reactions to it, and one that ultimately led to heartbreak. We end the book by looking at the impact these two marriages had on the royal family as we know it today, completing the saga of this branch of the royal family tree.

Never ones to let a good tale escape us, our research led us a merry dance back in time to an earlier marriage and to an eighteenth-century courtesan named Grace Dalrymple Elliott; our biography of Grace was published early in 2016 as *An Infamous Mistress: The Life, Loves and Family of the Celebrated Grace Dalrymple Elliott.* This is a continuation of the former book and alongside the two couples involved in the 'scandalous marriages' we also continue the life of their relative, Grace's granddaughter Georgiana, but both books can be read independently of each other.

So many interesting people form part of the backdrop to this tale of the marital exploits of two successive generations of the Cavendish-Bentinck family. To set the scene we have ventured a little into the histories of the

Wellesley family and of the British royal family as both are relevant and run parallel with our tale. It would have been incredibly easy to write much more on the life of Richard Colley Wellesley, 1st Marquess, and his wife Hyacinthe Gabrielle for they are fascinating characters. We have been able to add to what was already known in respect of Wellesley's oft-reputed son Edward John Johnston and we hope this will prove worthwhile to those interested in the wider Wellesley family. However, the 1st Marquess and Marchioness Wellesley are but supporting actors to the main drama in our book and so we have reluctantly glossed over much of their lives; likewise with Arthur, Duke of Wellington and the royals of the period. Should the reader wish to delve deeper into their lives we recommend the books listed in our bibliography for further research.

For the benefit of our readers, we must mention the confusing variations in the Cavendish-Bentinck surname. While this is now the accepted version, earlier generations used it in their own preferred manner. Hence we have Lord Charles Bentinck and his son Charley Cavendish Bentinck. Both seemed to view Cavendish as a middle name rather than part of their surname. However, various children of both these men used Cavendish-Bentinck. We have chosen to use the hyphenated full version when referring to the ducal family, but within the pages of our book we allow each participant to be known by the name they used in life.

After her marriage to Lord Charles Bentinck, his second wife Anne had the courtesy title Lady Charles Bentinck. During her first marriage she was Lady Abdy. For ease we have, however, also referred to her as Lady Anne throughout.

We hope you enjoy reading.

Joanne Major and Sarah Murden, 2016

Prologue

Intrigue and Gossip in Regency London

On the streets of Regency London in the autumn of 1815 everyone was talking about Arthur Wellesley, the Duke of Wellington. He was the hero of the hour following his victory at the Battle of Waterloo, which was fought just weeks earlier. Wellington, still in France, had triumphantly commanded the British forces at the battle and he was fêted not only at home but across Europe with balls, ceremonies and celebrations in his honour. Monuments to the battle and to the fallen were planned and subscriptions raised to help the wounded soldiers and the widows and orphaned children belonging to those men who never returned home.

Against this backdrop Lady Anne Abdy, Wellington's beautiful but self-centred niece, was surreptitiously entertaining her lover behind the closed doors of her elegant London town house on Hill Street in Berkeley Square, totally unbeknown to her husband. It was a scandal waiting to break and one that would occupy the newspaper gossip columns and the *haut ton* for some months. Instead of praising the duke, shocked tongues now wagged at the behaviour of his wayward niece. It was an unfortunate fact that the elders of the Wellesley family were no strangers to gossip about their private lives. Some society hostesses even whispered that it was no wonder Lady Anne had behaved in such a scandalous manner.

Lady Anne Abdy, née Wellesley, was the daughter of Richard Colley Wellesley, 2nd Earl of Mornington and 1st Marquess Wellesley of Norragh (both Irish peerages), an imperious man who had been eclipsed by the military successes and acclaim of his younger brother Arthur, Duke of Wellington. Her mother was Hyacinthe Gabrielle Rolland, a beautiful Frenchwoman and former opera dancer with whom her father had fallen head over heels in love during a stay in Paris as a young man before cruelly separating from her and setting up home in Kent with a *seraglio* of nymphs and courtesans.[1] Anne had inherited her mother's flirtatious nature and French gaiety in full and with it her father's horrendous temper and imperious demeanour. On the face of it she had made a splendid marriage to the spectacularly rich Sir William Abdy, a marriage made with her parents' full approval and one that gave her wealth, status and a title, but Sir William was dull and dim-witted and she had, in fact, been given little choice in the matter. The couple were ill-suited for a life together.

The Abdys lived in a large and sumptuous red-brick mansion on the corner of Hill Street and Waverton Street, just a short stroll away from Park Lane and Hyde Park. Six windows wide and three storeys high, along with its next-door neighbour the Abdys' house was much larger than those facing it.[2] Lady Anne wanted for nothing materially but emotionally she was very much adrift. Behind the façade of her fine house and perfect life she was unfulfilled and seeking a distraction; her life was starting to unravel.

Her lover was Lord Charles Bentinck, a younger and somewhat impecunious son of the 3rd Duke of Portland and a 34-year-old widower with a 4-year-old daughter. Handsome and charming, he was a confidante of the Prince Regent, one of the close-knit set around the prince that included the fashion icon and dandy Beau Brummell. A retired army officer, Lord Charles had a talent for little more than impressing a ballroom full of ladies with his elegant manner and graceful dancing but, nevertheless, he infamously captivated the bored Lady Anne Abdy in a way her husband had failed to do.

On a Tuesday morning in early September while Sir William was away from home, Lord Charles and Lady Anne made the fateful decision to elope. Lady Abdy stepped through the doorway of her marital home as its mistress for the last time with nothing more than her pet dog and the clothes on her back and determinedly walked into a new beginning. Stepping into her lover's new carriage that awaited her a short distance away, she allowed him to whisk her away to a secret bolt-hole in Greenwich. Within days the newspapers, instead of reporting on the successes of the Duke of Wellington, were busily employed in salaciously imparting the news of his niece's indiscretion to their readers.

The cuckolded and enraged Sir William Abdy immediately threatened to launch a Criminal Conversation (Crim. Con.) charge upon his rival, seeking damages of £30,000 for the loss of the rights to his wife; a staggering amount of money at that time. The laws of the day regarded a married woman as the property of her husband; hence Abdy was free to sue for the damage to his 'goods'. A full divorce allowing both parties to remarry could only be obtained via a parliamentary bill, and the crueller option of a legal separation was a distinct possibility, debarring any prospect of a remarriage. If Lady Abdy was neither reconciled to her husband nor freed from her marriage to wed again she would be irredeemably ruined in the eyes of society, and if Lord Charles was ruined financially in the Crim. Con. case then he would be unable to keep his lady in the style to which she was accustomed.

The stage was set. Reputations and fortunes were at risk: the lives of all involved would never be the same again and a new chapter of history was about to be written, one that would indelibly leave its mark on the future generations of several families along the social scale, all the way from British royalty to Romany gypsy.

Chapter One

Lord Charles Bentinck and the Prince Regent

Lord Charles Bentinck was of illustrious parentage. Born in the autumn of 1780, he was the third son of William Henry Cavendish-Bentinck, 3rd Duke of Portland.[1] His mother was Lady Dorothy Cavendish, the only daughter of William, 4th Duke of Devonshire and both Charles' father and maternal grandfather served their country as prime minister representing the Whig Party. He was nephew by marriage to the infamous Georgiana, Duchess of Devonshire who had married his uncle, the 5th Duke of Devonshire, in 1774, six years before Lord Charles' birth.

All the sons of the Duke of Portland were given William as a first name, something of a tradition in the family, but only one son used it. Lord Charles' full name was therefore William Charles Augustus Cavendish-Bentinck but he preferred to simply use Bentinck as his surname rather than the double-barrelled alternative favoured by his wider family. His siblings were William Henry, the heir to the dukedom who later added his wife's surname of Scott into his own making his triple-barrelled; another William Henry (confusingly the two eldest brothers were given the same Christian names); Frederick, the youngest child (just a year separated him and his brother Charles); and two sisters, Lady Charlotte (who married Captain Charles Greville) and Lady Mary. The four boys all finished their education at Westminster public school with the younger ones then entering the army as junior officers. Charles enlisted with the Coldstream Guards as an ensign at the age of 16.

Although he served with the army for many years across several regiments, Lord Charles was much more at home in a ballroom than on a battlefield, particularly noted as a fine and graceful dance partner. Along with his younger brother Frederick, he was a regular visitor to the house of the notorious Regency courtesan Harriette Wilson (although Harriette much preferred the younger brother to the elder, describing Fred Bentinck as her 'constant and steady admirer'). Lady Anne's mother Hyacinthe Gabrielle, Marchioness Wellesley, was later to describe Charles as a 'wretched roué, a man of no principle', although he was an inconstant visitor to Harriette's side, unlike his brother.[2] In the mid-1820s when Harriette wrote her *Memoirs* she blackmailed the men destined to be named within the pages, offering them the chance to buy themselves out and, perchance, save their reputation. The Duke of Wellington, another of Harriette's admirers, reputedly and famously told her to 'publish and be damned!' and she even attempted to blackmail the Prince Regent.[3] Whether or not Lord Charles and Frederick Bentinck were two of those who received such letters is not known, and perhaps Harriette wisely knew that the perpetually financially embarrassed brothers did not have the means to buy themselves out even if they wished to. At any rate, they knew they would appear in its pages and were content to let things stay as they were, with Charles shrugging off the whole debacle by saying:

> We are in for it ... my brother Frederick and I are in the book, up to our necks; but we shall only make bad worse by contending against it; for it is not only true, every word of it, but is excellently written and very amusing.

Harriette recounted Lord Charles Bentinck's sexual relationship with a young woman named Ann Rawlinson, a prostitute who was introduced to her line of business by a Mrs Porter of Berkeley Street (a brothel-keeper who, according to Harriette, filled the 'high situation of prime procuress to his Grace of Wellington'). Ann Rawlinson had been seduced by a Colonel Eden and, after falling pregnant, had been left adrift in the world with a child to support. She was 'rather pretty, with a little *néz, retroussé* [she had a nose that turned up at the tip in an attractive manner], and black eyes', and lodged above an umbrella shop in Knightsbridge. Harriette heard of her and introduced her to Lord Charles who took Ann into his keeping; he was generous enough to fit up her rooms with new carpets and decorations and eventually fell in love with her. Little Ann, as Harriette called her, forgot about her poverty and, thanks to her lover's purse, began to paint her face with rouge and to dress in the latest fashions. Lord Charles' patronage of her continued until Lord Burghersh (General John Fane, the future 11th Earl of Westmorland) visited Ann to let her know that a friend of his, an Italian nobleman recently arrived in England, required a 'temporary mistress' for the duration of his visit. It was only for a few days and the position promised to pay well, so little Ann accepted. As it turned out, the Italian gentleman was unable to perform in the bedroom, blaming his deficiency on the weather and lamenting that 'dis contree is great deal mush too cold' but Ann kept the money he had given her anyway. After this, Lord Charles' ardour cooled too and he turned his attentions to a lady of higher status, with drastic consequences for all involved.[4]

One episode in Harriette's *Memoirs* that took place shortly after Charles had eloped with Lady Abdy depicted his brother Frederick at Harriette's London house. The hapless young man was admiring himself in a new pair of leather breeches in her looking-glass when the Regency fashion dandy Beau Brummell was announced. Harriette called him over:

'Lord Frederick wants your opinion on his new leather breeches.'

'Come here, Fred Bentinck!' said Brummell. 'But there is only one man on earth who can make leather breeches!'

'Mine were made by a man in the Haymarket,' Bentinck observed, looking down at them with much pride; for he very seldom sported anything new.

'My dear fellow, take them off directly!' said Brummell.

'I beg I may hear of no such thing,' said [Harriette], hastily – 'else, where would he go to, I wonder without his small-clothes?'

'You will drive me out of the house, Harriette,' said Fred Bentinck; and then put himself into attitudes, looking anxiously and very innocently, from George Brummell to his leather breeches, and from his leather breeches to the looking-glass.

'They only came home this morning,' proceeded Fred, 'and I thought they were rather neat.'

'Bad knees, my good fellow! bad knees!' said Brummell, shrugging up his shoulders.

Frederick Bentinck was a visitor to Brummell's London town house, 4 Chesterfield Street, where Brummell held court in the front dressing room to a throng of young men about town, all in attendance to devotedly watch the dandy as he dressed. Perhaps Lord Charles Bentinck attended too with his younger brother? Even the Prince Regent himself was then in thrall to the splendid Beau Brummell, although they would later famously fall out (when the prince publicly and humiliatingly ignored him, Brummell pointedly turned to his friend Lord Alvanley and loudly asked him, 'Alvanley, who's your fat friend?').

Charles Bentinck was one of the innermost circle surrounding the prince, the future King George IV, serving in the capacity of equerry to his royal friend (then the Prince of Wales), a role that had somewhat been placed in jeopardy when Charles married the beautiful, haughty and possibly blue-blooded Miss Georgiana Seymour in 1808, shortly before being shipped off to the battlefields of the Peninsular War in northern Spain with his regiment. His life, both public and private, was already intricately bound up with the

Prince of Wales and his marriage to Miss Seymour made him personally related to his royal employer.

For Georgiana Seymour had two men who stood as a father to her and even today it is unclear which man, if either, was her true parent. Her mother was the well-born but infamous eighteenth-century courtesan Grace Dalrymple Elliott, who had enjoyed the protection of a British earl, a French duke and the Prince of Wales himself. Born illegitimately, Georgiana's father was reputed to be the prince, for Grace and her royal lover had dallied together in a short-lived but well-documented romance for a few months in 1781 and Georgiana was born nine months later. Grace had gained her notoriety and reputation as a courtesan following her starring role in her own Crim. Con. case and divorce from her husband, the society doctor John Eliot. He was many years her senior and much shorter in stature than his tall and elegant young wife and had discovered Grace in a most compromising situation in a London bagnio (high-class brothel) with the reprobate but handsome Viscount Valentia. Following her divorce Grace had, for many years, been the mistress of George James, 4th Earl (and later 1st Marquess) of Cholmondeley and she had hoped he would make her his countess, but once she realized it was never going to happen she took herself off to Paris and into the arms of Louis Philippe Joseph, the Duke of Orléans.[5] She then left her French duke to return to England and the charms of an English prince, judging him to be the better catch and she was perhaps correct in that assumption as the child born of the union gave her a permanent hold on the man who would become king and gained her an annuity from the royal purse.

However, the fickle Prince of Wales had moved on and with France and Louis Philippe once again beckoning to her, Grace left the infant daughter born of her regal union in the care of Cholmondeley, ever her most trusted friend and the prince's loyal servant and boon companion. Whatever public opinion might have been about the playboy earl, at his core he was an honourable and kind gentleman and he established a nursery for his newly-acquired ward. Little Georgiana was well looked after; she became part of his family, to all intents and purposes his own daughter and brought up along-side the earl's hotchpotch progeny, both legitimate and otherwise. If the prince was not Georgiana's father, then Lord Cholmondeley stood next in line in popular opinion. The earl was too financially astute to wed a penniless divorcée like Grace, despite his love for her, and so he eventually married a suitable and wealthy heiress who proved to be a remarkably dependable woman, mother not only to their children together but also to the ones his nursery had come ready stocked with upon their marriage. In time the couple were elevated in the peerage to a marquessate in reward for their steadfast loyalty and service to the British crown.[6]

After Grace, the Prince of Wales became enamoured of a Catholic widow named Mrs Maria Fitzherbert but the lady proved to be not such an easy conquest as Grace. She withstood his charms until he made a morganatic marriage to her, one that was unsanctioned by his father, King George III, and therefore not legal. Having married Mrs Fitzherbert primarily to bed her, once the object was achieved he soon tired of her and set his sights on the plump and middle-aged Countess of Jersey. A grandmother over the age of 40, Lady Jersey nevertheless captivated him and she ruled the prince's heart for some time thereafter.

It was Lady Jersey's idea that he should marry (ignoring his marriage to Mrs Fitzherbert which was, in fact, not a legal marriage at all) as the prince needed a boost to his income and his father was pressing him to produce an heir. Lady Jersey wanted no rival though, and she selected a German princess who she was sure would be an anathema to the fastidious prince. Lady Anne Abdy's father Richard Colley Wellesley, Earl of Mornington, was privy to the gossip surrounding the rupture of the union between the prince and Mrs Fitzherbert as well as the imminent marriage. He wrote from Brighton to his friend Lord William Grenville:

> I heard last night from no less an authority than Tom the Third [Thomas Coke, MP and future Earl of Leicester] that the Treaty of Separation and Provision is on foot (if not already concluded) between His Royal Highness and the late Princess Fitz [Mrs Fitzherbert]. I think you ought to marry His Royal Highness to some *frau* immediately; I am told he is very well disposed to take such a wife, as it may be His Majesty's pleasure to provide for him.[7]

Caroline of Brunswick, Lady Jersey's choice, was pretty enough and high-spirited too but the prince found her repugnant, complaining of her size (although Caroline thought him overweight!), her pungent aroma and her dress sense.[8] Lady Jersey was appointed, at her own instigation, as Caroline's lady-in-waiting and made the poor princess's life a misery. Caroline was, however, adored by the British public, even more so when she quickly fell pregnant and just nine months after the marriage produced a fine and healthy daughter who was named Princess Charlotte Augusta of Wales. The prince claimed he had been intimate with his wife on only three occasions and quickly separated from her, cruelly trying to prevent Caroline from seeing much of her infant daughter. Ten years later, the 'Delicate Investigation' examined scurrilous claims made by Lady Douglas against Caroline. She was exonerated of the claims but despite the investigation being held in secret, gossip leaked out.

By 1814 Caroline had taken enough abuse from her husband and she left England to live in Italy. The Earl and Countess of Cholmondeley were on good terms with Caroline, Princess of Wales (Lady Cholmondeley was one of her ladies before she travelled abroad), and they therefore walked a delicate tightrope between the two warring royal spouses. The novelist Jane Austen voiced her opinion on the affair:

> I shall support her as long as I can, because she *is* a Woman, and because I hate her husband ... I am resolved at least to think that she would have been respectable, if the Prince had behaved tolerably to her at first.[9]

Despite her Machiavellian wiles, Lady Jersey's reign over the prince's heart and household came to an abrupt end when he moved on from her to another matronly grandmother, the Marchioness of Hertford. The British public began to make clear their feelings regarding the prince's profligacy and his attitude towards his wife, and he was publicly satirized and mocked, both for his appearance and his behaviour.

Georgiana Seymour, the prince's privately if not publicly acknowledged daughter, had been on good terms with Lady Jersey and great friends with her daughter-in-law, Sarah Sophia née Fane. During Lady Jersey's tenure as the prince's mistress this could only have been of benefit in terms of enhancing the prince's benevolence towards her but by the time of Georgiana's marriage to Lord Charles Bentinck, Lady Jersey's reign was over and no help could be expected from that quarter.[10]

Blessed with stunning looks to complement her illustrious if scandalous ancestry, the union between Charles and Georgiana had been a love match, albeit one that had not initially been sanctioned by either family (the prince appeared rather aghast at the marriage and the wedding venue was hastily changed from Cholmondeley Castle at Malpas in Chester to the county town of Chester instead, suggesting that the Cholmondeleys were not fully on board either). Charles might have had the right background and connections but he had little in the way of fortune, and the same could also be said of Miss Seymour.

Once the pair were married though, there was little the two families could do other than make the best of it. With a belated marriage settlement made a year later, and after being posted overseas during the Peninsular War and the Walcheren campaign, Charles Bentinck took the opportunity to abandon his military career.[11] He retired with the rank of lieutenant colonel in the Guards and made an attempt to establish himself in a political vein, albeit with little success. His only lifeline was his continued employment within the royal household and the remuneration that came with it, although his brother, on ascending to the dukedom on the death of their father in October 1809, settled a sum of money on his siblings.[12]

Lord and Lady Charles Bentinck were happy enough together, although the couple suffered tragedy when their firstborn child, a son, lived but a few hours. A daughter followed two years later, born in 1811 and given the feminine forms of the prince's names, Georgiana Augusta Frederica Henrietta (as her mother had been before her, just in case anyone was to doubt their shared ancestry). The prince had by this time become the Prince Regent, on account of his father King George III's madness. Then came the misfortune of Charles' wife's untimely death; it was believed she fell while heavily pregnant and both she and the child within her perished. Lord Charles Bentinck was left distraught. He had not only lost his beloved wife and unborn babe, he also feared he had lost the patronage both of his supposed father-in-law and of the Cholmondeleys who had acted as Georgiana's guardians.[13]

However, the prince stood firm to his young friend, the pair united in their grief at the loss of Georgiana, and he continued to have Lord Charles by his side. When the Tsar of Russia, the King of Prussia and other European sovereigns landed at Dover on 6 June 1814 to celebrate the Peace of Paris and the abdication of Napoléon Bonaparte (who had been exiled to Elba), Lord Charles Bentinck played a prominent role in the proceedings. He is featured in a portrait of the Allied Sovereigns painted to mark the occasion which now hangs at Petworth House in Sussex. In the painting the young Prince Augustus of Prussia appears to be turning his head to speak to Charles who was standing directly behind him.[14]

The ship carrying the sovereigns docked at Dover and the crowned heads of state were met by Lord Yarmouth, the Earl of Rosslyn and Lord Charles Bentinck who then escorted their guests, together with a detachment of the Scots Greys, to a nearby house marked for their reception while the guard of honour discharged their cannons. The Prince Regent's younger brother, Prince William, Duke of Clarence was also in attendance and gave a sumptuous banquet. The next day the retinue started for London and more celebrations. Charles played a role in co-ordinating the festivities, particularly looking after the Prussian delegation led by King Frederick William III for whom he was appointed the temporary chamberlain and he must have been flattered in no small degree to be included so prominently in the arrangements. A court was held at Carlton House where the guard of honour marched into the courtyard alongside the band of the Coldstream Guards, Lord Charles' old regiment. All the great and the good were there including

Lady Anne's father (now the Marquess Wellesley) and the Prussian king and his family were conducted to the regent's side by Lord Charles Bentinck. Frederick William III wore his military regimental uniform, his hair cropped and without powder and, as the band played *God save the King* he repeatedly bowed; later that afternoon he was created a Knight of the Garter.[15]

The festivities continued with banquets and state visits as well as jaunts to the racecourse at Ascot, the Prussian party all the while chaperoned by Lord Charles Bentinck, until finally the sovereigns arrived at Portsmouth ready to embark on board their ship to return to mainland Europe. They were saluted with artillery, the roads were lined with troops and throngs of people had gathered to watch the spectacle. The Prussians arrived at 7.30 in the evening with Lord Charles still dancing attendance and the following morning the Prince Regent accompanied Frederick William III in his carriage to the dock-yard (and was Lord Charles inside too, one wonders?). Meeting the Tsar of Russia, they then continued in a fleet of barges on which the various Royal and Imperial Standards were raised. Even then the festivities carried on for some days and the Duke of Wellington arrived at Portsmouth in a coach and four to the sound of a band playing *See the Conquering Hero Comes* and shouts of 'Long live Wellington!' The duke looked well, if a little thin and sunburnt following months of campaigning on the battlefields of Spain and France. As he left England, the King of Prussia presented Lord Charles with a boxed set of diamonds worth £500 in generous gratitude for his attendance as chamber-lain upon him. It is not known what became of these jewels but perhaps, in time, they were worn by the second Lady Charles Bentinck?

Lady Anne Abdy was said to resemble Lord Charles' first wife and it was perhaps this similarity in appearance that drew him, like a moth towards a flame, into the orbit of his new paramour. Although everybody had assumed the Abdys' nine-year marriage to be a happy one, there had been no children born of the union and Sir William Abdy, reputedly the richest commoner in England, was no match for the spirited Anne. It was rumoured that he was impotent and Anne could no longer stand being in his bed. With no children of her own, Anne was touched by the plight of the little motherless Georgiana and it did not take much for her to be prevailed upon to offer a sympathetic ear to the young girl's widowed father. Their friendship quickly grew into something much more intense.

Chapter Two

The Wellesleys and the
Duke of Wellington

In 1784 the widowed Countess of Mornington took two of her sons to Paris: Richard, aged 24 and, since the death of his father Garret, the Earl of Mornington in his own right; and Arthur, younger than Richard by around a decade. Richard Colley Wellesley – witty, clever and ambitious for a political career – was the hope of his Anglo-Irish family. Following his father's death in 1781 the family finances were discovered to be in a state of disarray and Richard aimed to restore them.[1]

Arthur was not particularly academic and had just been taken out of Eton so there would be enough money for his more promising younger brothers Gerald Valerian and Henry to be educated in his stead. It would be a further two years before his older brother Richard wrote to the Duke of Rutland, recommending his younger brother for an army commission and starting him on his path to glory.

Following a visit by the threesome to the Palace of Versailles, Lady Mornington (a difficult woman at the best of times) became aware that her two sons had a shared secret, one she was not privy to; they were whispering and laughing together behind her back. She took Arthur to one side and demanded to know the secret but the steadfast young lad calmly informed his mother that had it been his own secret, he would have told her but it was not and he would not betray his own brother by divulging it. The furious Lady Mornington tried to force the truth out of him, denying him a place in her carriage for the journey back to their Paris *hôtel particulier* if he did not tell her everything. Arthur, with a certain degree of sauciness, replied he had no doubt that he could walk the distance and so he did. Richard and his still infuriated mother reached Paris way ahead of Arthur, even though the carriage had been instructed to drive slowly. Arthur eventually turned up, whistling nonchalantly, but from that date 'it was understood he retained a painful sense of his mother's tyranny and injustice'. For Richard, it was an indication that he could absolutely rely on his younger brother's loyalty and discretion, qualities that would be tested in full during the coming years.

Indeed, the Wellesley brethren ever presented a united front to the world, each assisting the other to achieve ever higher successes whenever possible.[2]

Arthur knew exactly what his mother's reaction would have been had he told her his brother's secret, for it threatened to destroy all her hopes for Richard's future. During their time in Paris he had fallen head over heels in love with Mademoiselle Hyacinthe Gabrielle Rolland, a beautiful young Frenchwoman with a disputed parentage who was reputedly either an opera singer or dancer, put on the stage by her mother. By the end of the year Richard was still in Paris and so enamoured with his mistress that he rarely appeared in public, preferring instead to stay by her side behind closed doors. It is possible that Mademoiselle Rolland appeared in performances staged at the Palais Royal and she may have had some connection to Louis Philippe Joseph, the Duke of Orléans. A miniature of Hyacinthe Gabrielle at Stratfield Saye has an inscription on the reverse indicating that she was pictured 'in the garden of Madame de Genlis' and Stéphanie Félicité du Crest de Saint-Aubin, Comtesse de Genlis, was governess to the Duke of Orléans' children and possibly mistress to her pupils' father.[3]

It was while Hyacinthe Gabrielle Rolland trod the boards of the Parisian theatres that she was noticed by the young and instantly smitten Lord Mornington. Nominally she was the daughter of Hyacinthe Gabrielle Varin, a Parisian actress, and a banker named Pierre Rolland but her real father was probably Christopher Fagan, an Irish chevalier and adventurer employed by the French army who, because of his royalist sympathies, had left France for England during the revolutionary years. The Chevalier Fagan died in London in 1816.[4]

Eventually the Earl of Mornington brought his *Gallic Cyprian of the first order* back to London, refusing to listen to any objections from his mother against such a move:

> Among the beauties who frequent the Opera this season, who have appeared the most piercing in the eyes of the *connoisseurs en beau sexe*, is a young French Lady (Madame Rolland), newly arrived from Paris, in this metropolis, whose waist, figure, and modesty, have attracted the glances of the eyes of the spectators to such a degree that we are obliged to give applause to the good taste of the happy mortal, who is in possession of an object, in which so many charms are united. Now, young Vestris cannot say as his father, *le grand Vestris*, '*je suis toute d'admiration de public!*'[5]

Madame Rolland was installed in a house at the end of Dean (now Deanery) Street, a narrow and discreet thoroughfare between Park Lane and Hyde Park. Her house had, a decade earlier, been occupied by another woman of dubious reputation whose titled lover had sought to hide her away from polite view but at a good address, for Grace Dalrymple Elliott had been housed there by the Earl of Cholmondeley following her divorce from her squat little doctor of a husband. Lord Cholmondeley had, by the time Hyacinthe Gabrielle was ensconced in Dean Street, moved on from Mrs Elliott to another mistress and, like Lord Mornington, he had chosen a Frenchwoman. A beauty like Hyacinthe, Cholmondeley's mistress, Marie-Françoise Henriette Laché, otherwise known as Madame Saint-Albin, was counted as the prettiest woman to be found in England and both he and Lord Mornington frequently appeared with their two fascinating French *inamoratas* on their arms. Madame Rolland and Madame Saint-Albin were the same age and had both travelled from Paris to London at around the same time and so were frequently thrown into each other's company. Both also gave their titled lovers children, albeit ones born out of wedlock.

Lord Mornington and Hyacinthe Gabrielle had five children together: Richard, Anne, Hyacinthe Mary, Gerald and Henry (the latter nicknamed 'The Tiddler' by his parents), taking in a tour of the Continent between the births of the last two for the sake of Mornington's health and leaving the children behind.[6] While in Italy, Lord Mornington referred to his offspring in a letter to his friend, the politician William Wyndham Grenville:

> Whatever may have been the folly which produced these little children, I am sure you have too much real feeling not to agree with me that they are a charge as dear and as sacred as if they had been born under the most solemn engagement.[7]

Then, not long after Henry's birth and while the country was agog with the news of the impending marriage of the Prince of Wales to Caroline of Brunswick, Wellesley belatedly married his mistress, finally giving her a title and a position in society. His family was largely aghast at his actions (Richard's mother had never visited Hyacinthe Gabrielle and the fact that she was now his countess had done nothing to change her mind), although Richard's brothers, with the exception of William Wellesley-Pole, were on good enough terms with their new sister-in-law. The couple applied for a marriage licence on 20 November 1794 and married nine days later in a quiet wedding that passed largely unnoticed at St George's in Hanover Square.[8]

The sudden impetus behind the marriage may have been the turmoil in France and a desire to safeguard his French wife and their children. His brother and sister, Henry Wellesley (the future Baron Cowley) and Anne Fitzroy had been captured off the French coast by revolutionaries while sailing back from Lisbon where Anne Fitzroy had been widowed (she had married Henry FitzRoy, son of the 1st Baron Southampton, in 1790), and were being held prisoner. Hyacinthe Gabrielle was a strong-willed and astute woman, able to manage her titled lover, and it was probably at her instigation that the wedding took place; she had the stronger character of the two and held sway over Richard's heart, at least for the time being. Iris Butler, in *The Eldest Brother*, references an intriguing letter in the Carver papers from a lawyer (named St Maur) in Paris dated October 1795 relating to money invested in Hyacinthe Gabrielle's name. Richard had settled £4,719-12s-3d on her before their marriage which, from January 1796, became legally hers as if she was *Femme Sole* (a woman without a husband). The letter is torn, perhaps intentionally, but tantalizing references to '*le cher Oncle*' [dear uncle] and '*le Beaupère*' [stepfather] can be seen.

The witty, charming and clever Hyacinthe Gabrielle was devoted to her children and husband but her unwillingness or inability to learn to speak or read in English hindered her socially, even among those who were disposed to overlook her exotic ancestry and reputation (contemporary gossip called her a courtesan). Despite this, many of high rank were glad to admit Hyacinthe Gabrielle as an equal and friend; her young daughter Hyacinthe wrote to her father in 1802 to complain that Brighton was full but dull, with no one her mama knew as Mrs Fitzherbert was in town and so people of quality had stayed away.[9] She was naturally vivacious, once describing herself in a letter to her husband as having quicksilver in her veins and remained very attractive.

Richard's opinion of his wife may have altered after their marriage, as her home, hearth and family naturally became the focus of her life now she had gained the financial stability she had craved during the days when she had merely been an easily discarded mistress, and some of the excitement and intrigue left their relationship. These domestic responsibilities (coupled with an abject fear of the sea) were behind her decision not to accompany her husband when, in 1797, he was posted to India as governor general, choosing instead to remain behind with her children.[10] While Richard reluctantly understood her actions, he was desperate for her to be by his side, telling her from India almost two years after his departure 'I assure you that this climate excites one sexually most terribly' and suggesting they would both be prey to the attentions of the opposite sex. (Hyacinthe Gabrielle's pithy reply to her husband's suggestion that the 'candle would burn at both ends' if they remained separated was for him not to light it at all! 'You can perfectly well exist without sex,' she wrote.)[11] For all her refusal to travel by his side, she was bereft without him and had a medallion made containing a lock of her hair coupled with that of their five children woven together and sent it to Richard, pleading with him to wear it under his shirt.

However, Richard Colley Wellesley had already strayed from his wife's side before he left for India and had sired at least two other illegitimate sons by a young mistress (perhaps still in her teens) named Elizabeth Johnston. An Edward John Johnston, born around 1796 in Middlesex and who later acted as a private secretary to Wellesley, was one of these sons.[12] He was later at the head of a group of young men who preyed on Richard and were strongly disliked by the Duke of Wellington, who referred to them as 'the parasites' or 'the *banditti*'. Does the fact that Hyacinthe Gabrielle was corresponding with a Paris lawyer in October 1795 and was granted the status of *Femme Sole* over her money in January 1796 have any bearing on this? Did she know and was making sure that she was financially secure in the wake of her husband's indiscretions and did he acquiesce to this to try to repent for his wrongs? It was hardly unheard of for an aristocratic married gentleman to take a mistress, but Hyacinthe Gabrielle with her Gallic temperament was not likely to turn a blind eye to her husband's indiscretions as other wives may have done. It presents another reason why the astute Hyacinthe Gabrielle may have been pressing for the security of a marriage late in 1794. However, if the existence of Johnston had initially been kept a secret from the new Lady Mornington, if she had indeed married Richard thinking him still faithful to her and her alone, she had certainly been made aware of her husband's indiscretions and Johnston's existence by 1816 when she referred obliquely to him in a letter as '*le J*'.

Richard made repeated attempts to lure Hyacinthe Gabrielle to India; if there were troubles in their relationship before he left then they appeared to have been mended and he did genuinely love and miss his wife, both her companionship and in his bed. He also trusted her implicitly and had left his private affairs in her hands (she held power of attorney over them together with William Wellesley-Pole). Lady Anne Barnard, the wife of the colonial secretary at the Cape of Good Hope, recorded in her journal that a Mr and Mrs Stokes (he had been a navigator on the ship that had brought Richard out to India) had passed through the Cape on their way to England to entreat Hyacinthe Gabrielle to make the perilous seven-month sea voyage to India.[13] Richard hoped she would overcome her fear of the sea, bringing their children with her if necessary (he thought it best to leave the boys behind at school, but if she had to bring them she should bring a tutor too):

If she likes to go to Queen it over the East instead of living in the more obscure view of a peeress in London – she shoud [sic] accept, Lord M woud

[sic] not press her to join him unless he saw that he can venture to bring her without fear of her meeting with mortification from the high mounted virtue of the Ladys who have carried their cut neat in order to dispose of it – the Happiness of Lord M: will be much increased by her coming, I hope she deserves him, his heart I am convinced is very good & his principles rigidly Honorable, he is certainly a pleasant and clever man too, with veins of little imperfections running thro the ability & the agremen [sic] so as to decrease its value a little but not very essentially.[14]

Correspondence was not easy for the couple, with letters taking many months to reach their destination and a similar amount of time for the reply to make the return journey, and then only if the ship carrying them successfully reached its destination.[15] Hyacinthe Gabrielle corresponded (in French) continually with her husband, her letters often grumbling about his absence or worrying he would fall in love with someone else while apart from her. Finally, she sanctioned him to sleep with other women if he had to, as long as he did not become permanently attached to them. It was a fateful decision and Hyacinthe Gabrielle seems to have at the very least been aware that her husband was becoming emotionally detached from her.

She wrote to him in September 1801 to complain that she had sacrificed her youth, beauty and health during the decade she had spent before their marriage supporting his misfortune, illness and bad humour, expecting nothing in return except to be a part of his life. Now, however, when he was rising high, she accused him of becoming ungrateful, of having cast her aside. Anonymous letters began to arrive at Hyacinthe Gabrielle's London town house on Park Lane, suggesting that her husband was being unfaithful to her. Although Richard strenuously denied the allegations in respect of the woman named in them – Madame de Cocremont, a French émigrée who had been abandoned in India by the rakish General John Hayes St Leger (possibly by the death of the general) – as the old saying goes, there is no smoke without fire. However, Richard never stopped loving his wife.[16]

Richard's younger brother Arthur had found success within the military and was now a colonel; he was already in India with his regiment.[17] He had been rebuffed in his plea for the hand of the woman he loved, a beautiful Irish heiress named Catherine (Kitty) Dorothea Sarah Pakenham. To add insult to injury, the refusal had been given by Kitty's brother, a man younger than Arthur. Her family thought his prospects insufficient for Kitty and Arthur was in India determined to prove himself a success and the Pakenhams wrong. Richard and Arthur's brother Henry was also with them in India, as Richard's personal secretary.[18]

The three brothers did find varying levels of success in their different fields in India but for Richard his return to England in 1806 was fraught. Although created Marquess Wellesley in the Irish peerage in 1799 as a reward for initial progress (Richard was affronted that it was an Irish and not an English peerage, referring to it as a 'gilt potato' and refusing the financial rewards that came with it at the expense of the army), his tenure in India had ended somewhat falteringly; he had changed the map of India but left his position as governor general under a cloud. He longed to see his family again and the last two loving letters between husband and wife, despite the rumours of Richard's affairs, reveal their enduring feelings for one another. Hyacinthe wrote that she 'lives for and longs only to find herself again in [Richard's] arms and to replace our five interesting and beautiful children under your protection.' Richard's reply was no less heartfelt: he was 'dying to embrace [his wife] ... *chère amie, toujours à toi et pour toi*.'[19]

The long-distance letters between the two had become more nagging, bristling with complaints and accusations, a situation not helped by the time lag between their epistles, but equally they had still written of their continuing love for one another. The enduring romance sustained through their letters during their many years apart faltered in the stark reality of their meeting. During his time in India as governor general, Richard had become used to a high status with people treating him accordingly. However, upon landing in England his imperious self-regard was quickly and fatally affronted when his wife, who had travelled to Portsmouth to greet him, made a joke at his expense over dinner. Accustomed to being treated almost as a king, he had barely contained his anger during that first day on shore; true, he had been the centre of attention but it had fallen short of the reception he felt he deserved. At dinner he had finally let his temper loose, startling the company around the table with the invectives he showered upon them. Hyacinthe Gabrielle, trying to restore peace to the room, instead set the death knell upon their relationship. Turning to her husband, she gave a hollow laugh and said: 'Ah! you must not think you are in India still, where everybody ran to obey you. They mind nobody here.'

Richard left the table in a rage and was never to live upon terms of intimacy with his wife again. During the long years of their separation both had changed: Hyacinthe Gabrielle was not the woman he had held in his memory and he could not bear the gentle teasing of his wife. Although she might have misjudged her husband, the marchioness could not be held responsible for their rupture. Richard wanted the sensual young woman he had fallen in love with in Paris and the reality of his wife as a still beautiful but middle-aged matron whose primary concern, despite all her love for her

husband, was the welfare and future success of her children who were ham-
pered by their illegitimacy, proved a stark contrast to the woman he had
imagined would still be waiting for him.

He had also returned with his reputation in tatters. In *The Eldest Son*, Iris
Butler says that Richard had left his luck in India as his wife Hyacinthe
Gabrielle had always prophesied, and indeed he had. The only improvement
was in the family finances and with the profits of his Indian governorship
Richard bought the magnificent Apsley House in London. He moved his wife
and children in with him but the warring spouses lived separately within its
elegant confines, the marchioness together with Henry when he was home
from Eton and her young namesake daughter on the upper floors and the
marquess on the lower, communicating largely by means of letters and notes
passed between them and delivered up and down the stairs by long-suffering
footmen. Still tainted by her years as a mistress and her obscure Parisian
origins, Hyacinthe Gabrielle was denied the social recognition she should
finally have been afforded by going forth in society at her husband's side as his
marchioness. Instead, Richard appeared in public with courtesans upon his
arm and took a house at Ramsgate in which he installed a mistress, reputedly
having a *seraglio* of concubines there over the years and needing to employ a
live-in *accoucheur* (male midwife).[20]

Richard cruelly deprived his wife of any control over the running or
finances of the household in London; she lived in luxury, it is true, but was no
more than a kept woman living in a gilded cage. With the Peninsular War
ongoing, the Marquess Wellesley was posted to Spain as an ambassador to
Madrid, sailing in the summer months of 1809 but not before a failed attempt
to take with him his mistress, the celebrated courtesan Miss Mary Ann
Leshley. Mary Ann was better known as Moll Raffles, supposedly due to her
being raffled off by members of the 7th Dragoons when they were quartered
at Rochester but actually because her mother, a cook at the Dolphin Inn at
Chichester, had remarried when Mary Ann was only 7 years old to a man
named Richard Reffell (her father had been 'pressed' into service with the
Royal Navy and had died at sea). It was the wounded Hyacinthe Gabrielle
who prevented Miss Leshley accompanying the marquess to Spain; she wrote
to the Foreign Secretary, George Canning and he prohibited the scheme; a
betrayal for which Richard could not forgive his wife and one that hardened
his heart against her even more.[21]

With Richard as inflexible and self-obsessed as ever and Hyacinthe
Gabrielle volubly critical of his behaviour, the couple formally separated in
1810.

Chapter Three

Unfortunate Marriages and Alliances

Hyacinthe Gabrielle had just wanted her husband to regain his senses and live once again in the bosom of his family but far too much water had passed under the bridge for that to ever happen. As she had no other option left to her, the wronged Marchioness Wellesley moved out of Apsley House almost immediately upon her husband's return from Spain, forwarding a scathing letter to her by now hated husband: 'Your unhappy daughter [Hyacinthe Mary] and I leave your house with horror ... Continue to live with vile and depraved characters who, by flattering your extravagant vanity, dominate you, dishonour you and ruin you.'[1]

Hyacinthe Gabrielle, although separated from her husband, was still his marchioness and able to use her title. Richard provided her with a suitable financial allowance and, feeling his duty was done, publicly embarked upon a series of affairs while his embittered wife retreated from public view. His brother Arthur, exasperated by Richard's love life which he thought was to the detriment of his political aspirations, was later to remark: 'I wish Wellesley was *castrated*; or that he would like other people attend to his business & perform too. It is lamentable to see Talents & character & advantages such as he possesses thrown away upon Whoring.'[2] In turn Richard, thwarted in his long-term ministerial attempts (although he did serve as Foreign Secretary for a little over two years from 1809 in the new administration following the resignation of Lord Charles Bentinck's father, the Duke of Portland), had to watch his younger brother take command of the allied armies fighting Napoléon Bonaparte in Spain and France, subsequently eclipsing his older sibling in the honours he received.

It was mooted that Richard Colley Wellesley would be appointed prime minister in 1812 following the assassination of Spencer Perceval. However, Richard was unpopular and the taint of scandal followed him; instead the position went to Robert Banks Jenkinson, the 2nd Earl of Liverpool. While Richard made do with the title of Marquess Wellesley, the 'gilt potato' of an Irish peerage, Arthur, who had been created first Viscount, then Earl and finally Marquess of Wellington, was elevated to a dukedom and so outranked his brother.[3] (Hyacinthe Gabrielle had, in error, rejected the offer of an English earldom for her husband while he was in India and instead accepted the Irish marquessate, thinking it the higher title, but Wellesley would have much preferred the former and did not hesitate to let his wife understand her mistake.) Arthur was also to serve as prime minister and was lauded with positions, honours and titles while Richard, the haughty older brother, never fully realized either his ambitions or his true potential.

For all his public honours, Arthur's private life was actually no less complicated than his brother's. On his return to England as a wealthy major general he found the ever-patient Kitty still waiting for him but much changed, having lost the bloom of her youthful beauty (Arthur reputedly cruelly remarked to his brother Gerald 'She has grown ugly, by Jove!'). An honourable man though (despite his comment on her looks), and recognizing that she had wasted years in waiting for his return, he duly married Kitty in Dublin in 1806 but could not return the adoration with which she still viewed him. Patently unsuited to one another, they lived separately for much of their married lives, Arthur's duties providing a perfect excuse to keep him away from home for protracted periods of time. Although his amours were on a far less public scale than his brother's, he did take several mistresses, although it does justice to his discretion that there remains to this day little evidence of them. Two sons had been born early on in the marriage and Kitty doted on them during her husband's absence on the battlefields of mainland Europe. Arthur was, perhaps, closer to Kitty's two younger brothers – Edward and Hercules Pakenham, who served beside him with distinction and honour during the Peninsular War – than to his wife.[4]

Richard and Arthur's younger brother Henry, who had returned from India early and in poor health, had a tangled love life too and Lady Anne Abdy's was not the first elopement within the Wellesley family. In 1803 Henry had married Lady Charlotte, daughter of Charles Sloane Cadogan, 1st Earl Cadogan (in its second creation) and the couple had four children before, in 1809, Lady Charlotte ran off with a dashing and brave cavalry officer, Lord Henry William Paget, the future 1st Marquess of Anglesey and eldest son of the 1st Earl of Uxbridge. Paget was also married and so two divorces swiftly followed. Lord Paget and Lady Charlotte were married but his military career temporarily suffered as a result of the displeasure of the Wellesley family and it proved impossible for Paget to continue to serve alongside the Duke of Wellington in the immediate aftermath of the scandal.

Charlotte's older sister, Lady Emily Cadogan, had married Gerald Valerian Wellesley, and both Gerald and Henry's marriages were strongly disapproved of by the dowager Lady Mornington who, with the exception of William and Arthur's wives, considered herself most unfortunate in her daughters-in-law (Hyacinthe Gabrielle meanwhile, in opposition to her hated mother-in-law, got on famously with Emily). There had been a scandal in the late eighteenth century when the Cadogan girls' mother had been divorced by their father following her affair with the married Reverend William Henry Cooper, and old Lady Mornington prophetically feared that history would repeat itself with the succeeding generation. Hyacinthe Gabrielle wrote to her husband while he was still in India, no doubt with a small element of satisfaction, noting 'it seems to be decreed that none of the Wellesleys should make grand marriages.'[5]

The Prince of Wales imparted his personal view of Gerald and Henry Wellesley to Hyacinthe Gabrielle, who he was in the habit of visiting to hear the latest gossip on the Wellesley family. Gerald, in his opinion, was 'one of the greatest roués he had ever met [and] Henry was infinitely amusing and knew all *"les filles"*.'[6] Lady Emily too was to prove an unfaithful wife but Gerald, to protect their children, did not seek a divorce. Iris Butler, in *The Eldest Brother*, pointedly says that while the Wellesley brothers were hugely attractive to women, they were also uncommonly bad at marriage. At least in Hyacinthe Gabrielle the marquess had met his match in a clever and feisty woman who chose to enter into the fray and match him word for word, whereas his brothers' wronged wives took their misfortunes more meekly.

Relations between Paget and the Wellesleys remained frosty for some years following the scandal but had recovered sufficiently by the time of the Battle of Waterloo for Paget (by then the Earl of Uxbridge) to be by the Duke of Wellington's side during the action and to get his lower leg shattered by a cannonball. The unfortunate event prompted the now famous exchange between the pair when Paget, in amazement, looked down and exclaimed to Wellington, 'By God, sir, I've lost my leg!' and Wellington replied with a wry, 'By God, sir, so you have!' Paget wrote to inform his wife the next day, instructing her to 'be bold, prepare for misfortune, I have lost my right leg.' Charlotte rushed to Brussels to be by her husband's side, arriving there a week after the battle with her 4-year-old son by Paget. No less a person than the Prince had helped her to get there, having placed the royal yacht at her disposal to carry her across the Channel. In the year following the famous battle, and in the midst of the scandal of his niece's own divorce trial, Henry Wellesley married for a second time to Georgiana Charlotte Augusta Cecil, daughter of James Cecil, the 1st Marquess of Salisbury.[7]

Richard's youngest children remained with their mother, who lived for a year in a furnished house in Grosvenor Square before leasing 12 Great Cumberland Place.[8] While their father grew to be a somewhat distant and slightly feared figure to them, the children, even into adulthood, continually strove to please him. Richard was the adored eldest son with the hopes and ambitions of both parents resting on his shoulders, while Gerald was over-shadowed by him. Henry, 'the Tiddler' and the youngest, was somewhat overlooked by his father, having grown up while the latter was in India. Hyacinthe Mary enchanted everyone who met her, but the spoilt and beauti-ful Anne was a mirror image of her mother with all her Gallic impetuosity intermixed with her father's bad temper; at the age of 11 she was already posing with her head held aloft in 'attitudes' because it was fashionable to do so. Both girls were well-educated, both academically and in more feminine pursuits. They shared a music master with the young Princess Charlotte of Wales (the German composer Louis von Esch who had been educated in France and had fled to England at the time of the French Revolution), sang in three languages and danced like 'little Frenchwomen' but did not have the recognition or titles of legitimately-born daughters of a marquess. As Hyacinthe Gabrielle pointed out, when she took her daughters out into society her calling card would look most odd:

The Marchioness Wellesley
The Misses Wellesley.[9]

The marchioness was under no illusions as to her eldest daughter's tempera-ment, remarking of the 16-year-old Anne that 'for all her pretty smile and big languorous eyes she is far from gentle ... She is a fine strapping wench who promises to be precocious and to have violent passions. I'm afraid when this girl falls in love, she will be untameable, impossible.'[10] She had been admired by no less a personage than the Prince of Wales when she came out into society in 1804 as a 16-year-old. Made two years later, Anne's marriage to William Abdy may have been an attempt to ingratiate herself with her father and to win his approval (with his own fortune far from secure, Richard would have been pleased to see his daughter wed to an independently wealthy baronet) as it was not by her own inclination that she made the match. She was far from being passionate or untameable with regard to Sir William Abdy.

The wedding took place on a summer's day in 1806 at the church of St Martin-in-the-Fields shortly after Lord Wellesley's fraught return from India and the two men who signed as witnesses to it were Anne's father (who had provided a handsome £11,000 as a marriage settlement for his daughter, a further diminishment of the ever-decreasing fortune he had brought home from India), and James Gordon junior, a relation of Sir William Abdy's mother. Anne was 18 years of age.[11]

The Abdys had been married for eight years when the widowed Lord Charles Bentinck began to visit their Hill Street home; Lady Abdy felt sorry for him and became interested in his poor, motherless infant daughter and so Sir William tolerated his visits. Lord Charles had just abandoned little Ann Rawlinson, the mistress who had temporarily filled the void in his life following his wife's death and, incapable of living alone, he now had his sights set somewhat higher than a courtesan who lived above an umbrella shop in Knightsbridge.

While the Abdys' marriage was outwardly content, gossip had reached the ears of Anne's father concerning certain indiscretions she was alleged to have been party to. Anne tremulously wrote from Hill Street to refute any reports of wrongdoing and the marquess agreed never to mention the subject again. Knowing that tongues had begun to wag, Lady Anne Abdy ought to have observed more discretion in her private life but, ever reckless and headstrong, she plunged headlong into her own downfall.[12]

In November 1814, with Napoléon Bonaparte in exile on the Mediterranean island of Elba and the Bourbon monarchy re-established upon the throne of France, the Abdys decided on a tour to Paris. They took rooms in a *hôtel particulier* on a fashionable Parisian street and it was there that Sir William's suspicions were first aroused for, shortly after their arrival in the French capital, Lord Charles appeared in the very same street, taking rooms in a nearby house and visiting as freely as he had in London. All the same, even after the event, the opinion of Anne's sister Hyacinthe was that 'no lady would have suspected [Lord Charles] of being in *the* least dangerous.'[13] Nor Sir William either, it would seem!

The threesome spent the winter in Paris, returning to London in February 1815 when the news broke of Bonaparte's escape from Elba and his reappearance on the French mainland. Just months later came the pivotal Battle of Waterloo (on 18 June) where the allied army, under Lady Anne's uncle, the Duke of Wellington, defeated the French forces. Napoléon Bonaparte subsequently surrendered to the British on board the HMS *Bellerophon* and amid jubilant celebrations the Abdys passed July and August, the 'watering season', at Worthing and Brighton on the south coast where Lady Abdy made the most of her familial connection to the hero of the hour. The *Bellerophon* brought Bonaparte first to the Devon fishing village of Brixham, anchoring off the harbour and attracting a flotilla of small sightseeing vessels once news leaked out about the famous prisoner held on board.

Shortly thereafter, when the throng of spectators became too large, the *Bellerophon* made for Plymouth where Bonaparte's infamy continued to attract the attention of eager sightseers and he was finally told that he would not be allowed to live out his days in exile in England as he had wished but instead would be sent to the remote British-owned island of St Helena in the South Atlantic Ocean.[14] Lord Charles, under the guise of his attendance upon the Prince Regent, also decamped to Brighton and a clandestine correspondence began between him and Lady Anne. There had been no children born to the Abdys; the rumour was that Sir William was impotent and unable to satisfy his gregarious young wife who was growing increasingly frustrated with her marriage.

Returning to London, the Abdys were invited by Sir William's sister and brother-in-law, Henrietta and Charles Caldwell, to a shooting party held at Bottisham Hall in Cambridgeshire. At Lord Charles' suggestion, Lady Anne persuaded her husband to travel there alone, even though the invitation and the acceptance of it had been of a long-standing duration. Mr Caldwell's father, Admiral Sir Benjamin Caldwell, was at Bottisham Hall and was known to be unwell so Sir William all too readily believed Anne's excuse that it would be an inconvenience to his relations if she accompanied him. In reality, Lord Charles had shamelessly used his young motherless daughter to bend Anne to his wishes, as proved by a letter that was subsequently found in her desk:

> If I die, Oh my love! I promise you the care of Georgiana. In a very few weeks, if you go into Cambridgeshire, this duty will devolve on you. Think, then, of your dearest Charles! This fills me with horror. How can I think you love me if you hesitate? Oh, that I was still as dear to you as ever![15]

Harriette Wilson had a conversation with Lord Charles' younger brother Frederick on the subject of his letters to Lady Anne Abdy, and she was withering in her opinion of the author of them:

> I only allude to the folly of a young man, like Charles Bentinck, sitting down to his muffins and eggs in a state of perfect health, and, with his mouth crammed full of both, calling for a half a sheet of paper to write to Lady Abdy, that he was, at that present writing about to die, and therefore took up his pen, to request her to be kind to his daughter Georgiana, when he should be no more.

Frederick's opinion of his brother was little better. He thought Lord Charles ought to be ashamed of himself, although in his muddle-headed way he too suggested little Georgiana should be left an orphan:

> 'I do not set up for a remarkable clever fellow,' Fred. Bentinck observed, 'but if I had made such a fool of myself as Charles did in that business, I would blow my brains out.'

'You are helping him out of it, nicely,' [Beau] Brummell observed to Fred. Bentinck.

The unsuspecting Sir William Abdy set out at the beginning of September to visit his sister, leaving his duplicitous wife alone in their Hill Street house with only her lapdog and the servants for company. Lord Charles had already discussed an elopement with Lady Anne, as another of his letters to her makes clear:

> By delaying [the elopement] for a few weeks, you put it out of the power of it ever taking place. You say he [Sir William] cannot regret it long. My thoughts tell me what I feel – but no words can express my wretched distress at being left thus dreadfully alone. I hate myself and, if I lose my dearest Anne, I shall be consigned to ever misery. Oh, it must not be. My love says she agrees with me. You must not go, love; Oh, promise me you won't – my existence depends on it.[16]

Was Lord Charles really contemplating (or threatening) suicide if Anne did not do as he wished? To use such emotional blackmail on the unhappy Anne, even allowing for his state of mind after the death two years earlier of his adored wife, was a pretty low trick. Lady Anne Abdy, stuck in an unhappy and (if rumours of Sir William's impotency were true) unfulfilled marriage, could not help but be swayed by Charles' desire for her. By nature she was impetuous and headstrong, acting first and thinking later. On the very day Sir William left for Cambridgeshire, Lord Charles Bentinck was once more admitted to the Hill Street house and this time to the lady's bedchamber.

Chapter Four

Elopement in High Life

Three days later and with her husband still absent in Cambridgeshire, Lady Anne Abdy left her London town house with her pet dog and walked determinedly along Dean Street towards Hyde Park and a pre-arranged rendezvous with her lover. A gig was waiting for her and Lord Charles Bentinck sat on the driver's seat. Lady Anne settled herself next to her lover and the couple quickly drove away, but for all their haste they had been spotted and it was only a matter of hours before Sir William's mother and sister were informed; they made straight for Hill Street and demanded admittance. Upon searching Lady Anne's bureau, the effusive and quite frankly laughable letters written by Charles were found and any hope of a satisfactory resolution vanished.

While Lord Charles had clearly been biding his time with only one object in view, that of an elopement, and although the plan had been discussed, it is likely that Anne acted with an impulsive, spur-of-the-moment impetuosity. One can imagine her pacing her drawing room, wondering whether to meet Lord Charles and, on a fatal and fateful whim, suddenly dashing from her home. She took nothing with her other than her pet dog; no clothes, jewels or money and, perhaps more importantly, left behind all the evidence of her affair in the form of the letters in her bureau. She also almost instantly regretted her decision and sent a letter into Cambridgeshire, post-haste and marked 'to be given immediately' to Sir William in which she confessed her rash action and begged his forgiveness:

> Oh! do not come to town. I am gone; I am a lost, miserable wretch; I have given up everything for Charles Bentinck. He has caused my ruin; he has made me wrong you so cruelly. I could never bear to see you again. Forgive me. I shall never forget your kindness to me; you have been indeed a kind husband to me. I am unworthy of you. I shall always regret you; always love you, as long as I live. Oh! may you be as happy as I am wretched and miserable. This is the only wish I can have upon earth. Bless you, my dear, dear William. Oh! I am distracted.[1]

Sir William came straight back to London with the intention of reclaiming his wife but went first to his mother's house where he found her in possession of the letters from Charles to Anne and in no mood to allow her son to admit his wife back into his house.[2] The two ladies, the Dowager Lady Abdy and Sir William's unmarried sister Harriet, schemed behind his back to this end. Harriet received a letter from her sister-in-law a day or two after the elopement in which Anne admitted her guilt and begged for forgiveness, pleading to be allowed to return to her Hill Street town house and roundly abusing Lord Charles, but the existence of the letter was kept concealed from Sir William. Harriet also wrote to Anne's mother, Lady Wellesley, to inform her of her daughter's disgrace and eliciting a flurry of letters written in the marchioness's interminable French to the rest of the Wellesley family.

A fully furnished house on Crooms Hill at the edge of Greenwich Park (where the Royal Observatory stands) had been taken by Lord Charles under the name of Captain Charles Brown (although he paid the rent with a banker's draft in his own name, a mistake that would later help to confirm his true identity), and Lady Anne passed as his wife for the time being. Walter Phillips, Lord Charles' valet, attended him but out of livery so no one would recognize him and even Phillips did not know who the lady actually was until she had lived in the Crooms Hill house for three weeks. The couple remained there, undetected, until late November, although the ton was agog with the scandalous reports of their elopement:[3]

ELOPEMENT IN HIGH LIFE! – A young married Lady of rank, and highly distinguished in the fashionable circles by her personal attractions, is said to have absconded from the neighbourhood of Berkeley-square a few days since, in order to throw herself into the arms of the brother of an English Duke.[4]

A married Lady has recently eloped with the brother of an English Duke. A female friend, on learning the story, coolly observed – 'Who could expect a tame duck out of a wild duck's nest?'[5]

Faux Pas – The Lady of a Baronet has eloped with a Noble Lord, and no less than five actions for Crim. Con. are to be tried the ensuing Term in the Court of King's Bench, four of which have originated in the intemperance of noble blood.[6]

Hyacinthe Gabrielle, the 'wild duck' referred to in the newspaper snippet above, was appalled by her reprobate daughter's behaviour which, if not managed correctly, would see Anne forever ruined in the eyes of society. It was what she had always feared. Two years before Anne's marriage when she was being courted by beaux and suitors, the marchioness was afraid her daughter would 'choose to be foolish', knowing full well that society would blame the mother for the daughter's indiscretions and point to Hyacinthe Gabrielle's own past.[7] For the Wellesley family, the preferred course of action was for Anne to be reunited with her husband with the minimum of fuss but otherwise a full divorce, which would allow her to marry Lord Charles Bentinck, would be the next best scenario. Only they had no idea whether Sir William, under the domineering influence of his female relatives, could ever be induced to take his wife back or whether Lord Charles would be willing to marry her. The fortune she had brought to her marriage as a dowry would be forfeited in the case of a divorce and Lord Charles could be financially ruined by damages awarded against him in a Crim. Con. action; even if a divorce was obtained and a marriage effected, Lord Charles and Lady Anne's scant finances could condemn them to a life lived in reduced circumstances.

Almost immediately after the elopement Harriette Wilson was surprised by a visit from Sir William Abdy, whom she hardly knew other than by sight and reputation:

> 'I have called upon you, Miss Harriette,' said Sir William, almost in tears, 'in the first place because you are considered exactly like my wife,' – my likeness to Lady Abdy had often been thought very striking – 'and, in the second, because I know you are a woman of feeling.'

Lady Anne Abdy was also considered to resemble Lord Charles Bentinck's first wife, Georgiana; if Harriette Wilson resembled Anne, then she must also have looked very similar to the first Lady Charles and this may suggest a further reason for Charles' attendance in her rooms. Suggesting his rival was even more stupid than he was himself (poor Anne! Neither man was particularly bright), Sir William explained to Harriette how it had come to pass that his wife had eloped:

> 'That Charles Bentinck,' said he, half angry, 'is the greatest fool in the world; and in Paris we always used to laugh at him.'
>
> 'But,' said [Harriette], 'why did you suffer his lordship to be eternally at your house?'
>
> 'Why, dear me!' answered Abdy, peevishly, 'I told him in a letter I did not like it and I thought it wrong, and he told me it was no such thing.'
>
> 'And therefore,' [Harriette] remarked, 'you suffered him to continue his visits as usual?'
>
> 'Why, good gracious, what could I do! Charles Bentinck told me, upon his honour, he meant nothing wrong.'
>
> 'Why did she run away from you?' said [Harriette]. 'Why not, at least, have carried on the thing quietly?'
>
> 'That's what I say,' said Abdy.

'Because,' [Harriette] continued, 'had she remained with you sir, you would have always looked forward with hope to that period when age and ugliness should destroy all her power of making conquests.'

'Oh,' said Abdy, clasping his hands, 'if any real friend like you had heartened me up in this way at the time, I could have induced her to have returned to me! But then, Miss Wilson, they all said I should be laughed at and frightened me to death. It was very silly to be sure of me to mind them; for it is much better to be laughed at, than to be so dull and miserable as I am now.'

'Shall I make you a cup of tea, Sir William?'

'Oh! Miss, you are so good! tea is very refreshing when one is in trouble.'

Struggling not to laugh, Harriette bitingly told Sir William that Lady Anne had good blood running through her veins from her mother's side of the family and then casually dropped the bombshell that she did not believe Lord Charles was his wife's only lover:

I think Fred Lamb was one of her seducers; but how many more may have had a finger in the pie, I really cannot take it upon myself to say ... I have seen Fred Lamb daily and constantly riding past her door. I know him to be a young man of strong passions, much fonder of enjoyment than pursuit; and further, my sister Fanny, one of the most charitable of all human beings, told me she had seen Fred Lamb in a private box at Drury Lane with your wife, and her hand was clasped in his, which he held on his knee!

Frederick Lamb was nominally the son of Peniston Lamb, the 1st Viscount Melbourne and his wife, Elizabeth Milbanke. Nominally as, due to his mother's numerous affairs, his parentage could never be definitively proved (it was thought that, along with his elder siblings William and Emily, his father might have been George Wyndham, the 3rd Earl of Egremont). Young, debonair and handsome, Fred was made in the mould of his mother and known for his many (albeit discreet) affairs. Lady Wellesley concurred with Harriette's opinion of Fred Lamb; she too thought he had seduced her daughter and she blamed a family friend for initiating and encouraging the situation, the exotically beautiful Madame Rosina Parnther.

Lady Wellesley had written an increasingly hysterical letter to Sir William's mother, believing their previous friendship would prevail upon her to accept Anne back into her family if she could only be induced to leave Charles' side. She implored Sir William 'on her knees' to be indulgent to her unfortunate daughter as he, as well as she, knew Anne had both virtue and a proper idea of her duties (the Dowager Lady Abdy and her son could perhaps be forgiven for not readily believing the marchioness in light of recent events). Hyacinthe Gabrielle put Anne's rash act down to her 'silliness, naughtiness and feather-headedness'.[8]

When the letter arrived Sir William's mother and sister were entertaining a guest, none other than Madame Parnther herself. Although it seems to have been assumed that this lady was also a Frenchwoman, possibly an émigrée following the Revolution, she was only born around 1789 and was formerly known by the name of Rosina Burrell, not a particularly Gallic surname. She was perhaps of Irish extraction and her marriage to the wealthy Robert Parnther, Esquire had produced two sons and established her as a society hostess; she was known to the diarist Fanny Burney and both Mr and Madame Parnther were intimate friends with Anne's uncle, the Duke of Wellington. Hyacinthe Gabrielle's writing, always in French, was hard to decipher and Madame Parnther was asked by the two Abdy ladies to help translate and to read it. Consequently Rosina, who also counted Lady Wellesley as a friend, had to unwittingly read aloud what that lady had written about her:[9]

> I am almost sure that there must have been some sort of argument between [Anne] and F. Lamb which resulted in a quarrel between her and Lord C.B., and that he took the opportunity to force her consent to follow him to prove that she loved him more than F. Lamb. And you know that she always acts on impulse and in a moment will have said the fatal 'yes' and 24 hours afterwards, would have been perfectly miserable and would not have dared to return home … Perhaps that Madame Panther [*sic*] has schemed all this to make certain of Lamb with whom she is madly in love. He is at her house every day. She is much more cunning than Anne and could trick her very easily. She has always been jealous of Anne and Hyacinthe. At any rate try to find out something on that score without however her guessing what has happened in case she does not know. We must keep this business as secret as possible … [Sir William] could see very well all that was happening and also, knowing that F. Lamb was in London, and that she could meet with him at any moment '*chez la Panther*', he should not have left her. I always told you that he should have been more firm and prudent.[10]

Anne's sister Hyacinthe and her husband came to London to meet with Sir William and try to discover Anne's residence so they could speak to her. Hyacinthe had been luckier than her sister in her own marriage for she had been allowed to choose her husband and had married for love, not duty, even though it was also a most suitable match in the eyes of her parents.[11] The handsome Edward John Walhouse Littleton, the future 1st Baron Hatherton, was both a wealthy Staffordshire landowner (he had inherited Teddesley Hall near Penkridge in 1812) and a Whig MP; he was born Edward Walhouse but took the surname of Littleton in compliance with the inheritance of his great-uncle, Sir Edward Littleton, 4th and last Baronet Littleton. Although noted as occasionally tactless, he was also a sensible man who was well liked and totally trusted by the Wellesley family. The couple had married just before Christmas in 1812 at St George's in Hanover Square and by the time of Anne's elopement they had two daughters to whom Hyacinthe was devoted.[12] The diarist Hester Piozzi thought Mr Littleton greatly preferable to Sir William Abdy. She knew people who were connected to the Abdys by marriage and wrote to her late husband's nephew and her adopted son, John Salusbury Piozzi Salusbury, giving her opinion on the ensuing drama:

> The Elopement of Sir William's Lady with Lord Charles Bentinck gives much Concern of Course. She is Sister to pretty Mrs. Wallhouse Lyttelton [sic], who must behave better, and not follow bad Example – *her* Husband is probably more amiable (you knew him) than the Baronet; and it behoves Gentlemen to make themselves beloved – when no stronger Tye [sic] than mere Preference restrains the Lady.[13]

With letters flying back and forth between Anne's siblings it was decided, as the affair was now becoming widely known, that their father must be informed and it fell to Richard as the eldest son to write. Lady Wellesley picked up her pen too. While the Wellesley siblings conferred with each other and with their father, all of a mind that Sir William should be separated from his female relations and induced to take back his errant wife, the marchioness wrote an ill-considered letter from her Brighton home to Lord Charles, threatening to bring down upon his head the full and frightful wrath of the Wellesley family if he did not return Anne to Sir William. Having no idea where Lord Charles was hiding, she sent the letter to Sir William's mother, the dowager Lady Abdy, in the hope that she would know and forward it on. Richard and his brother Henry, together with their mother, set off in a coach for London to attempt a rescue; they hoped to return Anne to her Hill Street home and the arms of her husband.

Upon arriving in London, Lady Wellesley found a reply from Sir William's mother. The rash letter to Lord Charles was returned with a terse note accompanying it that rejected any hopes of a reconciliation. The implication was clear: Sir William would do as his mother desired and his mother wanted nothing more to do with her disreputable daughter-in-law. Sir William dithered for a while in the middle ground, in turn influenced by his mother and then by the Wellesleys, but his overriding concern was always for his public image and he feared he would look weak if he forgave his errant wife.

Even as the Wellesleys futilely tried to effect a reconciliation, they were also busy on all fronts attempting to stop scurrilous articles appearing in the press, exploring the possibilities of a full divorce and scheming to extract a promise from Lord Charles Bentinck that he would marry his mistress. The ever-resourceful Hyacinthe Littleton had decided upon Bath House, the Duke of Portland's residence in Piccadilly, as a neutral place for letters to be exchanged between the parties (it was just a short distance from the Littletons' Arlington Street house) without revealing Lord Charles' hiding place in Greenwich and eventually the two sisters arranged to meet at the duke's house. Hyacinthe even persuaded her sister to accompany her to her former marital home on Hill Street but Sir William refused to see them and so Anne returned to the 'protection' of Lord Charles. With matters at an impasse, the Littletons set off for Teddesley Hall and Lady Wellesley, together with her sons Richard and Henry, made for Brighton.

With the Wellesleys clear of London, still unaware of Anne's 'amorous retreat', Sir William made one attempt to break free of his meddling mother (who had also conveniently left London). Somehow he discovered the whereabouts of 'Captain and Mrs Brown' and began to correspond with and even visit his wife; he also sent all her clothes and her harp to her. When they heard of this both Richard Wellesley and Edward Littleton wrote to Anne and Sir William, inviting them to Staffordshire for a visit, so hopeful were they now of a happy resolution to the saga. For Edward Littleton to invite his sister-in-law for a visit was truly generous on his part for he had an extremely low opinion of her and, to be blunt, hated the sight of the woman and this notwithstanding the present scandal. Littleton thought Sir William should take Anne back and the reunited couple should live abroad for a year or two while the gossip died down. However, all was not settled and with yet another twist Richard was informed by Sir William's mother and sister that they had found letters in Anne's former home proving that the elopement had been planned much longer ago than had first been supposed, dating from the time both were in Worthing. Anne's duplicity in concealing her plans for so long did not bode well for any reconciliation between herself and her husband.

Meanwhile, the Wellesleys, ever determined not to keep all their eggs in one basket, continued to make discreet enquiries relative to a divorce. Their most pressing concerns were to tie Lord Charles Bentinck down to a promise, on his honour (and preferably in writing), to marry Anne if a full divorce was granted and to minimize the financial damages that Sir William might seek to claim. Too high an amount and Lord Charles would be left with nothing to live on and then Anne would suffer as her marriage settlement of £11,000 was already forfeited to Sir William by her actions. Sir William's behaviour was alarming to the Wellesleys, blowing hot and cold on the idea of a reconciliation but intimating he would not allow the clause to stand that would enable the parties to marry again, should they divorce. A vague rumour of a cohabitation by Sir William with a 'former female connection' that may have been carried on alongside his marriage (and which would, if true, suggest the rumours of his impotence were false), gave hope to the Wellesleys that they might prevail in obtaining a full divorce for Anne.

If Sir William was blowing hot and cold, so too was Anne, to the absolute and utter despair of her family. She wrote to her sister Hyacinthe:

> As for him [Lord Charles] there is nothing honourable I am sure he will not do, and as for his family they have always been so famous for their honourable principles that he says that they would be the first he is sure to urge him to make every reparation should he ever be inclined otherwise, indeed the only thing he seems afraid of is losing me ... I have another plan in my head which I have not let him [Lord Charles] suspect. Only think yesterday I saw Sir William opposite my window in a state of phrensy [sic]. I flew out to him and did everything to calm and compose him. Oh Hyacinthe, if I had not been afraid of Lord Charles interfering I would never have left him ... Oh, if you had seen the delight he was in at seeing me again, he said it seemed as if I had come out of the grave to him. I left him with the hopes of meeting again tomorrow. Oh Hyacinthe, is it too late now if I was to go and stay with you? He would then I know take me back. He says he cannot live without seeing me now. And then I cannot either. And then it is dangerous. If Lord Charles's family were to know it might prevent the divorce. But I must see him. He is to write to me today after he has seen the lawyers to tell me if it is improper. And if I am *not* to see him again I shall go distracted ... he is afraid of what the world will say. I told him I would live by myself and he might come and see me, but he cannot bear that either and he is so afraid of his family. Think of his mother and sister leaving him in town by himself. He hates them.[14]

Lord Charles knew that his mistress was meeting with her husband but could not or would not stop her, even though it made him miserable to see it. Anne, with both men now dangling from her fingertips, magnanimously told Hyacinthe it would be a great sacrifice to give up Lord Charles and would undoubtedly send him mad but she would rather see Sir William happy. She ended by begging Hyacinthe to tell her what to do, 'for I have not a settled thought in my head. Wherever I turn, whatever I think of it is a distraction. To stay here or go away is both equally horrible. Excuse this scrawl, I hardly know what I have written.'[15]

Hyacinthe's opinion, in a letter written to her brother Gerald, was that Anne:

> feels too late the disgrace and misery she has brought upon herself and bewails her fault in agonies of grief . . . but I cannot help pitying her, when I think that Sir W. has been so much to blame for his silly management of her and I think that, with a man of the least sense, she would have turned out a very different person.[16]

Sadly for Anne, Lord Charles had no more sense than her husband and she was now doomed to either one or the other. With a change of heart, she swung her desire towards a full divorce; she told her family she thought she had persuaded Sir William this was now the best path for them both to follow.

Hyacinthe, seven months' pregnant with her third child, travelled to London and her brothers, Richard and Henry, met her there.

With the Greenwich house now fully discovered, Hyacinthe sallied to the door of her sister's love-nest and found both Charles and Anne at home. Mrs Littleton had evidently reached the end of her tether, for an argument ensued during which she gave Lord Charles a piece of her mind and left him in absolutely no doubt of her opinion of him. She succeeded in persuading Anne to temporarily leave him and place herself under her sister and brother-in-law's protection in their Arlington Street house, albeit with the freedom to write to whom she pleased and able to leave when she chose. Hyacinthe triumphantly sent a note to Richard who was at their mother's house in nearby Great Cumberland Place, saying 'She is here!' and asking him to come alone to dinner. She also wrote to Sir William and, after a bit of negotiation, he came to Hyacinthe's house to speak to his wife.

Sir William intimated he would allow Anne to return to their Hill Street home, but only if a suitable position could be found for him by Anne's father or by her uncle, the Duke of Wellington. He believed that this would deflect any ridicule attaching to him in appearing weak by taking her back, ever his main concern since the elopement; damage limitation was all, both for Sir William and for the Wellesleys, and only Charles and Anne appeared to act first and foremost with their hearts rather than their heads. Although Richard Wellesley visited Hyacinthe he declined to see his other reprobate sister and though he was loath to comply with Sir William's mercenary and self-centred request, he did broach the subject with both his father and his Uncle Wellington (his father wisely refused to have anything to do with finding employment for Sir William).

Lord Charles confirmed in writing that he 'engaged upon his honour' to marry Anne as soon as he was able, in the event of a divorce, and agreed not to contact her in the meantime. Sir William, who had papers ready to serve on Anne for a divorce, agreed to wait for a week or so before taking action. While the Wellesley family was waiting for the Duke of Wellington's reply to the letter Anne had written under Richard's hesitant direction (the duke was in Paris at the time), asking for a position to be found for Sir William, they resolved, if Sir William would not once and for all take back his wife, that they would encourage her to return to Lord Charles. Thinking that all eventualities were covered, Richard and Henry returned to Brighton to visit their mother who was unwell.

The Duke of Wellington had a busy schedule in Paris where he had been appointed ambassador to France. Peace treaties were ongoing following his victory at Waterloo and his own social life was a whirl of balls and parties. To these engagements, even though his wife had moved to Paris when he had been appointed ambassador, he was often accompanied by Lady Caroline Lamb (Fred Lamb's sister-in-law), Lady Frances Webster and Lady Frances Shelley who was the niece of Lord Charles Bentinck's former mother-in-law, the courtesan Grace Dalrymple Elliott.[17] However, the duke was an honourable man with a keen sense of family, and even though he was busy he treated his niece's request sympathetically and with thoughtfulness. He penned Anne a kind letter:

Dearest Anne, I received last night your letter of the 8th.
When I first heard of the misfortune which had occurred I had intended to write to you to offer any service which you might think I could render you, and I refrained from doing so only because I did not know where any letter could find you … you will readily believe, therefore, that your letter has not found me indisposed to do everything in my power for you.

I am quite certain, however, not only that I have it not in my power to prosecute Sir William Abdy's views of employment abroad, but that to attempt it at present would be highly injurious to his reputation and to yourself. I should not succeed because Sir William has, till now, had no experience in public business and it would naturally create suspicion in the minds of those to whom application should be made in his favour of the motive for making it, if it were brought forward at the present moment.

I therefore strongly recommend that all thoughts of this kind shall be laid aside for the moment, and that Sir William should be satisfied with the goodwill of all your family and with the desire which they cannot fail to manifest in every way to render him as happy as it is possible to make him.

Pray let me hear from you again, and believe me, Dearest Anne,

> Ever yours most affectionately,
> Wellington.[18]

However, before the duke's letter had been received back in London, Anne had once again had a change of heart: she now wanted to be with Lord Charles.

The ever-perceptive Hyacinthe, in a letter written to her mother and hand-delivered by Richard upon his return to Brighton, said she was certain Anne, however guilty she felt, would take little persuasion to finally sever all ties with Sir William. 'The very idea of going to bed with him again fills her with horror!'[19] Vacillation ran in the family for, with Anne now favouring a divorce, her father (who, up to this point, even though he did not preclude a reconciliation, had privately been staunchly for a divorce and remarriage) now wrote to his eldest son to say he had reconsidered and thought it would be best for Anne to return to her husband. Richard, upon receipt of the letter, must have felt he was doing little but banging his head against a brick wall in the midst of the drama. The marquess had been discreetly offering sage advice throughout from the safety of his Ramsgate *seraglio* and with his latest courtesan not far from his side; any irony in the situation was lost upon him.

Lord Charles, meanwhile, heightened the drama when he wrote to Hyacinthe to tell her he was about to confess all to his employer, the Prince Regent. He had already tendered his resignation from his household position, which the prince had refused to accept, and now felt the need to lay his conduct before the man who was simultaneously the regent of the realm, employer, friend and putative former father-in-law to Lord Charles, not to forget probably grandfather to little Georgiana who seems to have been over-looked in the middle of this chaos (she was no doubt safely ensconced in the Cholmondeleys' nursery, as her mother had been before her). The letter was twice rejected by Hyacinthe and the servant carrying it was sent away. On the third attempt she accepted the letter when the servant solemnly informed her that it concerned the prince. Anne demanded the letter but Hyacinthe refused to put it into her sister's hands and, moreover, refused to either read it or to send a reply. Unsure of the contents of the letter and desperate to know, Anne threatened to write to Lord Charles. In despair, Hyacinthe left her home, going to her mother's empty house in Great

Cumberland Place before, at Anne's request, calling on Sir William. Anne wished to see her husband.

With Hyacinthe absent, Anne pre-empted her sister. As soon as Mrs Littleton left Arlington Street Anne called a carriage and appeared at her old Hill Street address where she gave Sir William an ultimatum: either he agreed to take her back there and then and let her remain in her home, or she would that instant return to the protection of Lord Charles. Regardless of the pressing urgency in Anne's request and much as he had prevaricated all through the muddle, Sir William still declined to know his own mind. Faced with her husband's indecision, Anne made up his mind for him and, returning to the carriage, ordered it to drive to Bath House where she knew Lord Charles awaited her. From this second elopement there was no going back, especially as Anne, within weeks, found herself with child, Lord Charles Bentinck's child.

Hyacinthe was furious, writing to her mother to ask 'is it not maddening after all that we have done for her?'[20] Maddening it may have been, but the deed was done and the die was finally cast. All that was wanted now was a full divorce.

Hyacinthe wrote to the Duke of Wellington for advice on how she should behave towards her sister, and he replied advising her that the whole family 'must now make the best of it'. He continued:

> I am not astonished at your feeling for your sister; but you must not allow these feelings to keep you out of the World or to make you believe that people will on that account think the worse of you; nor on the other hand should you regret any good-natured act you may have done by her, or be induced to abandon her in her misfortunes.[21]

The duke ended his letter by affectionately begging Hyacinthe to tell Anne that if he could help in any way, she merely had to ask.

Chapter Five

Criminal Conversation and Doctors' Commons

The New Year of 1816 did not appear to offer a promising start for the Wellesley family. Anne's father was faced with mounting debts, disastrously for his estranged wife Hyacinthe Gabrielle who never received her allotted (and generous) £5,000 a year allowance from her husband with any great regularity. Reluctantly the marquess took the decision to sell his Irish estates, a bittersweet moment for his eldest namesake son who regretted the loss of them almost as much as he had feared inheriting the encumbered and debt-ridden lands. Anne, after a brief and very public sojourn in Marylebone with her lover at Harman's Hotel on Duchess Street, had taken herself off to Paris where the Duke of Wellington was still resident and she intended to remain there while the legal ramifications of her separation from her husband were discussed and debated in the courtroom. The problem now for her family was to secure a full divorce that would enable her to remarry, but it was by no means a foregone conclusion that this would be the outcome.

The action had begun on the first day of December 1815 in the Sheriff's Court with the Crim. Con. trial when Sir William Abdy had stunned the Wellesleys, and Lord Charles Bentinck too, by announcing to the courtroom that he was seeking damages to the tune of £30,000 for the loss of his wife. His counsel, Mr Topping, presented the Abdys' marriage as a love-match, saying 'they had lived upon terms of the most connubial harmony and happiness' until the villainous Lord Charles had shattered it.[1]

Sir William's relatives lined up to affirm that the couple had been happy together, as did Robert Parnther, the husband of Madame Rosina whom Lady Wellesley had accused of encouraging her daughter in an amour with Fred Lamb; then the Abdys' butler and two footmen to attest to the scandalous behaviour of their mistress with her lover while her husband was absent. Sarah Weston, who had been hired as a servant in the Crooms Hill house by 'Captain Charles Brown', proved that the couple shared the same bed and lived together as man and wife during their stay there. The love letters written by Lord Charles were read to the court, along with Mr Topping's opinion of them (he thought they were 'replete with balderdash!') and Lord

Charles could put up little defence to the claims. His legal team merely pointed out that there were no Abdy children to be deprived of a mother, that Lord Charles Bentinck and Sir William Abdy had not been particularly close and so there had been no breach of friendship, and they refuted the claim that the Abdys' marriage had been blissfully happy until Lord Charles' arrival in it.

At Lord Charles' insistence no witnesses were brought to put his case and no letters were read to the court, but it was pointed out that he was possessed of little wealth even though he was the younger brother and son of two successive Dukes of Portland. His counsel was Henry Brougham, legal advisor to Caroline, Princess of Wales, the estranged wife of the Prince Regent and a man also known to Harriette Wilson. In later life, after declining to buy himself out of the pages of her book, he instead offered her his legal expertise in recompense for her neglecting to mention him.[2] Harriette's opinion of his performance on the occasion of his defence of Lord Charles Bentinck was high indeed: 'In short never was Brougham himself more eloquent! Not even on that memorable day when he was employed by Lord Charles Bentinck to show just cause why Lady Abdy ought to have cuckolded Sir William as she did.'

Lord Charles must therefore have been somewhat relieved when the jury presiding over the case awarded damages of only £7,000; still a considerable sum of money but not nearly as bad for him as it could have been. He set off to join his lady in Paris and in April Sir William Abdy also visited the city. Back in London preparations were under way for the wedding of the Prince Regent's daughter, Princess Charlotte, to the impoverished but handsome Prince Leopold of Saxe-Coburg-Saalfeld (later known as Saxe-Coburg and Gotha); they married at the beginning of May 1816 in the Crimson Drawing Room at the regent's London residence, Carlton House. The young bride was heard to giggle during the marriage ceremony, which took place on 2 May 1816, when Prince Leopold promised to endow her with all his worldly goods.

Princess Charlotte of Wales had proved somewhat troublesome to her royal father. Inheriting both her mother's unruliness and her father's petulance in equal measure to offset her natural charm and gaiety, she had in turn infuriated and captivated a succession of governesses and annoyed the prince who resented his popular daughter. Pretty, if a little plump, both Princess Charlotte and her mother Caroline, Princess of Wales were loved by the populace, who by and large disliked and mistrusted the prince. Charlotte spent many months of her adolescence sequestered in seclusion at Windsor with Queen Charlotte and her maiden aunts, the three unmarried daughters of King George III. Interminable days were spent bent over embroidery while the old king could be heard wailing in his madness and Charlotte was desperate to escape from such splendid captivity.

When the question of her marriage reared its head her father settled on Prince William of Orange, heir to the Dutch throne and popularly known as 'Slender Billy'. Charlotte opposed the match as, once married, she would have to live in Holland for most of the year, something her father was all in favour of (the Prince Regent was ever wary of Charlotte eclipsing him in the public's eyes). For her part, Charlotte worried that if she left England she would also leave the way clear for her father to instigate a divorce against his hated wife and the last thing Charlotte wanted to see was her father free to remarry and able to father a male heir who would take precedence over her in the succession to the throne. She had been brought up expecting to be queen one day and she would brook no other direction in her life.

Desperately scheming to prevent her marriage to Slender Billy while still keeping her father's goodwill (which was ever on a knife-edge where Charlotte was concerned), she nevertheless managed to embark on at least two ill-fated and ill-considered romances. Neither of the objects of her affection would have been deemed suitable by her father and she lived in constant fear of him discovering her romantic escapades.

Finally, she alighted on Leopold – handsome and well-connected but utterly impoverished – and her father was persuaded to agree to the match. Although at the outset Charlotte's main attraction, in Leopold's eyes, was the possibility of a crown, he did quickly fall in love with his tempestuous tomboy of a wife and they were happy together.

As one marriage began, another approached its conclusion. Just over a fortnight after the royal wedding the proceedings that would enable the Abdys to divorce were heard in the Consistory Court at Doctors' Commons on Paternoster Row near St Paul's Cathedral. Around the middle of May the sentence of divorce was finally signed and that merely left the question of whether the divorce should be from bed and board only and the clause prohibiting both parties from remarrying should be inserted into the parliamentary bill that had to pass through the House of Lords. The bishops and some of the Lords, notably George Kenyon, 2nd Baron Kenyon, felt strongly that the clause should indeed be inserted, but most of the men to whom the decision fell looked to the Lord Chancellor (John Scott, later 1st Earl of Eldon) for direction.

The divorce bill was committed, leading to a brief and terse notice in the newspapers stating that 'after a short conversation, the allowance to the adulteress was fixed at £400 a year.'[3] On Monday, 10 June the Abdys' divorce bill received its second reading in the House of Lords. The Earl of Limerick,

Edmund Pery, stated to the House that Sir William was content to allow Anne to receive the full interest on the fortune she had brought to her marriage, should the Lords think it proper, and then the Earl of Lauderdale stood up and insisted upon a date being agreed for the third reading of the bill. He proposed 17 June, the following Monday. Lord Kenyon then stood to speak: he could not attend on that day and while he sorely wanted to be present, he did not feel that he could insist on the day being changed to suit him alone.

Wheels had been turning behind the scenes and Anne's father had been writing letters and begging favours, notably from James Maitland, the 8th Earl of Lauderdale. To have the bill read on 17 June achieved two objects: firstly to have it read when Lord Kenyon, the most vocal and strenuous opponent of allowing Anne the freedom to remarry was absent; and secondly, and perhaps more importantly, it was but a day before the first anniversary of the great victory at Waterloo. With the contingent goodwill towards the Duke of Wellington on that day, it would seem churlish of the Lords to refuse his niece a chance of future happiness. The duke himself, still abroad, had been approached for his assistance in speaking to some of his friends in the House of Lords and had replied: 'You may depend upon it I will do *all*, everything in my power to forward your wishes. God forbid such an affliction [i.e. not being able to remarry] should be added to what has already been suffered.'[4]

The ruse worked and the bill received its third reading without the insertion of the clause; both Sir William and Lady Anne were free to marry again if they so wished and it passed just in time too. Anne, back in London with Lord Charles, was almost at the end of her pregnancy and the urgent and pressing concern of the Wellesleys now was to get the pair married before history repeated itself and the child was born illegitimate. A licence was procured and the couple married the next day at the elegant church of St Martin-in-the-Fields, Westminster. With the divorced and heavily-pregnant bride described on the register as Anne Wellesley, single and unmarried, it was conducted on a cold and dismal summer day with little pomp or ceremony. To the relief of all concerned it was done; for better or for worse, Lord Charles Bentinck and Lady Anne were now man and wife.[5] Thoughts then turned to Anne's lying-in and less than two months after the marriage a daughter was born, named Anne Hyacinthe in honour of her mother and grandmother.[6]

While the courtroom drama concerning her daughter's divorce had been unfolding, Lady Wellesley had spent the summer travelling on the Continent with her son Henry, hoping that the warmer weather might improve her failing health. They made first for Brussels (which was crowded with people visiting the nearby Waterloo battlefield) where they took rooms in the hôtel Bellevue, a popular lodging for British tourists, before travelling on to Spa to take the waters. Hyacinthe Gabrielle remembered Spa as a fashionable resort from the heady days when her husband had still adored her and they had visited together, but now it was sadly altered and she was reluctant to mix with the English visitors there, fearing Anne's elopement would be the topic of conversation. Henry, however, thoroughly enjoyed himself, participating in picnics (when the dismal weather allowed), balls and visits to the theatre. Nevertheless, money was a constant issue and Lady Wellesley wrote to her son Richard, anxiously asking him to check if her allowance had been paid into her bank account and worried that her husband's mounting debts would mean she would suffer the consequences.

Her husband had been forced to sell the magnificent Apsley House to his younger brother Arthur, a humiliating necessity for such a proud man. In a satire written almost a decade later in 1825 it was suggested that the marquess had given his former paramour Miss Leshley (aka Moll Raffles) a bond for £7,000 on Apsley House during their time together and when the duke took possession his entitlement was disputed by the lady, by then the wealthy wife of a Spanish gentleman named Caballero. Wellington, it was reputed, was forced to pay Madame Caballero the forfeiture of the bond. Any financial gain for the marquess from the sale of Apsley House was swiftly negated when he discovered that the agents selling his remaining Irish estates on his behalf had vanished, taking with them the profits from the sale. Lady Wellesley and Henry decided it was time for them to return to England and they again stopped at Brussels during their journey.

The hôtel Bellevue was full to bursting and the landlord had not a room to spare. Leaving his mother in the coach, Henry disappeared into the city to find rooms elsewhere and while he was gone Lady Wellesley was interrupted by two gentlemen who walked up to her carriage to speak to her. She was most surprised to see they were none other than her former son-in-law Sir William Abdy and his travelling companion the Honourable Mr King, a close friend of Anne's supposed former paramour Fred Lamb; the pair had just arrived in Brussels.[7]

Tactfully neither Hyacinthe Gabrielle nor Sir William mentioned Anne, instead discussing the recent sale of Apsley House and Mrs Littleton's children before being interrupted by the landlord of the hôtel Bellevue who, reluctant to offend a marchioness by turning her from his door, offered Lady Wellesley the use of a suite of rooms he had been reserving for Prince Adolphus, the Duke of Cambridge, who had not arrived to take them. With that the former mother and son-in-law cordially parted, never to set eyes on one another again.[8]

Lady Wellesley was kept abreast of the news from home concerning her children and she wrote to her son Richard from Brussels before departing for England, commenting a little disparagingly on the news that Anne had been delivered of a fine and healthy baby girl: 'It's a bit soon after the marriage but she's lucky to have achieved that... [but] I would have preferred her having a son since he [Lord Charles] already has a daughter by his first wife.'[9]

Hyacinthe Gabrielle made straight for the Bentincks' new home in Brompton where, despite her disappointment in a granddaughter rather than a grandson, she cooed delightedly over the baby and made her peace with Anne. After spending some time there she decided on a fortnight's visit to her other daughter at Teddesley Hall, having never ventured into Staffordshire to stay with the Littletons before. Henry accompanied his mother and the first ten days of her visit passed pleasurably, if quietly, and Lady Wellesley was occupied with making plans for the future. She intended to return to London and had ideas about spending the winter in Paris; with the cessation of the war many of the émigrées who lived in London and with whom Hyacinthe Gabrielle had been great friends had returned to their native country. She longed to see Paris again and live, for a time at least, among her compatriots.

However, her plans came to nothing. What had at first seemed to be nothing more serious than a cold turned, within two short days, into a much more serious complaint and Lady Wellesley, her breathing laboured, was unable to leave her bed. Henry and Hyacinthe were by her side when the end came, as Hyacinthe related in a letter to her brother Richard informing him of his mother's death:

> At one o'clock she ate her soup heartily and drank a full glass of wine. At about two she had occasion to get up in bed and I supported her, when she said, '*Je suis bien faible* [I am very weak]' and laid her head upon my shoulder and expired without a groan so easily that I continued holding her for some time before I suspected the truth. Conceive my horror (as well as that of Henry) upon finding as I raised her that she was dead![10]

Hyacinthe Gabrielle, Marchioness Wellesley was buried by her bereft children in the Littleton vault at Penkridge Church (where a tablet was erected to commemorate her life). She had written her will in 1813 when Anne was still Lady Abdy and the wife of the 'richest commoner in the land' and had not stood in need of any financial help from her mother. As a result, and purely for practical reasons, Anne was not left as much as some of her siblings. However, during Anne's separation from her husband and the events leading up to the divorce, Lady Wellesley had added a codicil to her will which, in effect, wrote Anne out of it. This may have been intended only as a temporary measure to prevent Sir William from being able to claim any part of Lady Wellesley's estate on behalf of his wife while they were separated but still legally married but, if so, during the few months in which she would have been able to she did not revoke or alter the codicil. As a result, Anne was left little upon her mother's death and Lord Charles' bank balance was nowhere near the same size as Sir William's had been; an inheritance from her mother would have been a welcome boost to their family finances. The Marquess Wellesley too was left with nothing, despite making an attempt to stop the probate of the will and cutting off the allowance he paid to his sons Richard and Henry when they would not deliver their mother's papers into his hands. Hyacinthe Littleton kept a few mementos, including a treasured lock of her mother's hair, for the rest of her life.[11]

Sir William Abdy had withheld the annuity of £400 a year he should have paid to his former wife as a form of revenge and leverage because Lord Charles had neglected to pay the £7,000 awarded in damages, although in truth Lord Charles had neither the means nor the wherewithal to do so. Anne's brother Richard was once more brought into the fray and Sir William was finally convinced that, as it had been decreed in law, he had no alternative but to pay the annuity, irrespective of the damages still being outstanding. In fact, it would appear that Lord Charles never did pay a penny to Sir William.

The Bentincks' financial difficulties became all too apparent in an unseemly tug-of-war for possession of Lord Charles' 4-year-old daughter from his first marriage. Little Georgiana had, since her mother's death, lived mostly with the Marquess and Marchioness of Cholmondeley but after her father's second marriage she returned to his house on a protracted visit. Lady Cholmondeley now proposed to adopt the young girl (occasional visits to her father would be allowed), and in this event Lord Cholmondeley would settle £5,000 on her (a small fortune and one that her father would never be able to provide) but the new Lady Charles threw a spanner into the works. She proclaimed herself so attached to the child that she could not give her up, writing (in a cruelly detached way) to her brother Richard: 'I have been so harrassed [sic] about Ld. C's child. I don't know what to do. It makes me quite miserable the idea of giving it up, that I have been quite ill about it ...'[12]

Lord Charles' relatives were all strongly behind the Cholmondeleys' offer. The Wellesleys tried to remain neutral as much as possible (the young girl was, after all, a Cavendish-Bentinck) but Richard was one of the few people who could bring any influence to bear on his headstrong sister and so, against his better judgement, he was drawn into the affair. Lord Charles enlisted the help of his older brother Lord William Bentinck, an army officer and MP, to mediate with the Cholmondeleys.

The affair dragged on for some months with little Georgiana a pawn in a wider game; Anne indicated that she would be prepared to hand her over to the Cholmondeleys if some of the money to be settled on her could be diverted instead to her new baby daughter and to any other children she might have. With Lord Charles' finances in tatters, Anne was loath to see her step-daughter so well provided for when her own children would be left with nothing. She soon brought her weak-willed husband around to her viewpoint and he wrote to his brother, Lord William, pointing out that Georgiana was already amply provided for (with her mother dead she was a beneficiary from the marriage settlement made after his first wedding) and had 'great expectations' from her grandmother, Grace Dalrymple Elliott, who was living near the Bentincks in Brompton and possibly saw her granddaughter frequently during this period.

Mrs Elliott was, perhaps, the one person who was happy with the situation as it had unfolded with regard to Georgiana, one that gave her easy access to her young granddaughter upon whom she doted. Her views on who should ultimately care for Georgiana have not survived but as she gave over the care of her daughter to the Cholmondeleys, she probably also saw the benefits of her granddaughter living with them and knew she could trust them implicitly to love and care for her. As a woman with a scandalous past, and still notorious because of it, Grace herself would have been considered unsuitable as a permanent guardian of her young granddaughter. Lord Charles now wanted the Cholmondeleys' £5,000 to be settled on the children of his second marriage but Lord Cholmondeley disliked being held to ransom and was annoyed to see his kind-hearted wife, who was genuinely fond of the little girl as she had been of her mother before her, so broken-hearted over the whole debacle. He threatened to withdraw his offer and wash his hands of the whole affair, leaving everything at an impasse.

Chapter Six

The Birth of the Next Generation

On 6 November 1817 the young Princess Charlotte of Wales died following a complicated childbirth during which her son was delivered stillborn. The Prince Regent was distraught and the whole country was plunged into mourning.

On the same day the arguments over the money to be settled on Georgiana and her half-siblings, as well as the problem of where Georgiana should live, were finally decided once and for all. Georgiana had already been returned to the care of the Cholmondeleys and now two sums of £5,000 were settled upon her, one by Lord Cholmondeley and the other by Mrs Elliott (although Grace Dalrymple Elliott was to receive the dividends on her share during her lifetime) and the Duke of Portland settled a substantial sum of money on the children of Lord Charles Bentinck's second family (the young Anne and any further children to be born to the couple). Lady Cholmondeley was formally appointed as Georgiana's guardian and in the event of her death before Georgiana was of age or married, her sister, the 21st Baroness Willoughby de Eresby, or her daughter Lady Charlotte Cholmondeley would take over the responsibility.[1] After having made such a fuss of keeping her step-daughter by her side, in the end Anne had made little of giving her up. In a letter to her brother Richard, sent to the Steyne Hotel in Brighton where he had gone for his health, she wrote:

> For my part, I must say she has been a source of little comfort to me. I have had so much annoyance and unpleasant things to counterbalance the pleasure of her society that I think I shall not regret her loss as much as I should have done five months ago. I hope all parties will now be pleased tho' I daresay they will still find some new subject to complain of ... I rather dread the thought of it [Georgiana's departure], but one good thing is that I shall not feel a stronger feeling than that of missing her when she is gone, for she is so devoid of affection herself and so difficult a child to what she was originally. Besides, knowing that she has to leave me, I have not allowed myself to attach myself to her ...[2]

Hopefully young Georgiana was showered with love and affection by the kindly Lady Cholmondeley. Hopefully Anne was also more maternal towards her own offspring. Her sister Hyacinthe thought so, for she wrote to Gerald Wellesley (who was out in India) telling him Anne was 'doatingly [sic] fond' of her young daughter.[3] At the time Hyacinthe was writing, Anne was once more pregnant and on the same day the Princess died and the settlement was signed she gave birth for the second time to a fine and healthy boy, William Charles Cavendish Bentinck.[4] If the Bentinck household had been aware of the trauma suffered by Princess Charlotte who had been delivered of a still-born boy a day earlier (and as Lord Charles was close to the king he, at least, had possibly heard the news) and her subsequent death in the early hours of the morning, it must have been a day of trepidation for them. Anne would certainly have been unaware of another birth that took place in a setting far removed from these events but only weeks before them. In the picturesque chocolate-box countryside to the south of the Cumnor Hills in Oxfordshire, a young girl was born to a humble gypsy mother, a girl who would become pivotal in the life of the Cavendish-Bentinck family when their two worlds collided. She was given her mother's name, Sinnetta.

In London a constitutional crisis loomed: King George III had thirteen children but between them they had managed only the one legitimate child and she had just died. The remaining unwed princes began an unseemly scramble to produce an heir and the Duke of Kent and Strathearn, Prince Edward, won the race. He made a hasty marriage to the late Princess Charlotte's sister-in-law, the widowed Princess Victoire of Saxe-Coburg-Saalfeld and in 1819 the Princess Alexandrina Victoria of Kent was born, the heir apparent to the hopes of a nation. Victoire had previously been the wife of the Prince of Leiningen and had two children by him: a son who remained in mainland Europe and a daughter, Princess Feodora, twelve years older than her new baby half-sister.[5]

For Lord and Lady Charles Bentinck two more children followed in quick succession: a second son named Arthur born in 1819 just over two weeks before the young Princess Alexandrina Victoria, and a daughter Emily born in 1820. Arthur was named for his famed great-uncle and the duke stood as his godfather. The children were born in the Bentincks' snug, private and pretty little Brompton villa, accessed via its own narrow lane. Known as The Hermitage, it had formerly been occupied by the Italian opera singer and diva Madame Angelica Catalani until Lord Charles had bought it shortly after his second marriage and there the family lived in a form of contentment, even if Anne was a little piqued at not being invited to the kind of society events at which she would have taken centre stage before her elopement. After many years of childless marriage to Sir William she found herself, within five years of her elopement, the mother of four youngsters and so had plenty to occupy herself with in the hustle and bustle of family life.[6]

Despite the wedding and a clutch of new nieces and nephews, Anne's sister Hyacinthe still had no high opinion of her brother-in-law, saying of him in a letter to her brother Gerald: 'He behaves very well to her [Anne], but unfortunately is abominably stupid, which is a great pity for her to live solely with him.'[7]

Since the Wellesley children had been estranged from their father following their mother's death and their refusal to give up her papers, in 1819 the Duke of Wellington played mediator and hosted a dinner party at Apsley House where children and father could be reconciled, only to be enraged when the Marquess Wellesley arrived ingloriously at his former home bringing with him Edward John Johnston, now a handsome young man in his early twenties and the spitting image of his father.[8] The duke, who had a low opinion of Johnston, was horrified that he had turned up, unannounced and uninvited, to take his place alongside his Wellesley half-siblings and no seat at the table had been prepared for him. Lord Hatherton and his wife were there (Johnston was introduced to Hatherton, but not as Wellesley's son), as were Richard and Henry (Gerald was in India).

At the end of the evening Lord and Lady Charles Bentinck arrived and were received fondly enough by the marquess who had not visited his daughter since her elopement. The only male representatives of her family who had called on her since her second marriage were her brothers and the ever-kindly Duke of Wellington who had been most pressing in his invitations to her for his dinner party. If the duke had visited his niece, then he would no doubt have seen and played with his young great-niece and nephews. Hopefully the marquess asked after his new Cavendish-Bentinck grandson (Arthur's birth had been just under three months earlier) and even with the presence of the cuckoo in the nest, in the form of Johnston, the duke's scheme seemed to have worked.[9]

Living as a recluse in Windsor Castle, the old, mad King George III had been feeble for many years, blind too towards the end and also hard of hearing; he was largely unaware of the death of his wife, Queen Charlotte, two years earlier. He finally shuffled off this mortal coil in January 1820, six days after the death of his son Edward, Duke of Kent and Strathearn (father of the young Princess Alexandrina Victoria) and Lord Charles' patron, friend and employer ascended the throne. The Bentincks had every expectation of good fortune and a boost to their bank balance from this event.

At the Court held at Carlton House, the new king's grand London 'town house', on 12 February, among a select few present including the Archbishop of Canterbury, the Duke of Wellington and Viscount Castlereagh was Lord Charles Bentinck.[10] His name sat awkwardly in the list of those present, the majority of whom held a peerage or high political or ecclesiastical office (or both) and his presence in such illustrious company confirmed his status as one of the king's closest confidantes and allies. It was both a blessing and a curse: he could expect his position within the king's household to bring him great benefits but he was totally dependent upon his patron's largesse and good favour; with one ill-judged action he could find himself with neither employment nor prospects. Lord Charles was 'sworn in' to King George IV's Privy Council and later appointed as Treasurer of the Royal Household. As such he appeared in the funeral procession when King George III was buried and also played a part in the new king's coronation held in midsummer of the following year. With Lord Charles Bentinck's elevated status the family took up a new residence at Eaton Place in Pimlico.[11]

Upon hearing that her husband had ascended the throne, Caroline returned from her self-imposed exile in Italy, determined to be crowned as his queen. The new king moved quickly, beginning proceedings in the House of Lords that almost amounted to a state trial against his estranged wife. He wanted a divorce. Riding on a tidal wave of public sympathy, Caroline was ultimately jubilant when the bill was thrown out, despite the accusations of her immorality (it was suggested that she and her Italian servant Bartolomeo Pergami had been living as man and wife), although if Caroline had committed adultery then it was no more than her husband had done many times before. She was successfully represented by Henry Brougham, the same man who had defended Lord Charles Bentinck at his Crim. Con. case back in 1816.

The new king had a great love of costume, theatre and pageantry and he planned an extravagant and costly spectacle for his coronation, one he was determined would never be outdone by any future monarch. The total cost approached a quarter of a million pounds, around twenty times more than his father's coronation had cost in 1761. Ever a lover of fashion and frippery, George IV personally oversaw the design for the costumes of all the participants in the event, basing them on Tudor fashions; perhaps Lord Charles Bentinck, perpetually at George's side, played a role in suggesting and approving the outlandish plans? Certainly, as part of the inner circle around the king, he would have been privy to the preparations. Always ready to outshine Napoléon Bonaparte, the man whom he had viewed as his great rival and who had only recently died on St Helena never having regained his liberty (when the new king had been given the news that his bitterest enemy was dead his first thought was that it was his wife, and he replied to the messenger: 'Is she, by God!'), George was determined that his coronation should be more spectacular than the one in which Bonaparte was crowned emperor in 1804.

The king, worried that his disaffected wife would turn up at the coronation (she did!), had designed outfits representing Tudor pages for a collection of prize fighters whose function would be to prevent her entrance. Although she tried desperately to get into the Abbey, demanding to be crowned alongside her husband and crying, 'Let me pass, I am your Queen', Caroline was thwarted in her aims and retired.

One of Lord Charles' duties on the morning of the Coronation was to distribute medals to the judges in accordance with his position as Treasurer of the Royal Household. He duly turned up at the appointed time with a crimson bag containing silver and gold medals, specially minted for the occasion, solemnly handed them out to the assembled judges and then left. Shortly thereafter he returned, more than a little shamefaced, and admitted he was only supposed to have handed out the silver medals to the judges, the gold ones being intended for some slightly more illustrious recipients. The disgruntled judicial officials reluctantly handed back the gold medals, averting a potential disaster for the hapless Lord Charles Bentinck.

Later in the day, the incident forgotten, he took his place in the grand coronation procession from Westminster Hall which culminated inside Westminster Abbey, the route decorated to convey the old idea of feudal grandeur and chivalry set off by the Gothic architecture of the richly-decorated buildings lining it. Crowds of people jostled for the best view and the scene on that bright summer day did indeed remind them of the days of jousts and tournaments. The procession finally arrived at the Abbey and entered its venerable precincts at a quarter past eleven in the morning. James, Marquess of Graham (the eldest son of the 3rd Duke of Montrose), dressed in a scarlet mantle with a crown embroidered on his left shoulder and attended by an officer from the Jewel House, bore a cushion holding the ruby coronation ring that was to be placed on the king's finger and the ceremonial and bejewelled state sword (made especially for the coronation) that would be fastened around the king's girth. Behind him came, side by side, Lord George Thomas Beresford, Comptroller of the royal household and Lord Charles Bentinck as Treasurer of the Household, the latter bearing the crimson bag containing the remaining medals. Behind them, dressed in a tabard, was the Bluemantle Pursuivant of Arms and following him was John Bourke, the 4th Earl of Mayo, bearing the Standard of Hanover.[12]

It has not been recorded whether Anne managed to get one of the sought-after seats within the Abbey to watch the grand ceremony. Possibly her husband had managed to secure one for her as he was so blessed with the good favour of his Royal Highness, but if not she would have obtained a ticket to one of the seats in the stands erected outside (although she would have been extremely disgruntled to have had to watch from such a lowly position). Perhaps she also took her two eldest children with her, little Anne and Charley (as her eldest son was known to his family and as we shall henceforth address him to distinguish him from his father) who were then aged 4 and 3, to admire and watch their father play his part with pomp and ceremony?[13]

Some few places behind Lord Charles Bentinck in the procession was George James, Marquess of Cholmondeley in his state robes and with his coronet held in his hand. As he was the guardian of young Georgiana Cavendish Bentinck, possibly she too was present in the Abbey on the day with the Marchioness of Cholmondeley, watching her papa officiate at her putative grandfather's coronation. Anne's father, Marquess Wellesley, was one of the peers who carried the state regalia; the sceptre with the cross was borne by him. The Duke of Wellington was also there in his state robes, attended by a page who carried his field marshal's baton and, finally, the king himself surrounded by his bishops and Band of Gentlemen Pensioners and in his hot and heavy royal robes, adorned with jewels and under a canopy of cloth of gold that was supported by sixteen Barons of the Cinque Ports. The king's train was carried by eight eldest sons of peers, among them the Duke of Wellington's son Arthur Richard Wellesley, Marquess of Douro and the Earl of Rocksavage, the Marquess of Cholmondeley's son. Perhaps the new king had failed to realize quite how hot the elaborate costumes would be when he designed them, for the year had generally been cold, particularly throughout the spring and early summer, with a flurry of snow even being recorded as falling in London towards the end of May. They were far too heavy for the warm weather on the day of the coronation.

With the perspiring monarch crowned and shouts of 'God Save the King' echoing throughout the Abbey, the royal dukes and other peers of the realm advanced to kneel in front of him to do homage and Lord Charles scattered the medals he held in his crimson bag in profusion along the great aisle and among the seats of the peers and peeresses. He had also, during the crowning, presented an ingot of gold weighing one pound to Peter Drummond-Burrell, the 22nd Baron Willoughby de Eresby and the Deputy Lord Great Chamberlain, as a symbolic offering.[14]

In mid-afternoon the procession began again, leaving the Abbey and retracing its steps along the route where the spectators in the stands had endured the heat of the day rather than lose their seat. The newly-anointed king was steadily wilting in his overblown ceremonial costume, trussed up underneath with elaborate stays to hold in his girth and distressed almost to the point of fainting. 'Several times he was at the last gasp; he looked more like the victim than the hero of the fête,' according to Lady Cowper (formerly Emily Lamb, a noted beauty and the sister of Lady Abdy's putative seducer Fred Lamb). The king had to be discreetly revived with sal volatile (smelling salts), after which he recovered enough to flirt with the plump and middle-aged Marchioness Conyngham, his latest (and last) mistress, to the disapproval of the Archbishop of Canterbury and the notice of the Duke of Wellington who thought he behaved in a highly improper fashion during the ceremony, 'even in the most important and solemn parts.'[15] The society hostess (and Wellington's great friend) Mrs Harriet Arbuthnot, who was present at the ceremony, recalled the king taking a diamond brooch from his chest and kissing it while looking meaningfully at Lady Conyngham, and in reply she took off her glove and kissed a ring she was wearing. His appearance did not impress Mrs Arbuthnot, who said of her new monarch: 'Anybody who could have seen his disgusting figure, with a wig the curls of which hung down his back, and quite bending beneath the weight of his robes and his 60 years would have been quite sick.'[16]

Elizabeth, Lady Conyngham had set her cap at the prince two years earlier; she was thought to be a shrewd and greedy woman but could also be kind-hearted and she was still beautiful, if a little voluptuous. She was exactly the kind of woman the prince found most attractive and her hold upon him continued when he ascended to the throne. The Duke of Wellington loathed her. Harriette Wilson, in her capacity as a courtesan, knew all about Lady Conyngham's past indiscretions as the two women had shared the affections of the handsome John Ponsonby, 1st Viscount Ponsonby, and Harriette had managed to lay her hands on a cache of letters that Elizabeth had written to him. The unscrupulous Harriette would, in due course, use those love-letters to blackmail both the marchioness and the king.

However, for all the censure from those viewing from within the Abbey, most of the spectators outside were delighted by the pomp and ceremony and also by their king who had attracted neither their respect nor their love for some years. During the return to Westminster Hall Lord Charles amused himself by throwing silver medals into the air for the spectating crowds to scrabble over. A sumptuous banquet awaited the party where 336 guests sat down to dine and although it was still daylight a profusion of candles and chandeliers had been lit; an estimated 2,000 lights glimmered above and around the tables. With the sun gleaming in through the windows, the artificial illumination only served to detract from the overall spectacle and caused consternation to those seated below the candles; not only did it increase the heat but large globules of melted wax fell, without distinction, onto the heads of the great and the good. It was noted that 'the very great heat was nowhere more visible than in the havoc which it made upon the curls of many of the ladies, several of whose heads had lost all traces of the friseur's skill long before the ceremony of the day was concluded.'[17]

Following the coronation Lady Conyngham had arranged for the king to make a visit to Ireland, including a private visit to Slane Castle in County Meath, her husband's ancestral estate on the banks of the River Boyne where he would stay for a few days. However, her plans were thrown into disarray when Caroline of Brunswick died suddenly. Reeling from the refusal to grant her entry to the Abbey and denied the right to call herself a queen, Caroline had unwisely attended a re-enactment of the coronation at a Drury Lane theatre a few days later. Returning home, depressed and unwell, she took to her bed and after nine days and nights of intense pain she died at her residence in Hammersmith, Brandenburg House. The cause of death was recorded by her doctors as an obstruction of the bowels, attended by inflammation.

The king was conflicted by his emotions; he was moved by his wife's death, although clearly not bereft. Any show of false grief would be seized upon and the king would be mocked, but he still had appearances to consider and he could not simply ignore the event. He decided to go ahead with his jaunt but to spend the first few days on Irish soil in retirement as a mark of respect. Making arrangements for any of Caroline's jewels that belonged to him to be reclaimed and for her body to be shipped out of the country as quickly as possible (Caroline was buried in her homeland of Brunswick), the king put to sea. His courtiers were horrified to see him merrily disembark from the ship hours later, rolling drunk and enthusiastically shaking hands with a fisherman by the name of Pat Farrell. The Irish people loved him and he was enchanted by them.[18]

In anticipation of the benefits to come from their patron now holding the highest position in the land, at the end of 1821 the young Bentinck family moved once again, from Eaton Place to another small but elegant town house, 1 North Row, situated on the corner adjoining Park Lane and Norfolk Street (now known as Dunraven Street). An interesting coincidence, one of which Lord Charles was possibly unaware, was that the neighbouring house on that corner, 19 Norfolk Street, was for some years the residence of the eighteenth-century rake and politician Colonel Richard FitzPatrick, an intimate friend of Charles James Fox. Many years earlier, in the mid-1780s and over twenty years before he married Georgiana Seymour, Lord Charles' first mother-in-law, the courtesan Grace Dalrymple Elliott, had been living at

FitzPatrick's house as his mistress, 'azurizing' herself during April of 1784 by dressing in blue to proclaim her allegiance to his political party in the Westminster elections.[19]

From 1821 Park Lane and the surrounding area underwent refurbishment and improvements (only 100 years earlier it had been a simple trackway running alongside Hyde Park and known as Tyburn Lane). Benjamin Dean Wyatt had been commissioned to carry out work on Apsley House in Piccadilly at the other end of Park Lane, formerly the home of Anne's father but now owned by her uncle, the Duke of Wellington. Popularly known as Number One, London (due to it being the first house a traveller into London would pass by after entering through the Knightsbridge tollgate), Apsley House was actually 149 Piccadilly. Throughout the 1820s Park Lane was reconstructed with some of the older houses demolished and other existing ones enhanced with balconies and verandas facing Hyde Park to take advantage of the views afforded them. Even Hyde Park itself was given a facelift. Property values soared and Lord Charles Bentinck, so often derided for being something of a simpleton, on this occasion had proved himself astute in moving to the right property at the right time. Lord and Lady Charles Bentinck also maintained a country residence at Tunbridge Wells in Kent.[20]

Chapter Seven

Trials and Tribulations

In the summer months of 1822 Lady Anne Bentinck was once again pregnant. Always a little snappy, the discomfort of being *enceinte* in such hot weather only exaggerated the problem and she upset one of her servants with her rude and imperious behaviour.

Anne had been out in her carriage and had left her shawl inside the vehicle. Robert Manby, her footman, without being instructed took it upon himself to deliver the shawl to his mistress in her drawing room. Lady Anne was irate: he was a mere servant and had no business to meddle with her belongings without her orders and, with his ears ringing with her stinging admonition, he was told to carry the shawl back to the carriage that instant. Robert Manby, a man of spirit, took offence at her tone. He coolly informed her ladyship that, in his opinion, he had performed his duty properly and if she wished him to neglect his duty in the future he would do so but he flatly refused to take the shawl back to the carriage (perhaps anticipating that the haughty Anne would then command him to fetch it for her after all). Anne was aghast at her servant's disobedience and totally bewildered by being spoken to in such a way; did he not know his place? She repeated her instruction and, once again, Robert refused to do her bidding. At length Lord Charles was fetched and he tried, in vain, to persuade the footman to replace the shawl in the carriage. With everyone fully at the end of their respective tethers, Robert was ordered to immediately quit the house and his service but he stood firm. He would leave, he told his employers, only upon payment of a month's wages; it seemed the Bentincks had met their match. Charles, in a pique and fully enraged by his recalcitrant servant's insolence, manfully took him by the scruff of the neck and threw him out of the door, down the steps and onto the street below.

Knowing that he was now out on his ear without a reference or his outstanding pay, Robert Manby made straight for the local magistrate's office and lodged a complaint there, saying he had been assaulted by his employer. Lord Charles was duly summoned to attend and answer for his actions, although, due to his rank, he was afforded the courtesy of being heard in a private rather than a public room.

Seated in front of George Rowland Minshull, the sitting magistrate at Bow Street, Lord Charles got a sympathetic hearing, although Minshull offered as his opinion his regret that the Bentincks had not called for a constable rather than forcibly ejecting Manby from their home themselves. With matters as they were, Lord Charles admitted the assault and though the magistrate deferentially thought his heavy-handed approach totally understandable, given the circumstances he had to order him to enter into a recognizance to appear at the next sessions to answer any complaint that Manby might make against him. Robert Manby played one more throw of the dice, suggesting he would overlook the assault in lieu of a month's wages, but it was now Lord Charles Bentinck's turn to be imperious and he refused to listen, instead entering into the required recognizance which, luckily for Lord Charles, proved unnecessary. The whole affair paints a fairly accurate picture of the household in which young Charley and his siblings were growing up: one of entitlement and haughty impetuosity. It is a testament to Charley that, in later life, he showed he had not inherited his parents' attitude to those who they viewed very much as their 'inferiors'.[1]

It was in the North Row town house that Anne gave birth for the fifth and final time on 14 November 1822 to a son who was named Frederick William Cavendish Bentinck but who failed to thrive. The infant was buried one week later.

Anne's husband had been absent from her side for a great deal of time towards the end of her pregnancy, busy on official business and accompanying King George IV on his inaugural visit to Scotland in August, never far from the monarch's side throughout the trip. Stage-managed by the author Sir Walter Scott and containing a profusion of plaid (thereby overturning the censure on this material that had resulted from the Jacobite rebellions of the eighteenth century), the king was well received by his Caledonian subjects and thoroughly enjoyed his time there. The weather was terrible (it rained on most days) and John Murray, the old 4th Duke of Atholl, scathingly dubbed it 'one and twenty daft days', but overall it was a success. The flamboyant king appeared in full highland dress on just the one occasion during the trip, complete with a kilt that was a little too short and a pair of pink tights to hide his pasty white legs.[2]

The following year Grace Dalrymple Elliott, King George's old paramour from his handsome youth, died at the modest house in Ville d'Avray near Paris in which she had taken refuge during the last years of her life, years blighted by ill health. Her one remaining descendant was her young grand-daughter Georgiana Cavendish Bentinck and the two were extremely fond of

one another; Georgiana had often stayed in Paris with her doting grandmother. If Lord Charles was hoping that the faded courtesan would leave a
fortune to his eldest daughter he was sadly mistaken, as Grace could barely
leave more than her best wishes to her granddaughter. It was as well that the
money originally settled on the first Lady Charles Bentinck by her guardian
Lord Cholmondeley and by Grace had been protected, for there was precious
little else. Grace named the Marchioness of Cholmondeley as the executor of
her will, and the good lady patiently attempted to sort out Grace's affairs,
both in England and in Paris. Lord Cholmondeley, with less patience, had to
fund Grace's burial in Paris.[3]

The ageing Marquess Wellesley married for a second time in October
1825, a marriage that caused further divisions among his siblings and children. His choice of bride was a wealthy American lady, Marianne Patterson
née Caton. Marianne, born in Baltimore, Maryland in 1788, was the eldest of
four sisters, and with two of her sisters – Elizabeth (Bess) and Louisa – came
to England in the early summer of 1816 accompanied by Marianne's husband
Robert Patterson.[4] The sisters were instantly the toast of London society and
were courted by the Duke of Wellington who was struck by Marianne's
beauty. They would have heard first-hand the gossip surrounding the elopement of Wellington's niece Lady Anne Abdy and her subsequent remarriage
as they moved in the same social circles, fêted everywhere they went. A year
later they travelled to Paris as the guests of the duke and it was widely
believed that Marianne Patterson and the Duke of Wellington were carrying
on an 'intrigue' and were in fact lovers. No evidence remains to prove this
but they were certainly enamoured of one another, great friends and particularly intimate indeed. The Marquess Wellesley was infuriated by his younger
brother's good fortune, for he also had his eye on the beautiful Mrs Patterson
and he was widowed and free to marry. To escape the gossip, and at the
instigation of her husband, Marianne returned to Baltimore.

Robert Patterson then died of cholera in Maryland during the 'fever
season' of 1822 and two years later Marianne, a wealthy widow, sailed back to
England for the recovery of her health. During the summer months of 1825
Marianne Patterson and her sister Bess travelled to Dublin to fulfil a promise
to their grandfather to discover his Gaelic heritage and ancestry. The
Marquess Wellesley, described by Lord Clare at this period of his life as 'an
old ruined battered rake', had been appointed the Lord Lieutenant of Ireland
and the sisters dined at his magnificent Palladian mansion just outside the
city, the Viceregal Lodge in the Phoenix Park. Others had a different opinion
of the marquess: Lord Hatherton had known him since 1812 and believed
'both in character and in person, he was one of the most remarkable

individuals ever seen.' Standing 5ft 6in high (a Staffordshire gentleman once described him as 'the tallest man for his inches I ever saw') and always garbed in tasteful and expensive clothes, he had a bald head with silky fine hair around his ears and the back of his head, grey when Lord Hatherton first knew him but white as snow by the time the marquess wooed the widowed Mrs Patterson.[5]

Marianne had planned to return to America the following year but the 66-year-old snowy-haired marquess proposed marriage and everything moved so quickly that Marianne found herself married and a marchioness before the year was out. The marquess was an old fool in love but not such a fool that he had neglected to choose wisely, for Marianne brought her fortune as well as her charm and beauty to the union. The Duke of Wellington, still infatuated with Marianne but not free to marry himself, was horrified and tried to prevent the match (after years of seeing his younger brother triumphant it would not have escaped the marquess's notice that this time it was he who had ended up with the prize and Arthur who had ended up with his nose put out of joint).

The views of Richard's children towards his new wife were not overly enthusiastic and indeed they had heard little of it from their ever-distant father. Hyacinthe Littleton hinted that Marianne had settled for being a marchioness and Lady Lieutenant of Ireland only because there was no chance of the Duchess of Wellington's demise any time soon. Certainly Edward Johnston, the marquess's illegitimate son and, as his father's private secretary the one child closest to him, was deliberately obtuse to the new marchioness and he made her life a misery (one argument began because she did not bid Mr Johnston 'goodnight' before she went to bed and the young man felt slighted; his father agreed with him and took his side). Edward Johnston had married in London just eleven months before his father's second marriage and perhaps saw his prospects for financial security slipping away if his influence with his newly-married father diminished. He was later found a position, due to the influence of the Duke of Wellington who wished to help Marianne, with the Board of Stamps but remained largely absent from his desk and continued to be by the side of the marquess, much to everyone else's despair. It was generally believed by everyone except his indulgent father that he siphoned off large quantities of money in return for using his influence over the marquess. By 1833, finally realizing the truth of the matter, Wellesley called a halt to his relationship with his grasping son and banished him from his side.[6]

Lord Charles Bentinck was now once again placed in the public eye, this time in connection with the courtesan Harriette Wilson. In 1825 her

Memoirs featuring Lord Charles, his younger brother Frederick, Sir William Abdy and the Duke of Wellington among others were published in nine instalments between February and August of that year. If he was offered the chance to buy himself from the pages, Lord Charles refrained from doing so and sadly his wife's reaction to his appearance in Harriette's *Memoirs* has not survived. We would imagine it to be loud, scathing and voluble. In the autumn of that year he was in Paris, perhaps to escape the unwanted attention as another book reputedly authored by Harriette was also just published, a semi-fictional work entitled *Paris Lions and London Tigers* which was a satire featuring thinly-disguised portraits of celebrities of the day and written in the style of a novel. Lord Charles and his brother-in-law Edward Littleton, Baron Hatherton both got a less than flattering namecheck within its pages. The two unfortunate men were introduced to the readers of this novel thus: 'I remember my Lord Charles Bentinck, and that stupid young man, who married the Marquis of Wellesley's youngest daughter – I forget his name, but fancy it might be something Littleton.'[7]

The two men had been in Paris together some years earlier, according to the author, and had fixed on dining at Café Frascati, a gaming salon on the fashionable Rue de Richelieu where many a fortune had been lost and a reputation ruined, only they could not gain admittance without the introduction of a gentleman known to the house. Several well-to-do Englishmen had recently been turned from the establishment's doors and the pair knew not how to gain admittance. Then they had a brainwave. Harriette was in Paris and so Lord Charles wrote what was described as a 'very humble [and] pathetic epistle', imploring her to

> forward a character forthwith; forthwith being my Lord's favourite expression: 'For the love of Heaven, do, pray, dear, little, pretty Miss Wilson, forward me, forthwith, a couple of written characters, one for my friend, Mr Littleton, the other for myself: such as shall obtain us admittance into that highly respectable establishment.

Harriette claimed that she obliged the two men, penning a letter to the (probably fictional) Marquis de Livré to say that while she had been acquainted with the two gentlemen she had never had a reason to doubt their honesty, having never lost anything, and they were frequently sober, especially in the mornings. There would be no risk to the house, she thought, if the two gentlemen were allowed to sit at the bottom of the table.

Whether or not this account was false, combined with his appearance in Harriette's *Memoirs*, it presented an aspect of his personality that he would not wish to become public knowledge and, more importantly, left him open to the ridicule of society and his peers. Additionally, Lord Charles was possibly suffering ill health at the time and any stress caused by the publication of these two books can only have worsened his condition. He died suddenly, at his house on the corner of North Row and Park Lane, on 28 April 1826 of an aneurysm of the heart. He was aged only 45 and Anne was left a widow with four young children, the eldest of whom was approaching her tenth birthday. Charles had been feeling ill for a few days but had gone about his business on the preceding evening as usual and without complaint; he died while dressing himself at half-past seven in the morning, and his children had been running through his rooms just minutes before he fell to the floor. His footman, alerted by a strange noise from the dressing room, found Lord Charles lying prone on the floor and medical attention was swiftly summoned with Sir Henry Halford (a handsome doctor favoured by the Royal family) and Dr Warren arriving post-haste but to no avail, for there was no sign of life remaining.[8]

It is not known what caused Lord Charles' aneurysm and it could have been due to a variety of complications ranging from high blood pressure to a congenital condition, but it may also have been caused by syphilis. Syphilitic aortitis is a known cause of aneurysms of the heart in people under the age of 50 who suffer from tertiary syphilis (and this stage of the disease can occur up to three decades after the initial infection and after a period when the disease had lain dormant after the initial symptoms, i.e. the latent phase). Tertiary syphilis is not infectious, nor is it during the latent phase other than in the first couple of years, and it is possible that Lord Charles was suffering from syphilis without anyone knowing a thing about it until shortly before his death; perhaps if this was the case he had become infected in his youth when he served in the army and long before even his first marriage. Beau Brummell, who kept company with Frederick Bentinck at Harriette Wilson's establishment, was another famous sufferer; he died at Caen in northern France in 1840 at Le Bon Sauveur Asylum due to complications from tertiary syphilis.

That Lord Charles died suddenly and unexpectedly is partly evidenced by the lack of a will. Had he known that his death was near he would undoubtedly have written one but, instead, he died intestate leaving his distraught widow the additional problem of applying for probate and taking control of whatever estate he had owned at his death.

Lady Anne continued to live at 1 North Row during the early years of her widowhood, supported financially by her brother-in-law, the Duke of Portland. The Duke of Wellington was now prime minister, having been asked by King George IV to form a government (he resigned his position as commander-in-chief of the British army upon his appointment). However, the duke's tenure in office was marked by riots, he found himself an un-popular choice among many and his premiership lasted a mere two years. Being niece to the prime minister was of little use to Lady Anne Bentinck when, two years after the death of her husband, she found herself in front of the magistrates on a similar charge to the one that had years earlier been laid against her husband by their footman, Robert Manby. This time the accuser was Lady Anne's cook, a termagant-looking woman named Sarah Walker.

Sarah Walker had not held the position for very long; she was merely a substitute for the regular cook who was in the country with the rest of the Bentinck servants, and had been hired at 5s a week to look after the house in London while Lady Anne was on the Continent. One evening in October 1828, with Anne recently returned to London after a short visit to Bath following her continental tour, the two women found themselves under the same roof, a situation that resulted in the cook making a complaint to the Marlborough Street Magistrates Court that her mistress, without the slightest provocation, had chased her up the stairs brandishing a candlestick with which she had mercilessly set about the cook once she caught up with her. The cook alleged that she had been struck on her arm and on her head, with severe wounds inflicted by the heavy candlestick (although she would not show her injuries to the magistrate) before Lady Anne, her arm tiring from wielding her weapon of choice, had resorted to kicking the cook down the stairs, along the passageway and out of the house, much as her husband had previously ejected Robert Manby. She also claimed that Anne had threat-ened to set fire to her. The next morning the cook called at the house to ask for her clothes to be given to her (as Lady Anne, she said, had almost torn the ones she had on from her back in the fracas the day before), but this was refused.[9]

It is entirely possible to picture an enraged Lady Anne Bentinck chasing a servant around her town house; it is also plausible that she was rash enough, when angered, to strike a servant in the heat of the moment. However, that she would do so without provocation is hard to believe, even for a woman of her disposition, and not with a weapon that might have caused significant injury or even death. The magistrate determined to get to the bottom of the situation and Lady Anne was summoned to his office to answer the charge.

Her ladyship cut a sympathetic and aristocratic appearance before the magistrate and was described in the ensuing newspaper report in *The Times* as 'a lady of elegant person and amiable manners', which was perhaps stretching the truth just a little too far. She categorically denied ever striking her cook with a candlestick or any other implement that may have been to hand. The cook, Lady Anne told the magistrate, had behaved insolently towards her and had often been found at the bottom of a bottle, to the increasing frustration of her mistress:[10]

> *Lady Charles*: I assure you this woman was in a dreadful state of intoxication.
> *Mrs Walker*: Oh, you wretch! It is false, I never was drunk in my life.

Finally, on her return on the Sunday evening and with only two servants in the house, the cook and a little footboy, Lady Anne had had enough of her insolent servant and ordered Sarah Walker to immediately quit the house. This peremptory order had been issued in one of the bedrooms in the upper apartments of the house and Lady Anne had taken a candlestick, she said, merely to light the cook's path to the door of the house, but the tipsy cook refused to budge and dared Lady Anne to lay a finger upon her, saying she would have her mistress taken up for assault. Anne was having none of it and, laying hold of the cook's shoulder, forced her down the stairs, following behind with the lighted candle. The argument resumed in the hallway; the cook showered her mistress with abusive language and the poor little frightened footboy was ordered to open the front door and turn the cook out. The footboy wasn't strong enough to complete the task himself and so Lady Anne, as she herself fully acknowledged, gave him a helping hand. She might, she reasoned, have 'touched' the cook's body with her knee but if so that was all the 'kicking' that had taken place.

The footboy and the only other person present in the house at the time, Lady Anne's eldest daughter Anne Hyacinthe aged 12, were waiting outside the magistrate's office in the carriage (Anne Hyacinthe had accompanied her mother to London; the two were ever close and Lady Anne relied on her eldest daughter for companionship). When asked to produce a witness, Lady Anne, 'who was reclining against the Magistrates' table in a careless attitude' selected her daughter and Anne Hyacinthe was duly called into the building. Because of her extreme youth she was questioned without being required to take the oath and *The Times* waxed lyrical on the touching scene of the young girl being called in to defend her mother:

> The first person questioned on the subject was her ladyship's daughter, a beautiful and intelligent-looking child, displaying in every look and word an ingenuous simplicity that left no doubt of her veracity. She said, 'Oh, no indeed, my mamma did not touch cook with the candlestick.'

Miss Bentinck did finally admit that her mamma had frightened the cook with the candlestick. Sarah Walker remonstrated with the girl, saying she was lying for her mother on Lady Anne's instructions but Anne Hyacinthe was cut from the same cloth as her mamma and, with an air of confidence that belied her years, called for the footboy to be examined, sure he would back her up. Her mother echoed her request and as the footboy was outside he too was called to appear. This proved to be unfortunate for the two Bentincks as the footboy was a rather less reliable witness for Anne. His evidence was that 'cookey did not say a word in anger to my lady, but that my lady kicked cookey very much indeed.'

Lady Anne knew when to fight and when to retreat; she was, after all, the niece of the greatest military strategist of the age. With a smile, and echoes of the resolution to the complaint made against her husband by Robert Manby, she calmly remarked to the magistrates that she was much to blame in laying her hands on her troublesome cook and should really have sent for a constable but the cook's extreme insolence to her had made her forget herself momentarily. Sarah Walker could not resist one last taunt towards her former employer:

> *Mrs Walker*: It is no use for me to say what my Lady is, but the Lord, who searches out all secrets, will reward her.

Although it was thought that the cook had indeed been impertinent, her ladyship was convicted of the assault and fined £4 plus costs; a significant sum as the highest penalty for the most aggravated case of assault stood at £5. The magistrate suggested afterwards he had imposed such a high amount as money was no object to Lady Anne and a fine of a few shillings would have been a mere trifle to her. The poor footboy, with his account of Lady Anne kicking 'cookey', had undoubtedly sealed his fate within the household and was facing a long walk back home from Marlborough Street rather than riding on the carriage as he had done for the journey there.

Anne had been in London to make arrangements for leaving her London town house in the hands of an agent who was to let it for up to six months. She accordingly departed from London to stay in Brighton where she attended a December ball at the Old Ship Hotel on the seafront (at which Mrs Fitzherbert was a guest) and the house at North Row was taken, fully furnished, by a single gentleman named Macnamara whose family owned Llangoed Castle in Powys, Wales and his footman, William Phillips. Another servant of Anne's, Bridget Delaney, a young woman aged 28 and like 'cookey' only recently hired, was tasked to remain in the house until Mr Macnamara had taken possession and he decided to retain her services during his tenure there.[11]

Lady Anne checked all her drawers and cabinets before she departed and left some of her valuable jewels behind, securely locked away, or so she thought. These included a gold watch and appendages, alone worth upwards of 100 guineas, several brooches and some topaz and diamond ornaments. She left for Brighton, where her father and his new wife and her brother Richard and his wife Jane were residing. The new Lady Wellesley thought Anne 'in great beauty'. Richard and Jane Wellesley took Anne to a grand ball (probably Mrs Maria Fitzherbert's grand fancy dress ball, held at Steine House in Brighton and graced by all the attendant nobility), where she was 'well noticed and much delighted'.[12] If she had been shunned by society following her divorce, with the passing of time and as a widowed lady she once more had an entrance into the ballrooms of high society. The Marquess and Marchioness Wellesley left Brighton in early February after a five-month sojourn and Anne perhaps made a return visit to London with them, for she briefly called by the house and ascertained that her valuables were still under lock and key. However, on her next visit at the beginning of July, she found that her cabinet had been opened and was empty. Bridget Delaney had left two days beforehand.

A constable was sent for, who discovered the wine cellar and other places had also been broken into and, with suspicion inevitably falling upon the recently-departed Bridget, she was traced to her mother Anne's house at Johnson's Court near the New Road in Marylebone.[13] At first she denied knowing anything at all about the missing items but eventually she threw the blame onto William Phillips, Macnamara's footman. Phillips, she said, had been the one who had opened the cabinet (the constable thought a false key had been used, although the lid bore signs of force) and he had told her to take everything except the watch, assuring her that Lady Bentinck would never miss them when she returned. All the stolen goods, including some that Lady Anne had not missed such as wearing apparel belonging to her late husband, were found buried in the coal cellar at Anne Delaney's house and hidden at Bridget's home in Kendal Mews, except for the gold watch. Various portraits executed over the years by Lady Anne's own hand of her friends were also found, including one she had painted of Lord Byron, along with some items belonging to Dr Hill of London Street, Fitzroy Square, Bridget's former employer.[14]

It appears that William Phillips had indeed been involved in the robbery. Mr Macnamara had left for Wales expecting his footman to follow him and Phillips had spent the night before the constable's visit at Anne Delaney's Johnson's Court home. He turned up again to bid them farewell before setting off on his journey, only to find the constables still there waiting for him and all three were taken for questioning. The evidence against William Phillips was not enough to lead to a conviction but he was closely examined by Macnamara's brother and his explanation was found to be by no means satisfactory. He was warned by the magistrate that he was now known to the police and he could expect no second chance if he appeared before them again. The two Delaneys, however, who had confessed to their part in the crime, took their place in the dock before a judge and jury and were found guilty; Bridget for the theft and her mother for helping to conceal the stolen items.

Lady Anne was lucky in recovering everything but the gold watch which was never traced, but a mistake in the indictment meant that the capital part of the charge could not stand, luckily for Bridget who might otherwise have found herself swinging on the end of a noose. In a rare act of charity, Anne recommended Bridget to mercy as she had made such an ample confession and the jury extended their mercy to the mother, who had no former convictions. The pair were jailed for twelve months.

Chapter Eight

Belgian Revolution

To escape all her troubles, in the springtime of 1830 Anne decided to take a tour on the Continent accompanied by her two young daughters. The winter had been a severe one but when spring arrived it was unusually warm and Dover found itself thronged with passengers waiting for passage on one of the Calais packets. Staying at Wright's Ship Hotel on the waterfront for a day or two beforehand, the Bentinck party left England around mid-April intending to visit Paris and Brussels.

Back in England the 67-year-old King George IV was nearing his end. Bloated and nearly blind, his years of excessive living had taken their toll and the Scottish artist Sir David Wilkie (who had painted the king in his highland garb after the visit to Scotland in 1822) suggested the monarch looked like a sausage stuffed into its covering when squeezed into his corset. Suffering constant pain from swollen legs and a bladder infection, the king spent his days dosed with laudanum and almost insensible. He died in the early hours of the morning of 26 June 1830 with only two doctors present (one of whom was Sir Henry Halford, the same physician who had been summoned at Lord Charles Bentinck's demise four years earlier). Although Lady Elizabeth Conyngham had been playing the role of nursemaid during her royal lover's illness (much to her disinclination), the king died with a diamond locket around his neck which, when opened, was found to contain a miniature of Mrs Fitzherbert, perhaps his one true love.

The king's younger brother ascended the throne as William IV, reputedly showing scant sorrow for the loss of his older brother. On being informed of George's death he told the assembled courtiers that he was going to retire to his chamber with his wife, for he had 'never yet been to bed with a Queen'.[1] The new king paid all due respect to Mrs Fitzherbert with whom he was ever friendly and he ordered her to wear widow's weeds as if for her husband. For many years William, a naval officer who was known during his reign as 'the Sailor King', had lived with his own mistress, the actress Dorothea Jordan, and had fathered no fewer than ten illegitimate children with her (all of whom took the surname FitzClarence as William was, at the time, the Duke of Clarence).

In 1818, amid the scramble to produce a legitimate heir following the death of Princess Charlotte and her child, William had married Princess Adelaide of Saxe-Meiningen and this was the woman he bedded as a queen following the death of his brother. Adelaide was half the age of her husband and the couple had no surviving children together but lived happily enough despite this, and Adelaide proved a kind stepmother to her husband's illegitimate brood. She had four known pregnancies between 1819 and 1822: two resulted in stillbirths (one of twin boys) and two daughters died as infants. The tragedies of these births and deaths fostered a great sympathy for the unfortunate princess and rumours that she was again pregnant persisted for many years. Despite their personal tragedies and although perceived as slightly eccentric, the new king and his queen were considered a great improvement on the last monarch. The Duke of Wellington also approved of William IV, telling Mr Greville if he 'had been able to deal with my late master as I do with my present I should have got on much better ... [and] had done more business with him in ten minutes than with the other in as many days.'[2]

By September Lady Bentinck and her daughters were resident at the fine hôtel Bellevue in the Belgian capital city, an establishment well favoured by English travellers and where her mother and brother Henry had stayed in 1816. Her companions in the hôtel included, among others, Mr and Mrs George Harley Drummond and Captain William Siborne, a military gentleman engaged in constructing a model of the Battle of Waterloo. George Harley Drummond, a wild spendthrift, had been forced to sell his British estates to cover his debts (he was reputed to have lost £20,000 in one evening at White's to his crony Beau Brummell); he was the scion of a banking family who had wisely decided he should pursue a different career. After failing in his political ambitions, Drummond eventually deserted his wife and children for a mistress with whom he had a son. The Mrs Drummond at the hôtel Bellevue in 1830 was, therefore, merely pretending to that nomenclature.[3]

Unfortunately for the tourists at the hotel, unrest was brewing outside and in the nearby picturesque parkland (the Parc de Bruxelles) alongside the royal palace a mob was gathering. Following the French Revolution in the late eighteenth century, Belgium had been part of the French Empire and after Napoléon's defeat and exile to Elba in 1814 it became part of the 'United Netherlands' under Prince William of Orange-Nassau. When Napoléon Bonaparte escaped from Elba, Prince William, a ruler hugely disliked in Belgium, had proclaimed himself King of the Netherlands and Duke of Luxembourg. Years later, with resentment at a peak between the lower bourgeoisie and the tradespeople against the wealthier elite, the tensions tipped over into all-out rebellion with Dutch troops despatched to quell the unrest. Lady Anne had picked the wrong time to visit the city.

One side of the hôtel Bellevue overlooked the park and the guests inside were shocked to hear the sound of cannonades. Captain Siborne, together with a Captain Dent, rushed into the boulevards behind the Belgian palace to witness the bourgeoisie levelling a 9-pounder cannon at the advancing Dutch line. With grapeshot flying above their heads and shells landing close by, Dent and Siborne quickly made a dash back to the relative safety of the hôtel where, from one of the windows, they had a good view of the troops and the men who were firing on them from the windows and rooftops of the houses that lined the park.

The bourgeoisie had made a mistake in not occupying the parkland and the Dutch soldiers, with their superior numbers, soon rectified this error and took possession of both it and the royal palace. Four days of fighting were to follow, with little in the way of advance for either side following this first action.

The situation inside the hôtel Bellevue became critical. The small party of English ladies – Anne and her two daughters, the spurious Mrs Drummond and a Mrs Wollesley with her own beautiful young daughter plus their assorted servants – were trapped there under the guidance of Captains Dent and Siborne (and with the dubious assistance of George Harley Drummond). They had moved to a room on the second floor facing out onto the palace but found themselves in danger as, unbeknown to them, the bourgeoisie had scaled the roof of the Bellevue to fire upon the royal residence. The Dutch troops who occupied the palace now returned the fire with interest, putting the ladies directly in harm's way from a stray bullet.

With gunshots whizzing both from and towards the hôtel, coupled with cannonades from the artillery close to its gate and all manner of shouting and noise, the British party decided to make instead for the basement, thinking they would be safer. The journey to the cellar was a risky move, however, for they were temporarily exposed to musketry and at the mercy of a stray shot through the windows while rapidly descending the main staircase but they all made it safely to the basement which comprised a cook's pantry close to the kitchens. The pantry was vaulted and offered them a sanctuary with food and drink readily available so there they stayed, in good spirits, for two days until the afternoon of Saturday, 25 September.

Anne, with her feisty courage, tried to rally her anxious companions and keep them positive, absolutely in her element as a battle commander. Wounded men, members of the bourgeoisie, were brought into the upper levels of the hôtel and Mrs Drummond left the safety of the cellar on several occasions to see if she could help them. The ladies were also driven by curiosity and boredom to occasionally climb the stairs and sidle hesitantly towards the windows and doors to chance a peek at the chaos outside.

A Belgian gentleman, his wife and 17-year-old daughter made a dash into the basement looking for safety, closely followed by a bourgeoisie chief originally from the city of Liège, dirty and black from being in the thick of the fighting. The gentleman newcomer was suspected of being a traitor (it was believed he had passed food to the Dutch troops through the park railings during the night) and he and his entire family were peremptorily taken away for questioning.[4]

With more men pouring into the hôtel Bellevue and a cannon brought into the yard ready to pour grapeshot into the troops in the adjoining parkland, the British party realized the time had come to escape their situation before it totally overwhelmed them. The decision to abandon their refuge had been made by Anne, who imperiously demanded to know from the master of the hôtel if they would be safe in remaining any longer on his premises. The poor man hesitated for some time but Anne berated him until he told her that, in his opinion, they would be safer to quit his house (probably keen just to be rid of the vociferous and scary English lady). With that information Anne, an able a military general as her noble uncle in her own small sphere, readied herself and her daughters to leave and the rest of the party meekly followed her example. Five or six men were sent by the Liège chief to escort them to safety (he had earlier been embraced by Mrs Drummond and had promised to keep her safe when she begged him for his protection; possibly a clever and calculated move on her part to secure his sympathy and help).

Lady Anne, like a captain in charge of a company, sallied from the building at the head of the small party with her daughters. Captain Siborne had Mrs and Miss Wollesley on either arm and he was followed by Captain Dent with Mrs Drummond. George Harley Drummond brought up the rear with his young son. They hurried into the Royal Square (the Place Royale) as far as the church of Saint Jacques-sur-Coudenberg but then had to face a barrage of musketry and grapeshot. The men of their escort gave them some covering fire and, with the shots whistling past their ears, the terrified women could do nothing but make a run for it. Mrs Wollesley lost her footing and stumbled to the floor and her daughter broke down in hysterics, thinking her mother had been shot. Two or three men of the escort broke cover and carried Mrs Wollesley on their shoulders to safety while Captain Siborne held on to Miss Wollesley. By a miracle none of the party or their escort was as much as scratched and they hurried away from the chaos through the deserted back lanes of the city to a house of safety. The next morning they retreated still further, splitting up to travel to safer locations.[5]

After four days of fighting, a provisional government was established and Belgium declared her independence. Princess Charlotte of Wales's widower, Prince Leopold, who had influentially retained the goodwill and backing of the British, eventually accepted the throne of Belgium.[6]

Back in England, family concerns dominated the extended Wellesley clan in the early 1830s. After a lengthy illness Richard Wellesley, Anne's eldest brother, died leaving behind an impoverished wife and children. Richard had suffered greatly in his last months: he was probably suffering from tuberculosis, his mind began to wander and he attempted suicide twice. His younger brother Gerald was on his way home from India where he had spent most of his adult life in the employ of the East India Company. Travelling home across the Middle East and through Europe he fell ill in Belgrade and only just managed to complete his journey, arriving back in England during the spring of 1833. Gerald died months later at his brother Henry Wellesley's vicarage at Flitton in Bedfordshire (Henry had been ordained in 1823). Unbeknown to his family Gerald had fathered three children while in India to a native woman named Culoo; these children were revealed when they were sent to England in 1830 ahead of their father's return and were baptized in the church at St Marylebone as the children of 'Charles and Culoo Fitzgerald', a subterfuge to hide their true parentage.[7]

Lady Anne had relied on her older brother Richard to an inordinate degree. Her father had been largely unapproachable for many years and her relationship with her brother-in-law the Duke of Portland was on a more formal than cordial footing. Now she had only her sister Hyacinthe and younger brother Henry to turn to when she needed practical and friendly assistance, and Hyacinthe and Henry both provided a safe haven and a sympathetic ear for Lady Anne's brood of children.

Chapter Nine

The Summertown Gypsy

During the Regency and at around the same time as the *haut ton* in London were agog at the scandal of Lady Abdy's elopement and remarriage, but in the very different social setting of the racecourse at Warwick in the English midlands, another romance was blossoming.

One of the oldest in the country, the racecourse was built on common land bordered by the medieval town dwellings with the imposing Warwick Castle as a backdrop. It was always well attended with numerous people of quality there to gamble and enjoy the spectacle, and for those lower down the social order it provided an ideal environment in which to ply their trade and make money. The gypsy tribes had made their way to the racecourse, horse-dealers and trinket-sellers alike, to trade with the racegoers and to meet with old friends. One young gypsy woman, around 20 years of age, was slim and tall with rich brunette hair and piercing hazel eyes visible beneath her black beaver bonnet. She caught the attention of a young horse-dealer as she sashayed through the gathered horde of racegoers with her basket full of sundry wares and pretty baubles to sell on her arm. The young woman was one of the ubiquitous Smith gypsies and had an unusual forename of the kind so favoured by the Romany people. Her name was Sinnetta. *

James Lambourne had travelled to Warwick from his Oxfordshire home in the picturesque village of Cumnor. He was a horse-dealer, a trade that often brought him into contact with the gypsy people who also frequented the horse fairs and racecourses and one that gave him his nicknames of Gypsy Jim and Gyp Lambourne. The instant he set eyes on the beautiful young gypsy girl, James was smitten.[1]

Just over a month after their meeting at the racecourse the couple married, on 14 October 1816 at Shipston-on-Stour. It is an indication that Sinnetta's family were living in the Warwickshire area at the time but after their hasty marriage Sinnetta took the unusual step of turning her back on her people, instead following James back to his home in Cumnor where they settled.[2] Though Sinnetta moved away from her family she did not instantly turn away from her way of life for the young couple initially lived in an early form of caravan, described as a portable house fitted onto a horse-drawn cart with every necessary comfort, windows and a chimney. During the summer

* An Italian name - diminutive of Simonetta

months they travelled in this wagon, Sinnetta selling her wares and James continuing his trade as a horse-dealer, returning to Cumnor to overwinter. A gypsy named Gustun Smith remembered them travelling chiefly in the area around the market town of Banbury in Oxfordshire (and he believed that James Lambourne carried some gypsy blood in his veins). Sometimes, to protect themselves from the biting winter winds they encircled their primitive caravan with a barrier of long upright faggots (bundles of sticks, bound together and generally used for fuel), fastened securely together.[3] A year after their marriage their first child was born, a daughter who was named Sinnetta after her mother and who, for her first three summers, travelled with her parents in their 'portable house' to the fairs, carried in a papoose on her mother's back while Sinnetta Lambourne touted her basket of trinkets to anyone who would buy. Two more children followed: James born in the springtime of 1819 and William a year later.[4]

A discriminated-against minority, attitudes towards the gypsy and Romany people have ever been those of suspicion and mistrust and it was no different in the early years of the nineteenth century. Many gypsies did indeed commit crimes; it was hardly unknown for a few chickens or potatoes to go missing from the fields neighbouring their campsites, and not a few gypsies engaged in nefarious dealings when it came to horses and horse-theft but suspicion invariably fell on them for any crime committed in an area where they had been known to be camped, whether they were guilty or not. Conversely, they were also valued for their trades and as casual workers on the land, plying their vital and useful services (among these were knife-grinding, hop-picking and mending the seats of cane chairs) to grateful villagers, townsfolk and farmers who would watch out for the tribe, knowing they would be passing through at a certain time of the year on their circuit. As ever, there are two sides to every tale.

Most gypsy tribes were 'short-travellers' following a regular circuit each year and not journeying much beyond this. Sinnetta was unusual both in venturing so far afield and in leaving her family behind.[5] It might have been that her family had refused to allow her to marry a *gorja* (a non-gypsy) or perhaps her actions were indicative of a temperament that induced her to seek out adventure and a different life from the one into which she had been born. The gypsy tribes had (and still have) a wonderful sense of community, often very matriarchal, and it would have been more usual, if he had been accepted by them, to have seen James Lambourne join his wife's family and travel with them. Maybe it was James himself who refused to commit to such a life and instead wanted to return to his beloved Oxfordshire home? Whatever the true case may have been, James Lambourne offered an opportunity for a new life to Sinnetta and she fully embraced it. Their daughter and firstborn child would, in due course, follow her mother's example and follow her heart to leave her humble life behind for a bright new one.

Now with three young children and having made a tidy sum of money from their joint endeavours, in the autumn of 1820 the Lambournes felt it was time to put down some roots in preparation for giving up their travelling life. They bought a piece of land near to Cumnor upon which to settle. Their chosen plot was on the Banbury to Oxford Road, a short distance from the site of the old Diamond Hall public house that had been a notorious den of iniquity in the eighteenth century and a frequent haunt of the highwaymen who terrorized Oxfordshire travellers. With James often away following his trade, the resourceful Sinnetta travelled daily with a horse and cart to a stone-pit some miles away from the piece of land where they had pitched their caravan and brought back masonry with which she planned to build a cottage. Gradually other people also began to settle and build around them, but James and Sinnetta were the first and so were the founders of what would become a new village, one to which James gave its name. He went to Oxford and employed a sign-writer to paint his details on a board to advertise his horse-dealing business, a board that he could place outside his house, facing the road to Oxford and visible to anyone travelling in that direction: 'James Lambourne, Horse Dealer, Somers Town'.[6] However, the little settlement became known as Summertown; either James or the sign writer had misspelt the name for James had intended it to represent his favourite season, thinking the spot where he lived to be 'the pleasantest place in all England, nay, in all the world!'

The family was recorded in an unofficial census in the autumn of 1832, James and Sinnetta (recorded as Cynetta) described as middle-aged with three children. John Badcock, a Summertown resident who compiled the census, described them thus: 'Lambourne is a horse dealer. His family attend Church regularly but he is seldom there himself and is much addicted to that habitual profanes and Sabbath breaking too common with many in his line of life.'

Perhaps James Lambourne was fond of a tipple, a practice that Badcock abhorred, for Summertown was awash with inns and beer shops (six such establishments alone had sprung up within the two years Badcock had lived in the village). John Badcock knew the family very well indeed for he lived next door to them, in a house built in 1824 that he described as his little 'Nut Shell' as he only occupied one half of it. On the other side of the Lambournes' property was one of the inns, the King's Arms, although now both it and the Lambournes' cottage are sadly demolished; James and Sinnetta's cottage lay just past the inn's stable-yard gates and perhaps James used these stables in the course of his horse-dealing.

In his *Manuscript History of Summertown* that accompanied the census Badcock described James Lambourne as a 'tight, firm built, active man', around 5ft 4in tall and 'round as a baker's rolling pin ... now in the prime of life and increasing in wealth.' Better still, we have a description of his daughter Sinnetta, almost 15 years old and a 'little sprightly, but sensible well-disposed brunette'. The family sometimes had help in the house from a girl (named Emma Keil) and a lad occasionally worked in the stables. They also had a man living with them who helped James in his trade; William Cullimore who interestingly used the name Boss as an alias, another well-known gypsy surname. He had worked for James Lambourne since at least 1826 when he appeared at the Oxford Assizes to offer his testimony when James was charged with (and acquitted of) receiving a stolen horse.[7]

The family bore something of a bad character: an Oxfordshire resident who related her mother's memories from around the year 1816 onwards recalled that much being said about them. She also remembered the younger Sinnetta was known as a great beauty, just like her mother before her.[8] The rough and ready existence of the Lambournes was certainly far removed from the refined Mayfair life of the widowed Lady Anne Bentinck and her four children, in fact almost a whole world away but, unbeknown to either family and within a decade from Badcock's unofficial census, those two worlds were destined to become inextricably entwined.

Two more sons were born to the Lambournes: Samuel in 1824 (who died three years later), and finally, after a gap of many years, Esau, born in 1834. Upon Esau's birth, James Lambourne thought it wise to have his last will and testament drawn up to protect his wife and progeny financially in the event of his death. This document reveals the true extent of James Lambourne's prosperity for, as John Badcock hinted, he had steadily been increasing in wealth. Not only did he own the cottage in which the family lived and the land surrounding it, he also owned two cottages and gardens in nearby Wootton that were occupied by a Widow Bennet. He described himself as a horse-dealer and one other man named in the will, obviously one trusted by James, was George Randall who kept a livery stable on St Giles Street in Oxford; perhaps James supplied George Randall with his horses?[9]

While he might not have been a full-blooded gypsy, James Lambourne was certainly regarded and described as such in his immediate neighbourhood due to the origins of his wife, his trade as a horse-dealer and his prowess with his fists. Often he found himself only barely on the right side of the law. He was known to engage in bare-knuckle fights to settle disputes and he was also, on

Two miniatures of Anne Wellesley, Lady Charles Bentinck (formerly the wife of Sir William Abdy), (*left*) after Lawrence and (*below*) by Mrs Mee.

(*Left*) Hyacinthe Gabrielle Rolland, Countess of Mornington, with her eldest and youngest sons Richard and Henry. The original of this portrait was sent out to India to her husband.

(*Right*) Arthur Wellesley, 1st Duke of Wellington, writing the Waterloo despatch.

Richard Colley Wellesley, Marquess Wellesley.

ouble miniature depicting Lord Charles Bentinck and his first wife, Georgiana Augusta Frederica
ymour. Georgiana was the daughter of the courtesan Grace Dalrymple Elliott and reputedly the
ince of Wales, later King George IV.

reenwich, looking from the Observatory towards London, as it would have been at the time of the
opement. The houses on Crooms Hill where 'Captain and Mrs Brown' took refuge can just be seen
rough the trees on the right.

Doctors' Commons (*above*) and the House of Lords (*below*), where the criminal conversation case and the Abdys' divorce bill were heard.

The exterior and interior of the church of
St Martin-in-the-Fields as it would have
looked when Lord Charles Bentinck
married the newly-divorced Anne
Wellesley, formerly Abdy.

(*Left*) Princess Charlotte of Wales and Saxe-Coburg, heir to the throne. (*Right*) Her husband, the handsome but penniless Prince Leopold. Their short-lived marriage turned out to be a true love-match.

George IV, depicted in the early years of his reign.

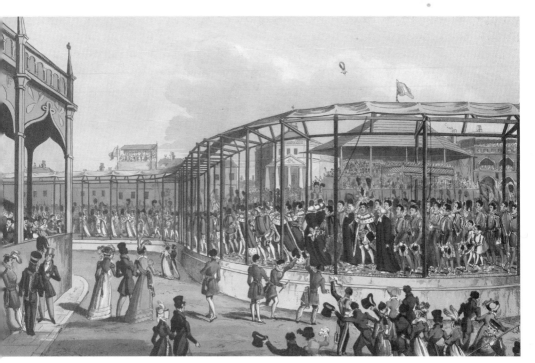

Coronation procession of
His Majesty George IV,
19th July, 1821.

Lord Charles Bentinck in his
coronation dress as Treasurer of
the Royal Household.

Apsley House was home to both Marquess Wellesley and the Duke of Wellington and the location of the duke's dinner held to reconcile the marquess and his children in 1819.

Bow Street Magistrates' Court in London, showing the queue of people waiting to put their case before the sitting magistrate. Lord Charles Bentinck, in 1822, was afforded the luxury of being heard in a private room.

Belgian insurgents behind a barricade at the Parc de Bruxelles on 23 September 1830 during the Belgian Revolution.

Hôtel Bellevue on the Place Royale in Brussels after the battle in 1830. This was where Lady Charles Bentinck and her daughters took refuge during the fighting. Marchioness Wellesley and her son Henry had also stayed there in 1816.

A scene at the races *c*.1820, similar to the one at which James Lambourne first met Sinnetta Smith.

A family of gypsies approach a gentleman on a horse and their tent can be seen in the background.

Panoramic view of Front Quadrangle, Merton College, Oxford University. This was where Charley attended and had rooms.

The coronation of Queen Victoria.

George Street, Hanover Square, showing the church where Charley and Sinnetta wed. Decades earlier, his Wellesley grandparents had also exchanged their vows at the same altar.

Fashion plate giving an idea of how Charley and Sinnetta may have appeared at their wedding.

he marriage of Queen Victoria to Prince Albert.

twick Manor in Bedfordshire, the home of John Thomas Brookes. Charley certainly visited there
d possibly Sinnetta too.

(*Left*) Charley's sister Emily Bentinck, later Mrs Hopwood, painted by her aunt Lady Hatherton.
(*Right*) Hyacinthe, Lady Hatherton when Mrs Littleton, probably painted by her sister Lady Charle
Bentinck (Charley's mother).

Miniature of Reverend
Henry Wellesley, who
tutored his nephew Charley
in order that he would gain
his degree at Oxford.

Foulislea: Charley and Sinnetta's grand house in Ampthill, Bedfordshire. Sinnetta died there in 1850.

The Duke of Wellington was godfather to Charley's brother and to Queen Victoria and Prince Albert's son, Prince Arthur. On 1 May 1851 he presented the prince with a gold cup (not a casket as depicted) and toys he had chosen himself to mark his godson's first birthday.

The christening of HRH Princess Elizabeth Alexandra Mary, 1926. Pictured are Charley's daughter (the Countess of Strathmore, seated second right) and his granddaughter (the Duchess of York, seated centre) at the christening of Princess Elizabeth (Charley's great-granddaughter and later He Majesty Queen Elizabeth II). The Earl of Strathmore is standing far right.

A postcard showing the coronation of George VI and his queen consort Elizabeth, née Bowes-Lyor Charley's granddaughter on 12 May 1937.

occasion, suspected of horse-stealing; a serious crime indeed and one for which, had he been found guilty, he could have seen himself transported across the seas to one of the Australian penal colonies in the best case, or facing the noose in the worst.

However, in 1836 it was not James Lambourne who stood charged of a crime but one of his servants. John Light, a young man only 16 years of age, had been employed by James as a stable-hand for around a month when it was found that several valuable items, among them three watches, two gold seals and a gold chain were missing. John Light had left the house just before the discovery and so suspicion inevitably fell on him. Enquiries revealed he had last been seen riding behind a chaise towards Cheltenham in Gloucestershire and the redoubtable Mrs Lambourne instantly took chase.

The elder Sinnetta was nothing if not intrepid. She took a coach and headed, unaccompanied, to Cheltenham in hot pursuit of John Light. Finding no trace of her errant employee in the spa town she visited Gloucester, Bath and Bristol in search of him but with no success. Exasperated by the wasted efforts of her fruitless search, she took a seat in the Royal Exeter fast coach to Cheltenham from Nisblete's in Bristol (where it stopped for dinner) and, while she was in transit, she happened to glance out of the coach and saw two men mounted on a horse riding past. By a total coincidence, one of the men was none other than the missing John Light. Shouting to the coachman to stop and crying out that the man who had just overtaken them was a thief who had robbed her of her property, she raised a considerable commotion within the coach. As the coachman pulled up, the two men on horseback heard Sinnetta's fulsome cry of 'Stop, thief!' and took off at full gallop. A gentleman riding up to the coach gave chase and, as one of the newspapers reported, quite 'a capital run now ensued.'

Even though John Light and his companion had a good half-mile start on their gentleman pursuer, he managed to make ground on them and, at last, brought them to a halt. By pure happenstance two Cheltenham police officers had been in the coach with Sinnetta and several other passengers offered their assistance too. The spirited Mrs Lambourne lifted up her skirts and ran with the policemen and others in the direction the chase had taken and still had enough breath left when she finally reached the dejected and captive twosome to identify John Light and to watch, with unfeigned satisfaction, as he was secured by the policemen and taken into custody. The party made their way back to the coach and resumed their seats, found space for John Light and continued their journey, Sinnetta no doubt with a triumphant gleam in her eyes as she surveyed the unhappy prisoner before her. He was taken to Oxford, examined before a magistrate and committed to the county gaol to await his trial.[10] John Light was duly brought up before a judge and jury at the Oxford assizes in July, found guilty and sentenced to be transported for the full term of his life. He saw out the rest of his days on the other side of the world.[11]

This was the world inhabited by the Lambournes: a humble working-class world of rural domesticity, punctuated at times by ugly reality and prejudice. A rough and ready world that was soon to collide with the aristocratic and genteel environment so familiar to Charley Cavendish Bentinck, with devastating consequences to all involved.

Chapter Ten

Passed from Pillar to Post

Lady Charles Bentinck had discovered a new life of independence in her widowhood and was generally to be found in full flight across the Continent or travelling the British Isles, visiting all the fashionable cities, watering holes and spa towns. Her adventures during the Belgian Revolution had not deterred her in the slightest and while her daughters were frequently to be found by her side, her two young sons could conveniently be left at their school during term time. Both Charley and Arthur were sent to Harrow in September 1831, one of the oldest and most prestigious of British schools, boarding in the Headmaster's House. The headmaster in Charley's time was Charles Longley (known to the boys as Jacob after his pet parrot), a polite and serious man but somewhat ineffectual in his position, and who was later to become the Archbishop of York. Numbers at the school had dwindled and when Longley took over there were only 120 boys but, by 1831 when Charley and his brother joined, the number had risen to 200. Around a quarter of those boarded in Mr Longley's house which was the cheapest at the school (as the Duke of Portland was no doubt picking up the bill for his nephews' education, an important consideration). In 1831 the half-yearly bill for one boy in Charley's position was almost £90, which did not include any luxuries or even necessities such as food and clothing.[1]

Both boys would have been subject to the often cruel initiation rituals and the practice of the younger boys 'fagging' for the older ones and Arthur, more rambunctious than the gentle Charley, was perhaps better suited to the rigours of public school life, excelling at sports and joining the Cricket XI. The school holidays proved a little more problematic for a woman on her travels like Lady Bentinck though, and 14-year-old Charley was forced to write something of a begging letter to his favourite uncle, the Reverend Henry Wellesley, pleading to be allowed to spend the midsummer holiday from school with him:

Dear Uncle Henry,
I am going to write instead of Mamma because she says she cannot write because your letter was so cross. We wanted to take a little trip and we asked Mamma if we might go to the inn at Selooe [Hurstmonceux] as it

was such a long time since we have seen you ... As you had never asked her she could not go to your house ... Mamma is rather offended that you should have asked Mrs. Wellesley, Aunt Hyacinth [sic] and Uncle Edward. Mamma is very angry with Hyacinthe for having written to you and made all this mischief. But as for us she has always been very grateful for asking us and if you could have us at Midsummer we should be very glad as Mamma is going abroad but we must know for certain if you cannot. Mamma must bespeak somebody else.[2]

Luckily the trip to see Uncle Henry went ahead and Charley thoroughly enjoyed himself when they stayed at Battle Abbey in Sussex with Lady Webster, her infant son Guy (he had been born on the preceding 5 November and named after the traitorous Guy Fawkes) and their pet dog, Snowball. The old abbot's hall at the abbey had been turned into a private home (and is now the Battle Abbey School), with the rest laying in a ruined state and Lady Webster, Charley noted, had 'a very pretty flower garden but a very bad husband and he left her for ten years and came to see her ... all at once she has got a new little child and he has left her for another ten years I believe.'[3] The errant husband was Godfrey Webster, 5th Baronet, an arrogant and cold man whose mother had been divorced by his father when she eloped with the 3rd Lord Holland, nephew of the politician and rake Charles James Fox (she had subsequently become Lady Holland). The Webster children remained with their father, to be further traumatized when he committed suicide, and Godfrey's unhappy marriage to Lady Charlotte née Adamson was a product of his dysfunctional childhood. Nevertheless, young Guy was the seventh son born to the 5th Baronet and his wife.

Lady Charles Bentinck, in the letter written by Charley, appears susceptible to being hurt by anything she perceived as a slight and she had obviously complained volubly to her sister about Henry neglecting to invite her and her children while extending invitations to the Littletons and to Richard Wellesley's widow. Sadly, it was all too true a fact that the Wellesley siblings more often than not found it easier and more pleasant to have Anne at arm's length rather than by their side and Edward Littleton, at least, must have been delighted to find she was not present to spoil his visit.

Georgiana Cavendish Bentinck, Lord Charles' daughter from his first short-lived marriage, was now grown up. Well-connected and a putative royal grandchild (even though her ancestry stemmed from an alliance on the wrong side of the blanket), she might have been expected to hold great prospects and be considered an eligible bride. If so, King George IV's death had indeed been untimely for with his passing she had also lost the promise of any favour or patronage from that connection. She was the niece of the Duke of Portland and was the treasured ward of the Dowager Marchioness of Cholmondeley (the marquess had died in 1827) but she was placed very much in the role of dependant upon these two families and she remained without suitors. Her modest fortune was secure and held in trust for her, but any potential husband could expect little beyond that.[4]

No portrait of Georgiana has yet been located. Her mother, the first Lady Charles Bentinck, and her grandmother Grace Dalrymple Elliott were noted beauties and if King George IV was her grandfather then he too had been handsome in his youth. In her later years though, Georgiana was known to the younger members of the extended Wellesley family as 'Hippo', one hopes affectionately! It appears that she was somewhat overweight and, to the children, resembled a hippopotamus (it is, unfortunately for Georgiana, the only clue we have as to her appearance). King George IV was certainly portly as he aged and her grandmother Grace Dalrymple Elliott had a maternal aunt (Janet Edmondes née Brown who married three times and almost snared a fourth husband) who descended into a wonderfully eccentric and obese old age. Reputedly Grace, when her glory days as a celebrated courtesan had faded into memory, was to be seen with her boon friend (who was also her aunt's maid) manoeuvring the rotund old lady into her carriage for visits to the theatre. Perhaps a thickening of the waistline was a trait from both sides of her family that was inherited by Miss Georgiana Cavendish Bentinck?

Georgiana split her time between the Duke of Portland's family and estates and those of the Cholmondeleys. With the death of the 1st Marquess (his eldest son George Horatio succeeded him in the marquessate) she was an invaluable companion to the ageing Lady Cholmondeley and was by the dowager marchioness's side at a great many gatherings, balls and parties. Georgiana had every opportunity to fall in love, if to fall in love was what she wanted, but she remained perpetually unattached. The pair were often to be found in Brighton with the royal family and in February 1832 were two of an extremely select party of dinner guests at the royal table, seated alongside King William IV and his queen. The king was known for his informality and was in the habit of sending to the local hotels for lists of their guests to invite to dine with him, stating that they should not stand on too much ceremony or worry about their clothes, for the 'Queen does nothing but embroider flowers after dinner'. Later in the year, for the Christmas and New Year holidays, everyone was once more to be found enjoying the society at Brighton. Queen Adelaide held a grand party with nearly 200 members of the *haut ton* invited and the 2nd Marquess of Cholmondeley, his wife, mother and Georgiana were among the guests that night. The dowager marchioness was the only steadfast and constant female presence in the girl's life; Georgiana relied on her and loved her and the old Lady Cholmondeley in turn doted on the girl she thought of as her granddaughter.[5]

Charley's uncle, the Reverend Henry Wellesley, had been appointed to the living of Dunsfold near Godalming in Surrey. Described as a 'cool, clever, elegant Jane Austen parson', Henry was a studious man, both a scholar and an antiquary and his family probably thought he would remain something of a dry old bachelor for the rest of his days. Luckily for Henry it was not to be so: it was at Dunsfold that he fell in love with the step-daughter of a neighbouring cleric, Miss Charlotte Anne Mackenzie Vandyck of Hascombe Rectory, a talented young artist more of an age with his nephew Charley. He wrote to his father to gain his approval for his marriage:[6]

> My removal to this neighbourhood has, among other advantages, procured me the intimate acquaintance of a very worthy and respectable family, Dr and Mrs Mackenzie, of the Rectory, Hascombe. They have a young and very pleasing daughter, to whom I have become deeply attached, and who accepts me for a husband with corresponding feelings. Her good sense, disposition and acquirements give me every hope of her proving a valuable wife and making the happiness of my life. As she is, of course a goddess, my report of her beauty and merits cannot be received; but Hyacinthe has made her acquaintance, and is willing and able to speak of her very highly. She thinks the match likely to be happy to myself, free from objections, and from any circumstances unpleasant to my family or friends ... In taking this step I trust and pray that I may obtain your approbation and sanction, and that your blessing will rest upon the happy prospect now before me.[7]

They married a little over a month later with Henry's sister Hyacinthe as one of the witnesses and by early July they were in London and engaged to dine with the Hathertons. Anne was living in Richmond and it was necessary to invite her to meet her new sister-in-law (although Edward Littleton's diary entry makes it quite clear he did so reluctantly and only because there was no way out of it). Lord Hatherton had managed to avoid his frequently bad-tempered sister-in-law completely for two or three years and he ruminated on the difference in temper and in character between his wife and her sister. Lady Hatherton was all kindness and grace, while Lady Anne was the complete opposite; her one redeeming feature, in Lord Hatherton's opinion, was that she often showed a great spirit of generosity.[8]

Charley made a trip to Dunsfold to visit his Uncle Henry later the same year, and was charmed by his new 'Aunt Chat'. He sent Henry a chatty letter from Harrow once he had returned to school (his younger brother, Arthur, who was not academically inclined, had left the school the year before to be schooled elsewhere and then to join the army; a partial echo of the great-uncle and godfather after whom he was named, who had been taken out of Eton to make way for his more scholarly brothers). He documented a disastrous coach journey back to Harrow via London. After missing the coach he intended to catch, young Charley was stung for 4d more than he should have paid by an unscrupulous London cabbie and only just made the Harrow coach. Boarding that, he spent a nervous and lengthy journey: the equipage nearly overturned on Oxford Street and then halfway to Harrow the splinter bar snapped, necessitating a repair.

Charley had hoped to spend the Christmas holidays with his Uncle Henry and Aunt Chat but he had received a letter from his mother and sisters, written from the port at Dover, telling him that they were visiting Brussels before overwintering at Paris where they wanted Charley to join them. He grumbled to Henry that if he had to go he hoped it would be better than a previous jaunt to Boulogne before finishing his letter in a rush as he realized the time: 'I must leave off soon as it is half past nine now and by half past ten I have got to learn 50 lines of Horace and do 30 Latin verses . . .'. While other public schools such as Rugby offered a much broader range of subjects, the curriculum at Harrow was almost exclusively classical, with only one half-lesson of European history a week. Mathematics and modern foreign languages such as French were treated much the same as dancing classes; additional extras that could be paid for if necessary.[9]

There was obviously a great deal of affection between young Charley and his uncle Henry and he preferred to be at Dunsfold when not at school rather than traipsing around in his mother's retinue. It was perhaps a combination of both Charley's regard for Henry and his own gentle disposition that led him in the same direction as his uncle and his heart was set upon a career in the church. The Duke of Portland held several livings within his gift and a particularly wealthy one in Northumberland was earmarked for Charley to succeed to in due course, once he had attained his degree at university and taken holy orders. His future was mapped out for him, or so he thought.

Chapter Eleven

Love amid the Dreaming Spires

On 1 June 1837, Charley Cavendish Bentinck entered Merton College at Oxford University. The handsome youth who, as a boy, had played with the great Duke of Wellington in the drawing room of the pretty Brompton cottage in which Lord and Lady Charles Bentinck had taken refuge following the scandal of their affair, and who was the grandson of one and the nephew of a successive Duke of Portland, had the promise of a successful career laid out before him. He was aged just 19 and preparing to study for a degree that would enable him to take holy orders, renting a room overlooking the Front Quad for the duration of his studies. Years later the gossip surrounding Charley's time at Oxford was still being told:[1]

> Not a few Oxford men, of nine or ten years' standing, could tell a tale of frantic passion for a Gipsy girl entertained by two young men at one time, one of them with ducal blood in his veins, who ultimately wooed and wedded his Gipsy love. So that it is no way impossible (the heirs to the dukedom being all unmarried, and unlikely to marry) that the ducal coronet of ____ may come to be worn by the son of a Gipsy mother.[2]

Sinnetta Lambourne, handsome, dark and lithe as her mother had been before her, captured the attention of Charley and his rival (whose name has been lost to the mists of time) and she aroused and entranced them in equal measure. The two young men strolled into the Cumnor hills to escape their studies and to gaze down upon Oxford (the view later described by the poet Matthew Arnold in *Thyrsis* as 'that sweet city with her dreaming spires'), and on to Summertown where they met the artless gypsy girl. John Badcock, the Lambournes' next door neighbour in Summertown, on the main road to Oxford, recalled how he watched numerous carriages rattling along and members of the university strolling in conversation outside his windows. Charley and his friend were two of those and they stopped to talk to the sprightly and beautiful young girl, captivated by her dark brunette hair and exotic features. Just like his Wellesley grandfather had done over half a century before, Charley fell head over heels in love with a woman of whom his family would most certainly not approve.

The story was no doubt still fresh in the mind of Matthew Arnold when, in 1853, he penned *The Scholar-Gipsy*. Arnold had attended Balliol College at Oxford as a freshman in 1841 when the gossip about the scion of a ducal family and the gypsy girl would have been at its height (and Arnold's great friend and fellow poet Arthur Hugh Clough was at Balliol at the same time Charley was at Merton and no doubt related the tale). Arnold's poem was based on an old seventeenth-century tale in *The Vanity of Dogmatizing* by Joseph Glanvill about a poor student at Oxford who left his books behind to join a tribe of gypsies and learn their secrets and he also referenced the Cumnor hills that had been home to Sinnetta's family, writing in 1854 to his wife to say he had explored the 'Cumner [sic] country ... and got up alone into one of the little coombs that papa was so fond of, and which I had in my mind in the *Gipsy Scholar*.' Arnold is often viewed as a link between the eras of Romanticism and Modernism and, as such, Charley Cavendish Bentinck's commitment to the gypsy girl he loved in the face of opposition might well have had a bearing on Arnold's poem. The 'scholar gipsy' of the title escaped modern life by joining with the gypsy tribes to learn their wisdom and travel with them. Charley's life was about to take a similarly fateful turn.

The romance between Charley and Sinnetta blossomed quickly, and a true love-match it was too, despite the vast gulf between their respective positions in society. Heedless of the reaction of his family but perhaps mindful of his rival at Oxford for Sinnetta's affections, Charley Cavendish Bentinck, nephew and great-nephew to two of the greatest dukes in the country, grandson to a marquess and half-brother to a girl who was reputed to have royal blood flowing through her veins, proposed marriage to Sinnetta. She accepted and we are left only to guess at her emotions and hopes (or fears) for the future in doing so. What a difference to his uncle Henry Wellesley's approach to his own marriage a few years earlier, when he had observed that his union would be 'free from objections, and from any circumstances unpleasant to my family or friends'; what counsel would Uncle Henry have given to his young nephew, one wonders? Viewed through the eyes of Charley's aristocratic family, a union to Sinnetta was unwelcome and unwanted, despite his love for her, and if Charley's desire for Sinnetta recalled the youthful passion of the young Earl of Mornington for his Parisian mistress, then his impetuosity in proposing marriage echoed his mother's fateful spur-of-the-moment decision to step into the gig and drive away with her lover into a different life. Like his mother and grandfather before him, Charley followed his heart and set his life upon a new course.

Certainly parallels must be drawn between Charley's infatuation for Sinnetta and his grandfather's earlier and similar attachment to Hyacinthe

Gabrielle Rolland. Both women could lay claim to a somewhat exotic background and both were considered unsuitable as wives by the extended families they married into, and both men completely disregarded their family's opinions. The real difference lay in the eras in which the two love stories were set: although only separated by just over half a century, the attitudes of the morally-relaxed Georgian years contrasted sharply with the more 'straight-laced' Victorian age. To add to that, Hyacinthe Gabrielle came with all the allure and mystique of a Parisian ancestry, while poor Sinnetta was solidly working-class and, even more importantly, with a gypsy heritage and all the associated prejudices that came with it. Where polite society had been divided in its opinion on Hyacinthe Gabrielle, even after her ascendancy to the peerage, it would undoubtedly turn its back on a poor gypsy girl once the initial novelty had passed. Charley's great-uncle, the Duke of Wellington, wrote to his eldest son some years earlier when the lad was at Eton, reminding him of what company to keep and who to avoid. The duke would probably have given the same advice to his young great-nephew Charley, had he been asked to do so:

> It is a common but true proverb, that a man is known by the company he keeps, and you may rely upon it, that if you keep bad company thus early, you will never be able to shake them off... good and wise men will shun you, and you will never become distinguished for anything excepting the low, vulgar, & contemptible pursuits of your companions, who, even if they should not have misled you, will have tarnished your Reputation.
>
> God forbid that I should be understood to advise you to keep company with none but persons of your own Rank and Station in life. In all stations there are persons of good and bad Education, manners and habits; and I earnestly entreat you to associate with the former alone, and to avoid the latter, be they of what Rank and Station they may.[3]

Charley had endured a somewhat lonely and loveless childhood, his overbearing and often hot-tempered mother often absent on her travels while he was passed from pillar to post among his relations. It is perhaps then no surprise to find him plunging headlong into a romantic union, seeking the warmth and security of knowing himself to be beloved. Sinnetta's parents, while obviously not at all blind to the advantages that would be given to their daughter following her marriage to a member of the aristocracy, also seem to have accepted Charley regardless of his elevated ancestry and he in turn appears to have enjoyed being part of the extended Lambourne family. It is unknown if he was aware of their true background, that the elder Sinnetta had been born in a gypsy tent and that James had gone by the name of Gypsy

Jim and had fought drunken bare-knuckle fights in his younger days. Possibly he initially just saw a hard-working family and found an element of normality with them that he had lacked elsewhere, and certainly he had not inherited the haughty pomposity with which his relations and forebears viewed humble country folk like the Lambournes. Perhaps it was a desire to conceal their origins that led the Lambournes to move from Summertown to London, a city where they could pass unnoticed and reinvent themselves. They settled in Paddington, their savings allowing them to rent a house in a decent street.

When Charley met his captivating gypsy girl it must have seemed like the dawning of a new age, a fresh beginning in which ideals could be challenged and where romantic possibilities presented themselves. Less than a month after Charley entered Oxford the old King William IV died and the crown passed to his young and beautiful niece Victoria who, like Charley, was still in her teenage years (she was just 18 years of age and dropped her first name of Alexandrina upon her accession to the throne). She had been brought up in Kensington Palace, closely guarded by her widowed mother and the man to whom the Duchess of Kent was in thrall, John Conroy, a darkly handsome but hot-headed and ambitious Welsh army officer who had been equerry to the Duke of Kent and comptroller to the household of the widowed Duchess; the pair harboured pretensions of ruling as regents on the occasion of their young charge ascending to the throne while still under age. They devised what became known as the 'Kensington System' of rules to bend young Victoria to their wishes and she later described her childhood years with some economy of sentiment as 'rather melancholy'. The young Princess Victoria hated Conroy with a passion.

In the event, the old king lived just long enough to thwart the Duchess and Conroy's ambitions and, when she became queen, Victoria was able to throw off the shackles of her constrained childhood and assert her own will. Coming from a family that had been close to the monarchy for successive generations, Charley could not have helped but be beguiled by the romance of the situation; in fact, people everywhere wholeheartedly rejoiced and Victoria's coronation provided a much-needed injection of festivity and joy into the country. The populace had, by and large, fallen out of love with the morally lax sons of King George III and although the steadfastness of William IV in his old age had gone some way to appease them, Victoria, with her naïveté and dignity, heralded a new beginning.

Queen Victoria's coronation (neither as grand as George IV's coronation had been, when Charley's father played such a prominent role, nor as frugal as the ceremony chosen by William IV) took place on 28 June 1838 and London was thronged with crowds who had taken advantage of easier travel to the metropolis thanks to the new railways and come to catch a glimpse of the day. Perhaps Charley and Sinnetta were two of those who made the journey and were there on the day to witness the occasion?

The Dowager Marchioness of Cholmondeley had not lived to see the coronation for she died just five days beforehand, leaving Charley's half-sister Georgiana bereft and adrift, dependent upon the goodwill of the remaining Cholmondeley and Cavendish-Bentinck families. The marchioness specifically named 'Miss Bentinck' in her will, leaving her £200 and a quantity of costly and valuable jewels and ornaments. These were doubly valuable as some had a sentimental connection to Georgiana's late mother, the first Lady Charles Bentinck, especially a gold heart set with turquoise that contained a lock of her mother's precious hair.[4]

Charley and Sinnetta's love affair was conducted with a degree of secrecy, known initially to only a select few and certainly not fully understood by his family who were unaware of the true reason for his failing performance in his academic studies. If his relations knew of Sinnetta at all they would have considered her a mere diversion, a pleasurable distraction but someone who would be abandoned when the time came for Charley to move on and look for a suitable wife. Although he had no great fortune nor a title (the 4th Duke of Portland had three sons living and so Charley had no expectations of ever succeeding to the Portland estate), he was well connected, held the favour of influential men and had the promise of an extremely beneficial living in Northumberland once he had gained his degree and was ordained. His mother and his uncle, the Duke of Portland, possibly already had had their eye on several well-to-do young ladies, their fortunes of equal consideration to their breeding. However, Charley chose to follow his heart, whatever the advice to the contrary.

Charley Cavendish Bentinck obtained a licence to marry from the Vicar General's Office in London. As Sinnetta was under the age of 21 she needed her father's permission before she could take her marriage vows and so old Gyp Lambourne, for the sake of polite convention, was named as an esquire on the marriage allegation and as a gentleman rather than a horse-dealer at the actual marriage (which took place on the next day, 26 September 1839, at St George's in Hanover Square). The youthful Sinnetta presented a pretty picture at her wedding in her best dress with the fashionable 'Victoria' sleeves of the day, her waist pinched in above her voluminous skirt and her dark curls peeping out from beneath her flower-trimmed poke bonnet. Charley was equally handsome in his frock coat and black top hat, gazing down upon his radiant bride.[5] On the marriage certificate Charley gave his address as Brook Street (possibly he had taken lodgings there to satisfy the requirement of

? according to Badcock (see bibliography)
she was born in 1817 so in 1839
she would have been 21 or 22

being resident in the parish for a period of time prior to the wedding), and Sinnetta was living at her parents' house on Southwick Street in Paddington. The two witnesses were John Henry Coole (the son of a greengrocer with connections to Oxfordshire who later followed his father into the trade) and a woman named Mary Baldwin.

The somewhat hasty marriage might have been partly influenced by the romantic fervour sweeping the country in anticipation of a much more public and prominent wedding. The young Queen Victoria had proposed (she had to as queen; it could not be the other way around) to Prince Albert of Saxe-Coburg and Gotha, the nephew of Prince Leopold who years before had been wed, for such a short space of time, to Victoria's cousin, Princess Charlotte of Wales. Prince Leopold, now King of the Belgians following the Revolution of 1830, had been the principal instigator of the union between the couple. It was Queen Victoria's wedding to Prince Albert on a rainy and blustery day in February of 1840 that began the tradition of white bridal dresses and the young queen's journal detailed her wedding day and expressed the emotions felt by any bride on such a momentous occasion since time immemorial. No doubt Sinnetta felt exactly the same as Queen Victoria when the latter recorded that:

> The Ceremony was very imposing, and fine and simple, and I think ought to make an everlasting impression on every one who promises at the Altar to keep what he or she promises. Dearest Albert repeated everything very distinctly. I felt so happy when the ring was put on, and by (my precious) Albert.

Victoria, like Sinnetta, felt all the happiness of finally being alone with the man who was now her husband; whether born a princess or a gypsy, the marriage night transcended class and social position. Although worlds apart in terms of their birth, they were also simply two young women who had just married the men whom they loved and adored:

> I never, never spent such an evening!! My dearest dearest dear Albert sat on a footstool by my side, and his excessive love and affection gave me feelings of heavenly love and happiness, I never could have hoped to have felt before! He clasped me in his arms, and we kissed each other again and again! His beauty, his sweetness and gentleness, – really how can I ever be thankful enough to have such a Husband! ... at 20 m[inutes] p[ast] 10 we both went to bed; (of course in one bed), to lie by his side, and in his arms, and on his dear bosom, and be called by names of tenderness, I have never yet heard used to me before – was bliss beyond belief! Oh! this was the

happiest day of my life! – May God help me to do my duty as I ought and be worthy of such blessings![6]

Sinnetta's parents knew of the wedding as James Lambourne gave his permission for his daughter to marry and the couple were more than likely present at the ceremony but, if so, the fact that neither of them was able to sign their own name precluded them from acting as witnesses to it. Although they could have 'made their mark' when required to sign the marriage register, James Lambourne was being passed off as a well-born gentleman for the day and so both he and his wife would have wanted to hide their illiteracy from inquisitive church officials.[7] However, while the Lambournes were privy to the wedding, the question remains whether Charley's nearest and dearest were aware that he was now a married man. Possibly one or two did know, for his sister Emily was keeping a 'secret' just weeks after the wedding.

Emily was now 19 years of age and the cause of much consternation to her mother. Family arguments about her wellbeing rumbled between Lady Anne and Emily's uncle, the Duke of Portland, arguments into which the Littletons were forever dragged as mediators and peace-keepers (now Richard was gone, Hyacinthe was always the first person to be turned to when Lady Charles Bentinck needed to be 'persuaded' into a certain way of thinking). The young girl was something of a handful and it was proving difficult to find someone to take care of her while her mother was traversing the country throughout the autumn of 1839, Lady Anne heading first to Edinburgh and then moving on to Teddesley for a visit to her sister (which Lord Hatherton was no doubt dreading). The Duchess of Portland offered to take care of her niece for six months but, much as little Georgiana Cavendish Bentinck had been used as a bargaining chip all those years earlier to secure a fortune for the children of Lord Charles' second marriage, now Emily was so used. The Duke of Portland offered Anne an annuity of £800 a year, taken from the money set aside for her four children but on the strict condition that Emily remained within his household.

The Hathertons had also offered to have Emily stay with them (with no financial strings attached) but the duke wrote from his seat, Welbeck Abbey, to Lord Hatherton to say, cryptically, that from what he had learned from their correspondence it would be impolite of Lord Hatherton to have in his house one of Lady Charles' children, other than as a visitor.[8] A few weeks later Lord Hatherton wrote to his wife, saying both he and the duke believed Emily should be placed in a good school in either Paris or Brussels to improve her so that, a year hence, she would be more ready to go into Lady William's household than she was presently. Was Emily a little rambunctious and unladylike? The impression given is that she required a little polishing before she could enter polite society as an eligible young woman.

Lord Hatherton then wondered if Emily had 'shared her secret' with the duke, before deciding she couldn't have done so as the duke would have invariably mentioned it in one of his letters. Unless it was regarding Emily's own romantic intrigues, could that secret have been the marriage of her brother, which had taken place just under three weeks earlier, perhaps known to Emily and to the Hathertons but not to the duke?[9] With Lady Anne and her children dependent upon the largesse of the duke, it was imperative that he especially remained in ignorance of the union his nephew had contracted, for no one was in any doubt of his fury should he discover it. Reading between the lines of Lord and Lady Hatherton's letters to each other dating from this period, it would seem that they and Lady Anne too were fully aware of the situation, with Anne terrified she would lose the income the duke allowed her. Anne also feared that her sister was taking the duke's part instead of hers.

The Hathertons were once again exasperatedly in the middle, trying to keep the peace whatever their private opinions on the matter, and mollifying any suspicions that the duke might be entertaining. Lady Bentinck must have felt that the disgrace Charley had brought on the family (as she saw it) would reflect on her own former behaviour, on her upbringing and management of her children and on Charley's siblings. The ripples from the marriage ran deep and wide; Charley, with the heedlessness of youth, possibly never gave a thought to how his marriage might affect his mother, other than incurring her displeasure. However, with the secret well-guarded from his extended family, it would seem that Emily escaped being sent abroad to school and, in May 1840, was presented by her aunt Hyacinthe, at St James's Palace, to the young Queen Victoria.[10]

To cement his marriage Charley had taken a house at 20 Pickering Terrace in Paddington, not far away from the Lambournes' Southwick Street home, although Charley, mindful of his aristocratic origins, described Pickering Terrace as being located in the neighbouring (and much more fashionable) Bayswater rather than in Paddington. He was not alone in describing Pickering Terrace as being situated in Bayswater as several of his neighbours did likewise, and indeed the houses were situated so close to the boundary between Paddington and Bayswater that it was not too much of a stretch of the truth. Pickering Terrace (now part of Porchester Road) was backed by a double row of houses called Pickering Place, the whole forming a compact block of cottages situated in a rural setting amid the fields of Westbourne Green with some detached villas built alongside.

Relatively new, the terrace had only been built some fourteen years earlier and as late as 1837 some houses were still unfinished and empty. An ideal and quiet spot in which to hide away his wife and to commence family life at a distance far enough away from the prying eyes of London society gossips (the semi-rural location attracted many artistic and literary residents who would be more sympathetic to Sinnetta's origins). It was reasonably cheap to rent too; an important point as Charley was still studying at Oxford and splitting his time between his lodgings there and his home with Sinnetta. While the new Great Western Railway was almost on his doorstep in Paddington, the tracks visible from the fields bordering the front of the house, he could not yet take advantage of convenient and discreet train travel directly to Oxford as it would be some years before the line to that city opened, meaning that Charley had to rely on travelling by the mail or stage coach. As might be predicted, with his attention elsewhere and stuck between two parallel lives, his studies suffered in consequence.

It was at Pickering Terrace that Sinnetta gave birth to their first child, a son named Charles William Cavendish Bentinck. Born on 24 June 1840, he arrived almost exactly nine months after his parents' wedding. Charley's extended family remained silent on the new addition, if indeed they knew of it. Lord Hatherton recorded in his diary four days later that Charley's younger brother Arthur had arrived at his London house to pick up letters of intro-duction for him to take to Dublin where he was to be quartered with the regiment he had joined. As the godson and great-nephew of the Duke of Wellington, it was perhaps ordained from birth that Arthur would enlist as an officer in the armed forces. Charley and Arthur's older sister Anne wrote the following day from Grosvenor Street West asking for the release of her share of the money set aside for the four children, complaining that neither the duke nor her mamma gave her any allowance or pocket money and, understandably at 24 years of age, she wished for some independent income. With Charley's siblings preoccupied with their own lives, no one mentioned the new little Bentinck boy or reached out to him or his parents who soon needed some support, for Charley had but a short and anxious time to enjoy being a father. His newborn son was sickly and died of convulsions, having lived for less than three weeks. The babe was buried at All Souls Cemetery in Kensal Green.[11]

Perhaps it was Sinnetta's grief that persuaded Charley to give up his rented rooms at Merton College at the end of July, for Sinnetta had more than just her son to grieve for and cope with. Her father had been admitted to the Bethnal Green Asylum (a madhouse for lunatics) and he died there, on

6 January 1841, of a palsy. His body was taken back to his birthplace of Cumnor for burial.[12]

The 1841 census reveals the vastly different living standards between Sinnetta and her new in-laws. While Charley's spinster half-sister Georgiana Cavendish Bentinck was living in the luxurious setting of Houghton Hall in North Norfolk, the seat of the 2nd Marquess and Marchioness of Cholmondeley and with seventeen servants listed in attendance, Sinnetta was staying in a humble cottage with her aunt, Nancy Drewitt (James Lambourne's younger sister), in Cumnor. Strangely, Sinnetta was recorded under her maiden name. Did her aunt and uncle Drewitt know of her marriage? While Charley was striving to keep his personal life away from the attention of his ducal uncle, perhaps Sinnetta was facing the same problem but from the opposite direction. Was she worried that her relations would think her too grand a lady now she had married out of her station in life? It is also an indication that she had not yet totally embraced her new way of life and was somewhat adrift between her past and her future. With Charley away at university she must have felt lonely. Charley's friends and family were closed to her but at the same time she must have been wary of getting too close to her mother's new friends in London, lest they jeopardized her position in Charley's eyes.[13]

Sinnetta soon found herself once again with child and another son was born on the evening of 24 July 1841 and given the same name as his unfortunate and short-lived older brother: Charles William Cavendish Bentinck. He survived longer than his sibling, living just over seven months before succumbing to convulsions that led to his death. He died at Hanwell with his gypsy grandmother by his side and was buried at Kensal Green. Sinnetta Lambourne registered the death of her grandson, stating she was present at the time; unable to sign her name, she instead made her mark on the official paperwork.[14]

The death certificate of Charley and Sinnetta's second son shows, perhaps more than any other document, the gulf between their two families. Charley, recorded on the certificate as a gentleman, descended from aristocratic forebears and classically educated at Harrow and Oxford University, contrasted sharply with his mother-in-law who had gypsy rather than ducal blood flowing through her veins and was uneducated, unable to even sign her name. Yet still the gentle and intuitive Charley loved his wife and respected his mother-in-law, happy to live in the same house as her and be counted one of her family. For while he paid lip service to the conventions of the Victorian age, he quietly lived his life on his own terms and according to his own principles and desires. Richard Colley Wellesley may have married a woman who his family and the world at large deemed unsuitable, but he would have baulked at living with her lowly relations – had that been the likely outcome, Charley's grandfather would never have married his Parisian mistress – but Charley, almost modern in his approach, had no such qualms.

There are similarities between Sinnetta and Jane Burden who married the designer and poet William Morris. Jane was born in Oxford in 1839, the year in which Charley and Sinnetta wed, and her later experience somewhat mirrored Sinnetta's. Jane, the daughter of a stableman and a laundress, had a similarly humble and poor working-class upbringing before she was noticed by the Pre-Raphaelite artist Dante Gabriel Rossetti at the age of 18, for whom she became a muse and a model. It was through Rossetti that she met his friend William Morris who, captivated by her beauty, fell in love with her and, like Charley before him, proposed marriage but unlike Sinnetta's love-match, Jane Burden was not enamoured with William Morris (she later became Rossetti's lover). Between her engagement and marriage she received a private education designed to give her the knowledge she lacked and to recreate her as the wife of a rich gentleman. Highly intelligent, she excelled and did become accepted in later life within upper-class circles. Maybe Sinnetta too had been educated at the time of her wedding to help raise her from her humble origins?

Sadly, Sinnetta did feel she had to become the wife that society deemed right and proper for a gentleman of Charley's standing, and not only with regard to her education but also in her appearance, possibly with fatal results. In her desire to disguise her background and look more like a refined English lady, it was asserted that Sinnetta habitually whitened her skin using lead-based cosmetics; she was later described as 'enamelled to her waist'.[15] Unwittingly, if she did indeed do so she was possibly damaging her unborn children by using toxic creams on her skin while pregnant and this may have had a catastrophic bearing on the health of her two babes, hastening their untimely and early deaths, but she was also damaging her own health. The irony is, of course, that Charley had fallen in love with her and married her despite her background but neither of them quite had the absolute courage of their convictions to take the final step and appear fully as they were to the world. While Charley hid his marriage from his relations and Sinnetta tried to hide her dark skin and lied to her extended family back in Cumnor, they were both unconsciously set on a path that would lead them from the happiness they sought.

Sinnetta Lambourne also tried to hide the fact that she was a gypsy; while she did not attempt to lighten her skin she later described herself on census returns, when she was asked for her birthplace, as a British subject born in

Italy; a handy ruse to make her background appear Mediterranean rather than Romany.

Charley's aristocratic links came back into sharp focus later that year with the death of his grandfather, Marquess Wellesley, who died on 29 September 1842, aged 83. For the last eighteen months of his life he had been a virtual recluse and if any of his family knew of Charley's marriage they would not have thought to tell the irascible old man; somewhat ironic given his own youthful insistence upon marrying the woman he had loved despite her origins. Notwithstanding his waspish nature, the marquess was mourned by many including his son-in-law, Lord Hatherton.

After a rather shaky start, the Hathertons had got on famously with the second Marchioness Wellesley. Marianne had been named the beneficiary of her husband's will to the detriment of any expectations from his children, but in the end that counted for nothing once the extent of his debts were realized. The marquess was buried at Eton as he had wished (or at least in accordance with his second choice of resting place, for he had really hoped to be buried at Westminster Abbey). Wellington had his emotions well in check on the day; he was noted by young Richard Wellesley (son of Anne's brother Richard) who recorded the day's events in a letter to his brother Edward: 'The Iron Duke folded his arms and looked sternly on the whole scene, what he felt he was determined not to show.'[16] Charley Cavendish Bentinck would have attended the funeral alone, being careful not to give away anything about his personal life and fending off awkward questions about his studies at Oxford. With his delicately juggled roles of husband, father and bachelor scholar, he was still nowhere near gaining his degree.

Life passed quietly for some time until disrupted by the discovery that Sinnetta Lambourne had been guilty of a deceit. Esau, her youngest son, had been living with a Miss Johnson who kept an establishment on Cambridge Terrace off the Edgware Road in London (possibly he was sent there at the onset of his father's illness to protect him from witnessing the descent of his father into madness). Miss Johnson had educated and boarded Esau for about five years and the bill for his keep was steadily rising. To avoid settling it Sinnetta Lambourne had fabricated a spider's web of lies and half-truths; she claimed that her husband was still alive but insane and upon his death she would inherit some property and be able to settle all her bills. In reality, of course, James Lambourne had already died in the asylum and his wife had taken over the ownership of his property for herself.

Miss Johnson eventually discovered that she had been duped and James Lambourne had lain in his grave for at least three of the five years Esau had spent in her establishment (did Esau know of his father's death and was he complicit in his mother's deceit?). She pressed for payment of the outstanding bill that totalled £120. Quite what Charley made of his mother-in-law's glib and lying tongue is unknown and perhaps she spun stories to explain her predicament which he all too readily believed. Whatever the true case of the matter, Charley steadfastly stood by her, a godsend as she quickly needed every ounce of his help and support. The household was plunged into mourning when Esau died suddenly after returning home, aged only 10, from an inflammation of the bowels (probably a ruptured appendix). Charley took upon himself the responsibility of registering the death and Miss Johnson bided her time, empathizing with a mother's loss even while she remained determined to eventually reclaim the money due to her.

The Reverend Henry Wellesley, now the vicar of Woodmancote in Sussex, felt it was prudent to now take his nephew under his wing. Charley was 27 years of age and had been studying at Oxford for over seven years; it was high time he passed his examinations and obtained his Bachelor of Arts, a necessary qualification if he wanted to be ordained. The two worked daily on Charley's Latin in preparation for his examination and although Uncle Henry was ever a confidante for Charley, he seemed to be unaware of the extent of his nephew's domestic distractions.

Gossip was nonetheless starting to circulate (it must have been common knowledge in the precincts of Oxford University) and Charley was forced to refute allegations of misconduct in a London park where he had presumably been spotted in company with Sinnetta. She was a wife but no wife and gossips would have thought her Charley's mistress or worse. Perhaps he had thought himself safe among the throng, unlikely to be recognized, and with a guilty conscience he denied being there, for as soon as he heard the name of the park mentioned he knew what the inference would be. Henry Wellesley, more concerned with his nephew's poor grounding in Latin grammar which, for all Charley's hard work, was holding him back, wrote to his sister Lady Hatherton about the gossip. Charley was shocked, Henry declared, to have been suspected of such conduct and denied ever having set foot in Richmond Park since the time when he lived nearby with his mother. Henry readily believed his errant nephew, for Charley had denied being in the park before Henry had told him why he was asking. In truth, we suspect Charley's guilty conscience got his rebuttal in quickly before any awkward questions could be asked, forcing him into greater untruths.[17]

Narrowly avoiding wider discovery of his marital affairs, Charley at last achieved his Bachelor of Arts but not at Merton College. He instead took his degree at another of the colleges at Oxford, New Inn Hall, usually known for law and not for the Classics at that period; it was used on this occasion as a quiet corner in which to tuck him away while he finished his studies. He was presented with his degree in a ceremony held on the last day of the Easter term.[18]

Finally, with his degree in his pocket, Charley could look forward to being ordained and granted the lucrative living at Bothal in Northumberland that was in the gift of the Duke of Portland. There was only one thing left to do: the duke would have to be informed that Charley was married before Sinnetta could appear at Bothal as the new vicar's wife, and Charley hoped that his uncle would not pry too deeply into her family connections.

Chapter Twelve

Ducal Discoveries

With the cat out of the bag, the Duke of Portland wasted no time in making his own investigation into the matter at hand. Predictably, he was horrified. Convinced the whole extended gypsy family would pitch up to camp at the rectory door, he was furiously adamant that the living at Bothal could no longer go to Charley. Henry Wellesley made his own enquiries and sadly forwarded the results to his sister Hyacinthe, Lady Hatherton in a letter dated 17 June 1845. The information he had uncovered about the Lambournes matched that found by the duke and he had to agree with him that there was 'no way of patching up the respectability of the connexion, or making a decent defence it is as bad as possible.' He was prepared to allow that the two Sinnettas' moral characters were correct (presumably he had not uncovered evidence of Mrs Lambourne's deceit towards Miss Johnson), but Charley's wife's relatives were gypsies and horse-dealers and the duke would not consider giving the living of Bothal to Charley. Henry felt helpless, not knowing how to persuade the duke to change his mind, 'yet I do not like to see Charley so completely dished by his family.'[1]

Henry had tried to present the matter to the duke in a different light, suggesting that it was Charley who had been deceived by his wife's family rather than he who had intended to deceive his uncle, and stressing to the duke that Sinnetta's relations would not come to live at Bothal; that yes, she had gypsy blood but was not one of a tribe of travelling gypsies. It was all to no avail.

No one had yet dared to tell Charley's mother about the duke's decision. Furthermore, Emily, in the care of the Cavendish-Bentinck family at Welbeck Abbey, was to be married to the Reverend Henry Hopwood, a clergyman who no doubt had one eye on the generous living that had become unexpectedly available to someone in the duke's good books and Anne was in ignorance of that fact too. Did Emily, to further her future husband's prospects, encourage her ducal uncle in his tirade against his unfortunate nephew? In the midst of the secrets and lies spun like a spider's web around the family, it was Lady Hatherton and her brother Henry who struggled to keep the peace and untangle the chaos that was unfolding around them. Again Henry Wellesley wrote to Hyacinthe, unsure of how much their sister

Anne knew of Charley's indiscretions, and he added a postscript to his letter. He thought that either Emily herself or the duke should write to Anne to inform her of the impending wedding and he worried that if Anne was unaware of Charley's marriage then she would think the duke had broken his promise on the living purely to provide for Emily who was under his care. Henry ended by saying 'it is a tad harsh but when once there is mystery it is like one lie necessitating another, there is no seeing one way.'[2]

Nothing has survived to record who was finally brave enough to tell Lady Anne that because her eldest son had married a gypsy he had therefore lost Bothal, or that her youngest daughter had contracted an engagement to a man who now hoped to gain the living, but it is safe to say that Anne would have been incandescent with rage at such an injustice to her eldest son. For all her anger, however, she also wanted to see her children financially secure and the Duke of Portland was persuaded to make a final division of all the trust funds and additions relating to the four children; under the terms of the settlement the fund had to accumulate until the youngest of the children was 21 years of age and that milestone had been reached some four years earlier.[3] Charley wrote to his Uncle Henry with the news and Henry forwarded on the information to Lady Hatherton: each of the four siblings was to have a capital of about £6,000 value and £3,000 at a further time and interest besides. In addition to this, the duke had granted each of them an annuity of £600 in place of their former allowances from him. Henry ended his letter to his sister by noting it was 'all very liberal and satisfactory and places Charles at his ease ... Charles is all gratitude.'[4]

Indeed, it was much more favourable than Charley had dared to hope and a great deal of the credit for that was due to the conciliatory actions of Henry Wellesley (and aided by the duke's wish to appease the vociferous Lady Charles Bentinck). Henry's efforts on behalf of his nephew are all the more touching as he was beset by personal grief himself at the time: 'Chat', his beloved wife and mother of his young children, was dying of consumption and passed away later that year. She was buried at Offley, a pretty village just outside Oxford.[5]

The newspapers made the whole debacle over the living at Bothal even worse when they incorrectly printed that it had gone to Charley after all, the news item running over several days the length and breadth of the country and finally printed in the *Morning Chronicle*:

UNIVERSITY INTELLIGENCE, Oxford, October 18, Preferments.
The Rev. C.W. Bentinck has been presented by his Grace the Duke of Portland to the lucrative rectory of Bothal, near Morpeth. Value £1,307.

These details were followed, a few days later, by a more accurate report in the papers, naming the actual new incumbent and an increased value to the living:

> THE CHURCH – The following appointments have taken place: The Rev. Henry Hopwood, of Queen's College, to the rectory of Bothal, Northumberland. Value £1,507.[6]

Emily had managed to take precedence over her brother and obtain the living for her betrothed. The Reverend Henry Hopwood was, however, required by the duke to sign a deed of covenant promising to resign in favour of either the Honourable William Charles or the Honourable Charles Arthur Ellis, should either of them take holy orders and want the living. The two Ellis boys were the duke's grandsons; his daughter Lady Lucy Joan Cavendish-Scott-Bentinck had, in 1828, married the diplomat and politician Charles Augustus Ellis, 6th Baron Howard de Walden and 2nd Baron Seaford. The living was highly regarded and the duke was determined to see it eventually go to a member of the family related by blood rather than by marriage.[7] That, however, was an event far in the future as the two Ellis boys were only 10 and 6 years of age respectively and so Henry Hopwood gained not only the temporary incumbency of Bothal but also Emily's hand in marriage in quick succession. The couple married in a grand ceremony far removed from Charley's low-key and secretive wedding to Sinnetta. The Duke of Portland took centre stage, signalling his approval of the union, and both he and his eldest daughter Lady Harriet signed the marriage register as witnesses. The *Morning Post* newspaper trumpeted the details:

> MARRIED
>
> On Saturday, the 8th inst., in the parish church of Norton Cuckney, near Welbeck Abbey, the Rev. Henry Hopwood, M.A., Rector of Bothal, Northumberland, to Emily Cavendish, youngest daughter of the late Lord William Charles Augustus Cavendish Bentinck, and granddaughter of his Grace the late Duke of Portland. The bride was given away by her noble uncle, the Duke of Portland. There were also present Lord Henry Bentinck, Lady Harriet Bentinck, and Lady George Seymour. After the ceremony the party returned to Welbeck Abbey.[8]

Still reeling from the recent loss of his aunt Chat with whom he had spent so much time in his childhood and from his ducal uncle's anger at finding out about his union with Sinnetta, Charley was most likely left off the guest list. Even though he was a compassionate man, he would have been a saint indeed not to have felt the injustice to himself and his wife in the proceedings. He could not in truth have attended even if he wished to, with gossip circulating around the wedding feast at Welbeck speculating as to why the duke's nephew had been so publicly debarred from the living. Other events preoccupied Charley's mind, however, of more personal importance to him than the disapproval of his relatives: Sinnetta was pregnant again; an event which, after the two former tragedies, was simultaneously a happy and fearful prospect for the couple.

The child proved to be another son and he arrived in the world and departed from it on the same mild winter's day, 23 December 1845. Born prematurely, he survived for a mere four hours. The sorrowful father registered both the birth and death of his tiny son, who was unnamed, at Hayes in Middlesex, Charley and Sinnetta's new home. Their desolation was complete. All their tentative hopes for their future remained unrealized and all their fears had proved only too accurate.

After some months and as a temporary respite after all the tragedy, a little light now briefly shone into Charley's world. He was ordained as a deacon at the Parish Church of St John the Evangelist on Smith Square in Westminster on Sunday, 31 May 1846 and in the same year he gained his Master of Arts at New Inn Hall.[9] However, that light was all too quickly extinguished. The Hathertons suffered a dual tragedy: their daughter, named Hyacinthe after her mother but known to her family as Cynthy, became ill and deteriorated quickly. She died in the summer of 1847. In the nearby cemetery the family vault was reopened and Cynthy was laid to rest next to her maternal grandmother, Marchioness Wellesley, whose coffin was starting to decay although the velvet surrounding it was still stout, if turned brown through age. Before her daughter's death Lady Hatherton, who had done so much to hold all the branches of her family together, had confessed to her husband that her breast had been painful for some time. Refusing to see a doctor, Hyacinthe declared she would rather die than submit to an operation. She struggled on but both she and her husband knew that there could only be one outcome.[10]

It was probably through the influence of his uncle, the ever-kindly Reverend Henry Wellesley, that Charley gained the position of curate to the Reverend John Hodgson at the village of Lidlington in Bedfordshire.[11] By the summer of 1847 Charley and Sinnetta had taken a house in nearby Ampthill and had made the acquaintance of John Thomas Brooks, a Bedfordshire 'squire' or landowner and a friend of Henry Wellesley's (they had attended Oxford together in their younger days). Brooks' estate was the nearby Flitwick Manor, a fine red brick house surrounded by pleasure gardens and the two families were instantly on visiting terms. Sinnetta was accepted on her merits as Charley's wife by the Brooks family and the Bentincks rented a house in Ampthill on Church Street, a commodious two-storey eighteenth-century property.

John Thomas Brooks kept a diary from which Charley and Sinnetta's joint social life in the early months of 1848 are revealed. He wrote appreciatively that Sinnetta looked 'handsomer than usual' and his daughter Mary Ann called on her during a visit to Ampthill a few days later. Later Brooks stayed for a dinner party at the home of Mr and Mrs George Maule (Maule was the Ampthill vicar) and the other guests were Mr and Mrs Bentinck and Mr and Mrs John Eagles. After dinner there was conversation and music (Jane Maule played the *Elphin Waltz*) and Brooks was entranced by some caged gold-finches that Sinnetta demonstrated, painstakingly trained to perform and 'drilled to trick' (it was something of a Victorian obsession to keep caged finches as pets). A week later John Thomas Brooks, his daughter Mary Ann and the Reverend and Mrs Charles Cavendish Bentinck found themselves guests at an evening party given by the neighbouring Dawsons at their vicarage in Flitwick. Brooks recalled there was dancing from half-past nine until the early hours of the morning, and the assembled guests waltzed and danced polkas; Mary Ann Brooks described the evening as one of 'conjuring and dancing'. After the tribulations of the preceding years it is heart-warming to know that Sinnetta was invited, without prejudice, to join the local gentry at their dinner parties and evening entertainments, and they in turn happily took their place in her drawing room. It was, perhaps, the happiest period of her married life.[12]

Sadly, shortly after a few tantalizing diary entries in the early months of the year mentioning Sinnetta and Charley, Squire Brooks' daughter Mary Ann became ill and he largely gave up socializing with his neighbours; his diary falls silent on the Bentincks' daily activities. Mary Ann died in the August of 1848, plunging the Brooks family into mourning and Charley and Sinnetta's life back once again into the shadows.

Charley Cavendish Bentinck was ordained as a priest in August 1848 but continued as the curate of Lidlington in Bedfordshire. It was a living in the gift of Francis Russell, the 7th Duke of Bedford, who became Charley's patron after he was abandoned by the Duke of Portland and perhaps the patronage of the Duke of Bedford came about at the prompting of Squire Brooks of Flitwick Manor.[13] Tellingly, the Duke of Bedford was fully aware of Sinnetta's ancestry and, as it was something he could not influence or change, he chose to pay no regard to it and instead judged her upon her own worth. He was repaid in full: Sinnetta proved to have a gentle connection with Charley's parishioners who trusted and respected her.

Rather than live in Charley's parish, the couple retained their home in Ampthill where the bustling life of a market town offered more distractions than a small village and where they were happy. Perhaps this was a deliberate decision upon the part of Charley and Sinnetta to protect their privacy, for they would have been fearful of the reaction they might encounter if their story became common knowledge, even with the Duke of Bedford's support in the local community. Did they feel on safer ground having their home at a little remove from the village Charley served? Sinnetta was now truly caught between two worlds, simultaneously the sprightly gypsy girl from the Oxfordshire countryside with whom Charley had fallen in love and a respectable vicar's wife with a hidden ancestry.

The curacy at Lidlington was by no means as impressive a position to hold as the one at Bothal in Northumberland would have been, neither in terms of the salary it offered nor in the fabric of the church. The Duke of Bedford's librarian, John Martin, penned a series of often scathing articles on Bedfordshire churches that were printed in the *Northampton Mercury* newspaper under a pseudonym to hide his identity from his employer. His article on the church at Lidlington dates from June 1845, just three years before Charley's time. It would appear, from Martin's account, to be a shabby little church to which Charley was appointed:

> The exterior view of this church placed in a commanding situation, is extremely unpicturesque, nor is there anything in the internal fitting to redeem it ... The floor [of the chancel] was extremely dirty, and it appeared to be selected as the lumber room for benches and boxes, which were piled up against its side walls. The font, a miserable modern imitation, was misplaced in front of the rails. Within the railing was an iron chest, one of the most glaring instances of desecration that has fallen under our notice. The table itself would have hardly been deemed worthy admittance to the humblest cottage of the village. There was no handstile by which access to the church yard could be obtained, it was therefore necessary to clamber over the gate to obtain entrance into the church. Sheep were grazing, rendering the pathway very disagreeable in consequence of their admission, the feet of those who entered the building depositing their impurity upon its floor ...[14]

Still, it was a safe haven, it paid a wage and offered a position in society. The couple resided among friendly folk in a pretty village setting and Charley and Sinnetta counted their blessings. Meanwhile, the news from Teddesley Hall regarding Charley's aunt Hyacinthe continued to provide a gloomy prospect on the horizon for her condition was worsening day by day.

It was from the house at Ampthill that Charley wrote on a cold, dark January day to offer his uncle, Lord Hatherton, his sincere condolences and sympathies. Hyacinthe, Lady Hatherton had finally succumbed to her illness on 6 January 1849 in the southern bedroom at Teddesley Hall. She had known she was dying: her breathing had been laboured and difficult for many months and she had suffered other setbacks too, including losing the sight in her right eye. Arthur Cavendish Bentinck had been to see her a month earlier and she had taken an affectionate farewell of him and given him a present for one of his sisters. Charley, like everyone who had known Hyacinthe, was bereft.

Charley arrived at Teddesley Hall on the day before the funeral and was met by his brother Arthur and his Wellesley relatives, including his uncle, Henry Wellesley. Sinnetta Bentinck did not attend but it was not unusual for the mourners to be predominantly male so this should not necessarily be considered a slight upon her. Universally mourned, the Right Honourable Hyacinthe Mary, Lady Hatherton was laid to rest in the family vault beside her beloved daughter Cynthy and her mother, Lady Wellesley. She had planned her own funeral including ordering mourning for the children of the National School who stood in the chancel near to the vault during the service. Her husband's heart-breaking diary entry, written later in the day, recalled that he 'took of each [coffin] a last painful look, and kissed them both.'[15]

If the Duke of Portland had been suspicious of his nephew's in-laws, he need not have worried. The widowed Sinnetta Lambourne remained in London, living at 43a Grosvenor Mews near to fashionable Grosvenor Square in Mayfair and had not, as the duke feared, insisted on remaining by her daughter's side and scandalizing Charley's parishioners. Miss Johnson, the lady who was still owed £120 for young Esau Lambourne's education and upkeep, had continued to hound the elder Sinnetta for payment of the debt and Sinnetta had continued to avoid paying it. Even a decision in a court of law that had added a further £39 in costs to Sinnetta's bill had been ignored. Finally, Mrs Lambourne declared herself bankrupt, regardless of the properties she had inherited under her husband's will and which she still owned. She was summoned to appear in the Insolvent Debtors Court in Portugal Street where she applied for an interim order for the protection of process. The Reverend Charles Cavendish Bentinck and his wife wisely refrained from any involvement; it was not the scandal the duke had feared but, all the same, they would not wish it to come to his ears. Sinnetta Lambourne claimed to be 'out of business' and her financial woes rumbled on throughout the year.[16]

Grosvenor Mews might have looked, on paper, to be a desirable address close to Grosvenor Square but in fact the maze of narrow mews was home to poverty and disease. The small living quarters of the buildings were located over sundry workshops or over the stables and coach houses that belonged to the neighbouring gentry and were overcrowded by unscrupulous landlords.[17] Sinnetta Lambourne was more at home in the fresh country air enjoying village life or on a gypsy encampment than in an overcrowded and unhealthy city environment, but she neither returned to Summertown in Oxfordshire nor seems to have attempted to lodge with her daughter and son-in-law. Perhaps she knew that her daughter would suffer and have little chance of being accepted by Charley's Bedfordshire parishioners should she attempt to move in to their Ampthill home.

After spending so long away from her former gypsy family she was no longer one of them, even supposing she did wish to return to the old travelling life she remembered from her childhood years. Therefore Sinnetta Lambourne remained in London on her own, trying as best she could to resolve her problems and keep her head above water. It was a sad end to the bright future she had seen for herself when she turned her back on her old way of life and her gypsy tribe. For some years she must have felt justified in her brave decision for all had been happiness and prosperity but now, with the sole exception of her daughter's elevated marriage, she had been brought low. Living far away from her few remaining children, she eked out a reduced existence in the shadows of the London slums.

The Reverend Charles Cavendish Bentinck left his curacy at the rundown church at Lidlington in August 1849 for new and better prospects. He was presented with a handsome silver inkstand to place on his desk by his parishioners who were sorry to see him leave. It was engraved with the following inscription: 'Presented to the Rev. W.C.C. Bentinck, as an affectionate token of their grateful attachment and esteem by his parishioners at Lidlington, August, 1849.'[18]

Charley had been appointed to the livings of nearby Husborne Crawley and Ridgmont by his kindly patron the Duke of Bedford, but still the Bentincks continued to live in Ampthill. The duke was having a vicarage built in both of these two villages at the time when Charley took over the livings, hoping to encourage proper support for both the churches and to reinvigorate the two parishes. Husborne Crawley was a pretty and rural little village, bordering the Duke of Bedford's stately Woburn Abbey and with a population of just over 600 inhabitants.[19] The church in which Charley ministered was St James, located half a mile to the north of the village; a fine, venerable building dating from the medieval era. It was a clean and tidy church but one that was in a somewhat dilapidated state of repair. John Martin again gave us his opinion on the church in August 1845, four years before Charley was appointed to the living:

> The fine tower of this church is a well-known object from various points. It has happily escaped the hands of modern improvement, at least they have been very gently imposed. Not so the interior, which has undergone such mutilation that little vestige of its former beauty remains... The noble owner of the living, whose restorations in others in his gift have called forth the praise in all capable of appreciating them, may perhaps one day give the minister and churchwardens a gentle hint as to the state of the interior of this church ... The porch was in a very decayed state; the windows were not entirely blocked up. The churchyard was in tolerable condition, cattle were grazing, and the nettles flourished, but the gates were open, and facility to enjoy the very agreeable prospect from this spot thus provided for. It is but just to say that the interior as to cleanliness was all that could be desired.

The ancient church at Ridgmont (it dates from the eleventh century, before the Norman Conquest, and was originally the church belonging to an Anglo-Saxon settlement named Segenhoe) fared little better. John Martin was pleased to note that the building was in a decent state with the churchyard in good order, but he was equally scathing about the fabric of the church as he had been regarding Husborne Crawley and Lidlington:

> This as little resembles a building for the Church of England as any that we have seen in this country ... The western entrance and window are entirely blocked up ... The font, though miserably encrusted with white-wash, was apparently, a very good one of the period, and occupied its proper position ... A mean altar table, and the railing to match.[20]

While the churches themselves may have been unimpressive, Charley's new appointments brought with them a bigger stipend allowing the couple to move slightly further down the road upon which they lived in Ampthill to a bigger mansion house.[21] Their new home, built in 1742 and known as Foulislea, was constructed from the local orange-coloured brick to a London 'square' design and cleverly converted into a prominent town house by the addition of supporting red brick 'book-ends' to its façade. Standing three storeys high, it had a square bay running up the whole height of the house over the grand Ionic porch and was a suitably grand house for the nephew of a duke to live in. Sinnetta was now very much a well-to-do lady with servants to take care of the day-to-day running of the house, a far remove from her childhood years.[22]

Squire Brooks began to pay social visits once again, a year in mourning having passed, and he noted in his diary several visits to the Bentincks' new Ampthill home. On one occasion in September 1849, he went straight from the Bentincks' home to visit the Duchess of Bedford at Woburn Abbey. Born Anna Maria Stanhope, the daughter of the 3rd Earl of Harrington and Jane Fleming, the Duchess of Bedford had served as Lady of the Bedchamber to the new Queen Victoria and remained a good friend of the monarch. How strange and wonderful to think of a grand duchess hearing an account of Sinnetta, the daughter of a gypsy, from the gentleman seated in her drawing room and taking an interest in her welfare.[23]

Chapter Thirteen

The Love Story ends in Tragedy

Charley and Sinnetta's love story was about to play out to its tragic conclusion; the year 1850 broke upon the couple in their Ampthill mansion with a barrage of emotions.

In the first few days of the year Charley's younger sister, now Mrs Emily Hopwood, gave birth to a daughter at the vicarage in Bothal; a happy event but one tempered with longing regret for Charley and Sinnetta for it had been their intended home and the place where they had imagined themselves bringing up a much-longed-for family. The Hopwoods were steadily filling their Northumberland rectory with a brood of noisy children, two sons already present in the nursery there. The Bentincks' nursery in their grand house at Ampthill remained resolutely empty. More worryingly, Sinnetta was battling with ill health, a doubly cruel blow with the couple finally settled and embarked upon a new happy chapter in their lives as a much-respected country vicar and his wife. Sinnetta was experiencing severe abdominal pain and losing weight, almost wasting away although her belly was swollen. Did she perhaps initially wonder if she was once again pregnant, hoping against hope for a positive outcome to her suffering?

If any doubts had been entertained as to her true condition, they were quickly put into sharp focus. No sooner had the news of Charley's new niece been received in Bedfordshire than it became clear that Sinnetta Bentinck was seriously ill. The doctors diagnosed mesenteric disease and could do nothing for her. It was soon realized that she would not live much longer. Charley was distraught.

He had sacrificed everything to live his life by Sinnetta's side and now he was about to lose her. In the midst of all his troubles, the displeasure and censure of his family, the loss of Bothal and, most significantly, the shared grief of their lost children, Sinnetta had been there to comfort him and provide a reason to continue. When the shining light of her love for him was finally extinguished, when she no longer lit up his home and life with her mere presence, he would be on his own to face the bleakness of an existence without her.

Sinnetta died, aged just 32, on 19 February 1850 in her Ampthill house. The few people who had truly known her had all, unfailingly, been touched by her kind thoughtfulness and they loved her regardless of her origins, as had Charley. It was a tragic end to a love story that had broken the rules and crossed class boundaries, a union for which Charley had fought bitterly despite all the objections raised by his family. He had loved Sinnetta with all his being and now he was alone.[1]

The Duke of Bedford, Charley's patron, was the one who told Lord Hatherton of his nephew's bereavement. He wrote from Woburn Abbey of 'Mrs Bentinck's very alarming illness'; the duke had travelled to London and, upon his return, learned of her death. He praised Sinnetta as a clergyman's wife and was fully appreciative of her help in the regeneration of his neglected villages where her influence with the labourers and their families in Charley's parish had been a boon. The duke ended his letter with a plaintive appeal on Charley's behalf which reveals the torment the poor widowed man was enduring: 'I know not what he will now do, but I almost fear that I shall lose him.'

However, when the Duke of Bedford wrote to Lord Hatherton again four days later, he was already thinking about the future. With a practicality almost bordering on heartlessness, he opined that Charley should marry again and that his next wife must be acceptable to both his ducal uncle and to his family. For all his approbation of poor Sinnetta, the Duke of Bedford had already written her off as Charley's youthful folly now the way was clear for him to make a more 'respectable' union. Charley was lost in his own personal torment for it was a view that was shared by Charley's wider family: Sinnetta's death, sad as it was, offered him a chance to atone for his marital indiscretion and appease his family.[2]

Sinnetta had been ignored by the wider public in life, for with Charley's relationship to the Duke of Portland, one could have expected an announcement of his marriage in the newspapers and also news of the births (and deaths) of his children. No such public announcements had been made but in death, and as a clergyman's wife, Sinnetta was recognized and a notice was printed in various publications. The *Gentleman's Magazine* was one such source, lauding Charley's illustrious connections and incorrectly ascribing four children to the couple.[3] Her long-dead father was once again raised in rank to an esquire rather than a much lowlier country horse-dealer; in death just as during her married life, Sinnetta was denied her true birthright: 'Feb 19. At Ampthill, Sinnetta, wife of Rev'd Charles W.F. Cavendish Bentinck, nephew to the Duke of Portland. She was the daughter of James Lambourne esq., was married in 1839 and had issue four children, all who died infants.'[4]

With no surviving image of her and little trace left behind, it is tempting to view Sinnetta Bentinck as almost ethereal, a beautiful nymph who had captivated Charley, bound him to her and then suddenly faded from his life. For Charley, however, her presence in his life had been all too real, both in its pleasure and in its pain and he was now left alone and grief-stricken to face a future that looked bleak without his wife by his side. His faith was the only beacon left to him and he threw himself into helping his parishioners, dedicating himself to his religious calling. It was one small comfort to him.

Sinnetta's unusual name lived on, given to several successive generations of girls in the village of Ampthill and the immediate vicinity, the tradition being that they were descended from Sinnetta Bentinck's maid and had all been named in her honour.[5]

It was not at Ampthill where Sinnetta was buried, nor in the churchyard of the two churches where Charley ministered but at Lidlington where Charley had initially held his curacy. Perhaps Charley and Sinnetta both felt an affinity with the church and the parishioners where they had first been accepted. Her resting-place was a handsome marble tomb, surrounded by tall iron railings and standing on the north side of the church. At least two of Charley's relatives attended the funeral – his uncles the Reverend Henry Wellesley and Lord Hatherton – and John Thomas Brooks was also present to pay his respects.[6]

There is a curious entry some months later in the diary of John Thomas Brooks. Towards the end of September he mentioned meeting Henry Wellesley at the train station alongside a woman whom Henry introduced as his mother. Perhaps Brooks was unaware of the death of Hyacinthe Gabrielle, Marchioness Wellesley some thirty-four years earlier and Wellesley, diplomatically and to prevent untoward gossip, told a small white lie and hoped to pass off one lady of exotic heritage for another? Could the woman he was there to meet possibly have been Mrs Sinnetta Lambourne, on a journey from London to visit her daughter's grave and comfort her bereaved son-in-law? Charley had never shunned his gypsy mother-in-law in the past when his wife was alive; why would the two not stand together at Sinnetta Bentinck's grave to mourn her?

Sinnetta Lambourne was to live for more than two decades after her daughter's death and eventually died at her home on Euston Road of chronic bronchitis in early 1871, aged 87, without her family by her bedside and with few people left to care either for or about her. Her death, which took place on 23 January 1871, was registered by a family friend, Matilda Elizabeth Anderson née Carnegie whose mother had been born in Cumnor and whose family lived in the same area (St Pancras) as Sinnetta Lambourne in the 1850s. There was no one left to take her body back to the Oxfordshire countryside to be buried in Cumnor alongside her husband James. Instead, Sinnetta was buried in the cemetery at Kensal Green where the bodies of her little Bentinck grandsons lay.

Foulislea, the Bentincks' grand house in Ampthill, now rattled with empti-ness; any hopes of sons and daughters to fill the many rooms in the house with laughter and happiness had died along with Sinnetta. The mansion stood as a symbol of all that Charley had loved and lost and he could remain there no longer. He moved with just two servants to the newly-built rectory at Ridgmont instead: a seven-bedroomed house complete with a prospective nursery, four drawing rooms, servants' quarters, a stable-yard, coach house and substantial garden. In all likelihood Charley had intended to share this new and modern home with Sinnetta upon its completion. Now it offered a chance to escape the continual reminders of her presence and to attempt to make a new beginning.[7]

As if life had not already thrown enough at the Reverend Charles Cavendish Bentinck, just months after the death of his wife his sister Emily Hopwood died at the Bothal rectory. Her widowed husband was left to bring up their three young children and Charley must have envied his brother-in-law this small comfort that had been denied to him. Although Emily had clashed with her mother in her youth (Lady Anne had made little secret of the fact that she preferred the company of her eldest daughter to that of her youngest), Emily's death left Lady Anne bereft. Even with the holes left in their lives by all the myriad deaths of their nearest and dearest, it is still somewhat surprising, given his former total abhorrence of her, that Lord Hatherton now found a great deal of pleasure in his sister-in-law's company and he began to call frequently on Lady Anne and her namesake daughter (who was settled into the role of middle-aged spinster and reluctant com-panion to her still often irascible mother).

Lord Hatherton had begun, almost too late, to see the similarities between his late and adored wife and his sister-in-law, even though they were possessed of very different characters. Their shared tragic losses threw the two old protagonists together and in their older age they began to build bridges in their relationship and try to ease each other's grief. Lord Hatherton was also instrumental in supporting his nephew Charley in collusion with the almost fatherly Duke of Bedford. The two men encouraged Charley to pay a visit to Teddesley Hall during the late November of 1850 to lift his spirits and to try to mend the poor broken man. The waspish Lady Anne must have struggled somewhat to share in her son's grief at Sinnetta's death, however much she might have felt sympathy for his pain.[8]

It was during the following year that the London Illustrated News ran its article in the 'Gypsey Experiences' column written by Tom Taylor under the pseudonym of 'A Roumany Rei' in which the tale of a 'frantic passion for a Gipsy girl [was] entertained by two young men ... one with ducal blood in his veins' was told. If gossip had not fully picked up on Sinnetta during her lifetime, it obviously had quickly caught up since her death. It was doubly cruel for Charley to see his life laid bare for the entertainment of others when his grief was still so raw and his family would have despaired still further to find the whole affair public knowledge when they had tried so hard to keep it quiet. They had thought the scandal buried along with Sinnetta.[9]

The widowed Reverend Cavendish Bentinck lived in a solitary way with just two female servants in the rectory at Ridgmont, hoping that the interest in his love life stirred up by the Roumany Rei would be of short-lived duration. The females of his family carried on with the social merry-go-round. In the early 1850s his mother and sister Anne were staying in rooms at fashionable Brighton, at 2 Junction Road West. At no. 4 was Augusta Ada, Countess of Lovelace and Lord Byron's only legitimate daughter, together with her mother and youngest son. Charley's half-sister Georgiana was in even grander surroundings. She was visiting her uncle, the Duke of Portland, at Welbeck Abbey in Nottinghamshire with a veritable army of staff at her beck and call who would indulge her every whim. Arthur Cavendish Bentinck was with his regiment and Henry Hopwood was at Bothal, with a nurse and nursemaid living in to help look after his young family. Their lives were interrupted a year later with the state funeral of Charley's great-uncle, the mighty Duke of Wellington.[10]

Wellington died on 14 September 1852 at Walmer Castle in Kent where he held the position of Lord Warden of the Cinque Ports. His funeral took place a little over a month later in St Paul's Cathedral in London. With barely any standing room left, London was brought to a standstill on the day and the streets were lined to watch the coffin wend its way to the cathedral upon an enormous funeral carriage drawn by twelve horses, the design of which had been specifically chosen by Prince Albert (and which caused confusion and chaos: its wheels got stuck on The Mall and it took an hour to get the duke's coffin into St Paul's when they arrived as the mechanism on the carriage that would transfer the coffin to the bier failed). The duke had been kinder to Lady Anne in her hour of need than her own father had been; if it was a sad occasion for the country at large, it was even more so for those who had known the great man intimately.[11]

Back in Charley's Bedfordshire parish of Ridgmont a new church was being built. The Duchess of Bedford laid the foundation stone and Charley's mother paid for two magnificent stained-glass windows as a benevolent gift. The church was consecrated on All Saints' Day, 1855. Charley threw himself into his vocation and managed to find some comfort in ministering to his parishioners and wholeheartedly serving in his churches; life passed by quietly for some years. The Reverend Henry Wellesley and his eldest son (when not at Eton) paid the occasional visit to Ridgmont and Squire Brooks eagerly pressed them to visit Flitwick Manor and to dine with him whenever he had the chance.[12]

In what seems like one long list of deaths in the family, Charley's uncle the 4th Duke of Portland passed away in 1854 aged 85. His eldest son had pre-deceased him and so the title and the estates passed to the second son, the eccentric William John Cavendish-Bentinck-Scott who, at the age of 54, was unmarried and something of a recluse; his obsession with building tunnels beneath Welbeck Abbey earned him the nickname of 'the Mole'. As neither the new 5th Duke of Portland nor his younger brother Lord Henry Bentinck had any legitimate heirs, Charley now stood second in line to the dukedom (which could only pass down the male line and so bypassed the 4th Duke's many daughters). With Charley also being childless, his younger brother Arthur was placed in a most fortunate position and both Charley and Arthur began to appear as a good catch on the marriage market to parents who were keen to see their daughters married well.[13]

Arthur Cavendish Bentinck had continued steadily in his military career and by 1857 had risen to the rank of lieutenant colonel with the Dragoon Guards. He was dashing, handsome and still a relatively young man of 38 when he finally married at St George's in Hanover Square. His chosen bride was Miss Elizabeth Sophia Hawkins-Whitshed, daughter of Sir St Vincent Keene Hawkins-Whitshed, Baronet, of Killincarrick in County Wicklow in Ireland. The two families had been on friendly terms for many years and had intermarried previously; the Hawkins-Whitshed family were both descended from and had married into the Dutch branch of the Bentinck family. The wedding ceremony was conducted by the Dean of Ripon who was Elizabeth Sophia's great-uncle, and he was assisted by Charley who was keen to play a part in his younger brother's wedding day.[14]

Sadly, Arthur's marriage was doomed to end in tragedy just as Charley's had been. Elizabeth Sophia quickly fell pregnant and was delivered of a son on 28 December 1857 at her father's Scottish estate of Kinnaird in Perth-shire. The child survived the birth but Elizabeth Sophia did not. She died exactly one week later.

Chapter Fourteen

A New Beginning

With all the quiet rebelliousness of his youth now over, the Reverend William Charles Cavendish Bentinck slowly closed the chapter of his life that had contained his passionate love for his gypsy bride and all the combined sorrows and joys that their union had brought to him. Steadily he began to be accepted, once more, back into the folds of his aristocratic family. His presence at the wedding of his brother Arthur bore testament to this fact.

Their father's elopement with their mother in 1815 and the subsequent Crim. Con. trial had rightly scandalized Regency high society and their families, but the couple had lived together happily enough after their hurried marriage once they were free to do so. Charley's first marriage had likewise scandalized his family but for very different reasons; this time it had been the disgrace of marrying beneath him to a girl with gypsy blood flowing through her veins. However, Charley and Sinnetta's union had been a true love-match and only her death had brought an end to it. Now, after many years of solitary widowhood he chose to marry again, this time to a woman of whom his family fully approved. This second marriage was, perhaps, no less a loving one but its difference lay in the fact that not a whiff of scandal could be attached to it for the bride was eminently respectable and suitable in every way. In stark contrast to Charley's first secretive marriage, this one was announced to the world, doubly lauding the forthcoming nuptials and announcing that Charley had regained his footing within the social elite:

APPROACHING MARRIAGE in HIGH LIFE.
A marriage is arranged, and will shortly take place, between the Rev. Charles William Frederick Cavendish Bentinck, first cousin to the Duke of Portland, and Miss Louisa Burnaby, youngest daughter of Mr. Edwyn Burnaby, of Baggrave Hall, Leicestershire.[1]

Caroline Louisa Burnaby was 27 years of age when she married Charley on 13 December 1859, some fifteen years younger than her new husband.[2] Her father, Edwyn Burnaby, was a public-spirited man, serving as Deputy Lieutenant and High Sheriff of Leicestershire, and her mother Anne Caroline née Salisbury was the daughter of a Dorset solicitor. A talented artist in her own right, two religious paintings by her are held within the Royal Collection at Windsor. The Burnabys' family estate, Baggrave Hall, was a fine eighteenth-century Palladian-styled mansion standing at South Croxton to the east of Leicester. Possibly the couple had been introduced by Caroline Louisa's uncle, the Reverend Gustavus Andrew Burnaby who was the rector of St Peter de Merton Church in Bedford from 1835 to 1866 and who would therefore have been known to Charley from the days of his first marriage and afterwards. The Reverend Burnaby officiated as a visiting minister at the wedding of his niece to the Reverend Charles Cavendish Bentinck.

Although Charley's family had been pushing for a remarriage to a suitable lady since poor Sinnetta's death, Charley had proved by his past actions that he knew his own mind and would not be swayed from his designs. His second union should therefore be viewed in this light; it must have been a relief to him that his family were more than willing to take Caroline Louisa into their hearts but he was not a man to marry purely for the sake of respectability or to conform to the wishes of others. It may have been a more sensible union in the eyes of his peers, but it need not have been any the less heartfelt than his first.

The marriage took place at St George's, Hanover Square; that parish having, over the years, borne witness to the wedding of Charley's Wellesley grandparents and to his own first marriage to the beautiful Sinnetta Lambourne in 1839. This marriage did not take place in St George's church itself though, but instead in one of the district churches to be found within the ecclesiastical boundary of the parish. Perhaps it would still have been too painful to have stood at the same altar where Charley had exchanged vows with his first bride?

Charley and Caroline Louisa married at St Paul's, a relatively new church on Wilton Place in Knightsbridge, one of the most beautiful of the Victorian churches in the whole of London. It was also, even if he meant it unwittingly, a nod back to Charley's Oxford days when he first set eyes on his gypsy love for it was the first church in London to evince the principles and ideals of the 'Oxford Movement' (something of a Catholic revival that had steadily gained ground during the years of Charley's attendance there). St Paul's had been enhanced to suit High Church conventions and Caroline Louisa was later described as being 'very religious and rather too High Church' by her niece, Lady Ottoline Violet Anne Cavendish-Bentinck Morrell.[3] The new Mrs Bentinck and Charley seem to have been well-suited to one another in respect of their religion and Caroline Louisa made a quintessential Victorian clergyman's wife. Charley's ancestry was illustriously confirmed in the marriage register where the description of the rank or profession of his long-dead father was given simply as 'duke's son'.

Standing as he did, second in line to becoming the Duke of Portland, a probability that looked increasing likely due to the continued bachelorhood of his two cousins, Charley was a most eligible husband. Certainly he appeared a much better prospect than he had at the time of his marriage to Sinnetta all those years earlier, for then it would have been expected that the three sons of the 4th Duke of Portland would supply enough heirs between them to provide claimants to the title. To cement his return to his proper social standing, on the arm of his new wife Charley was presented by his father-in-law to Queen Victoria and Prince Albert at a levee held at St James's Palace.[4]

Queen Victoria's own happy marriage to Prince Albert ended with his death in December 1861, plunging Victoria into a grief from which she never recovered; she remained in mourning for her husband for the rest of her life. At least Charley had grasped a second chance at happiness and was fully rewarded for doing so.

The new husband and wife lived, when in London, with the Burnaby family in fashionable Belgravia, at 50 Eaton Place (Charley's parents had lived on the same street around the time of King George IV's coronation). It was in that London town house that their daughter Cecilia Nina Cavendish-Bentinck was born on 11 September 1862. The birth, unlike those of his sons which he had been forced to keep from public knowledge, or at least from his uncle the duke's eyes, was announced in the newspapers. The little girl was baptized back in Charley's Bedfordshire parish of Ridgmont just over a month later and named after her aunt Cecilia Florence Burnaby who had married George Onslow Newton of Croxton Park in Cambridgeshire. The baptism of little Cecilia was an occasion to cement the new-found family goodwill: her godparents were the Duke of Portland and his sister Lady Charlotte Denison, and it was conducted in the new parish church.[5] A few months earlier, in the early summer, Charley's portly but handsome brother Arthur had also married for a second time after resigning his army commission. His bride was Augusta Maria Elizabeth, daughter of the Reverend Henry Montague Browne, Dean of Lismore in Ireland. Arthur's wedding, which took place in Weybridge in Surrey, was conducted by Charley.[6]

Finally, after all the tragedy that had played out in their earlier married lives, both brothers were settled and happy with all the love of a growing family around them. The reclusive 5th Duke of Portland was delighted to reclaim the Reverend Charles Cavendish Bentinck as a relation and began to send down hampers and produce from Welbeck as gifts.[7]

Edward Littleton, Lord Hatherton, that old adversary turned fond and beloved friend of Lady Anne Bentinck, died at Teddesley Hall in May of 1863. He had married again, three years after being widowed, to Caroline Davenport née Hurt who belonged to a Derbyshire family. Caroline was herself widowed and during her first marriage to Edward Davies Davenport she had become good friends with the author Elizabeth Gaskell. It was to Mrs Gaskell that Caroline Davenport turned a week before her marriage when she found herself alone at Capesthorne Hall near Alderley Edge in Cheshire, her former marital home (she had expected Lord Hatherton for company but he had been detained). So Mrs Gaskell travelled to be by her friend's side and on the way she met Lord Hatherton, who jumped out of his fly (a 'nice-looking elderlyish gentleman') and introduced himself to her, saying he had come down from London via an express train to pay a surprise visit to Mrs Davenport as she had told him she was unwell. At Capesthorne Hall, Caroline Davenport displayed the trousseau for her forthcoming wedding to her friend:

> A set of diamonds and opals, and a set of diamonds & emeralds – (the first far the most beautiful & far the most expensive too,) a green velvet cloak down to her heels lined & trimmed with miniver, 6 Indian shawls of various kinds ... *oh dear!* They were so soft and delicate and went into such beautiful folds ...[8]

Elizabeth Gaskell was one of the first visitors to the new Lady Hatherton and her husband at Teddesley Hall. There she made the acquaintance of the head gardener John Burton who had travelled to Tehran in modern-day Iran to take up the position of gardener to the Shah of Persia (Mohammad Shah Qajar, 1808–48) a lucrative opportunity that soon turned sour upon the death of the Shah. He returned to England and was taken on at Teddesley, a far cry from his Persian adventures. Mrs Gaskell interviewed him and then published an account of his experience titled 'The Shah's English Gardener' in Charles Dickens' magazine *Household Words* in 1852. It was at the instigation of the 2nd Lady Hatherton that the gardens at Teddesley that were tended by the well-travelled Mr Burton were opened to the public.

The new Lady Hatherton had also made the acquaintance of Elizabeth Gaskell's fellow author Charlotte Brontë, who thought her beautiful and kind. Did Charley Cavendish Bentinck and his new wife ever meet any of these literary figures at Teddesley Hall, one wonders? Lord Hatherton's second marriage was a contented one but when he died he was buried by the side of his beloved first wife and their young daughter in the family vault at Penkridge church, with his former mother-in-law, Hyacinthe Gabrielle,

Marchioness Wellesley lying close by. Charley attended the funeral service; his uncle had been a firm and good friend to him throughout his life and Lord Hatherton would have been pleased to finally see his nephew settled, happy and with a family.[9]

In December of 1863 Charley performed a baptism ceremony for the baby daughter of his distant relatives, General Charles and the Countess Aldenburg Bentinck, at their house in Grosvenor Street. The Princess Mary was to be a godmother and she arrived at the house with her Royal Highness the Duchess of Cambridge. Also in attendance was the Prussian Ambassador and the Crown Prince and Princess of Prussia (the Princess was Queen Victoria's eldest (and namesake) daughter) sent their representative to the ceremony, the Countess Bernstorff. The Crown Prince was the grandson of Frederick William III who had presented Charley's father with the splendid diamonds in grateful thanks for his service at his side during the visit of the Allied Sovereigns in 1814. Illustrious surroundings and company indeed, all of which had previously been denied him. Did the self-effacing Charley reflect on this, one wonders, and feel a pang for the life that had been barred to him and his first wife by polite society? Despite everything, he must also have felt that he was back in his rightful sphere.

Two further daughters – twins – were born to the Reverend Charles Cavendish and Mrs Caroline Louisa Bentinck and baptized at Ridgmont on 26 March 1864; Violet Anne and Hyacinthe Mary, their names given in remembrance of Charley's mother, sister, aunt and grandmother with Violet a neat counterpart to Hyacinthe. They were known to their closest family and friends by their nicknames, Vava and Cinty.

Sadly, Charley had but too little time to enjoy his new life, the renewed affections of his extended family or the pleasures of being a father to three happy and healthy little girls. He died, just five years into his second marriage, on 17 August 1865. He was only 47 years of age but had endured enough grief and heartache to fill double those years, with only a few years of happiness to offset them.

Charley passed away at his Ridgmont vicarage; the cause of his death was a tumour and dropsy (we would now term it an oedema) of the abdomen. His death was registered by a woman named Charlotte Barwell, maybe either a servant or a nurse who was by Charley's side when his life ended. Charlotte Barwell made a mistake though when she gave the registrar the details and Charley was recorded as Charles William rather than William Charles Cavendish Bentinck. Many years later one of his twin daughters, together with a loyal family friend, applied to have the names on the certificate corrected. It obviously meant a lot to this daughter, who had not had the chance to grow up knowing her father, that she was able to perform at least this duty for him. Charley was not buried in his Bedfordshire parish nor by Sinnetta's side but at Croxton in Cambridgeshire close to the country estate of Croxton Park, home of his sister-in-law, Mrs Newton. He was buried in the church-yard there in an ornate tomb on 22 August 1865. His distraught young widow, with three infant children to care for, made her home for the imme-diate future with her sister and wanted her husband buried close to her.

Caroline Louisa Bentinck not only had to cope with the death of her husband and the care of her three infant daughters; she was with child at the time of Charley's death and the newspapers speculated how, if the child was born a boy, there would be but one elderly bachelor standing in between the babe and the dukedom of Portland. However, it was not to be. The child was a girl and stillborn, perhaps this sad event brought on by the grief borne by Caroline Louisa.[10] The widowed Mrs Bentinck had been named as the sole heir in Charley's will and she arranged for the contents of the Ridgmont vicarage to be sold by public auction. The Duke of Bedford was kind and liberal in his concern for her, arranging for her buildings and greenhouse to be taken care of in her absence. Her brother-in-law George Onslow Newton also assisted, writing on black-edged notepaper from Croxton Park and Eaton Square to direct proceedings on Caroline's behalf and to offer his own bid on Charley's excellent wine cellar (bidding £24 for the 'very good light claret' that had been especially imported from Bordeaux, but instructing the agent to get more for it if he could).[11]

The sale took place towards the end of September at the vicarage, begin-ning at 10 o'clock in the morning and continuing throughout the day. No personal items were included, no portraits or miniatures, no ornaments or jewellery, but all the household furniture and kitchen utensils were for sale, as were the contents of the greenhouse and sundry garden implements. From the stable-yard were added a hunting saddle and two lady's side-saddles, a 'very excellent double-bodied four wheel phaeton by Deane', a 'handsome grey harness horse' and a 'twelve hand iron grey pony, quiet in harness, five years old.' The proceeds of the sale cleared Charley's debts and the remaining money was deposited with Caroline Louisa's bankers, Messrs Drummond of Charing Cross.[12]

We hope, for Charley's sake, that his marriage to Louisa was a happy one. She offered him the chance to start anew, a chance to overcome the grief he had felt at the loss of his adored Sinnetta and their infant sons. We hope he had at least a few years of bliss and contentment. We wish, for his sake, that it had been of longer duration. Sadly, history can merely be recorded, not changed to suit our whims, and we must leave Charley to rest in peace having lived the life he chose to lead despite the obstacles and prejudice placed in his path. He was an honourable man, an enlightened man and a kind, gentle and considerate soul, if quietly rebellious. While his public persona was a staid and devout Victorian cleric, Charley was at heart a passionate and almost modern man, way ahead of his time in his liberal views and disregard for social class and norms. His memory deserves to live on.

Chapter Fifteen

Victorian Values and Sensibilities

To conclude the saga of these two generations of the Cavendish-Bentinck family we must now turn to the other members, both those in the extended family and Charley's widow and three young daughters.

The Reverend Henry Hopwood died in his Bothal vicarage on 25 February 1859 during Charley's lifetime and naming his brother-in-law as one of the two executors to his will. Following Hopwood's death the lucrative living was occupied for only two years by a temporary incumbent before being given to the Reverend William Charles Ellis, the old 4th Duke of Portland's grandson. Even though Sinnetta was no more and he was respectably married in the eyes of his family, Charley never did gain the living once destined for him.[1]

It was now the turn of Charley's half-sister, the seemingly sedate Victorian spinster Miss Georgiana Augusta Frederica Henrietta Cavendish Bentinck, to shock her noble family. Hippo, as she was (we hope) affectionately termed, had matured into a plump maiden aunt much beloved by the younger members of the family but something of a burden on the older ones. She remained on reasonably good terms with her stepmother and often stayed with her when in London. Never used to a great deal of independence, she flitted from the London and country houses of both the Marquess of Cholmondeley and the Duke of Portland along with visits to various titled and well-to-do friends, but all the time with an ever-decreasing grip on their largesse and generosity.

Georgiana had inherited the money that had been placed in trust for her by her old guardians, the 4th Duke of Portland, the 1st Marquess and Marchioness of Cholmondeley and her infamous grandmother Grace Dalrymple Elliott, but that fortune quickly disappeared in the hands of a woman not used to the responsibility of managing her own finances. Before long, Georgiana found herself in desperate need of an income. She owned some items that had belonged to her late grandmother, including a journal penned in the years immediately following the French Revolution. It had been written by Mrs Elliott when she was safely back on English soil and living with her widowed aunt in Twickenham, and recounted her adventures and experiences during those terrifying years in France when she lived in fear of the notorious prisons and a close shave with the dreaded guillotine. Despite more than half a decade having elapsed since, interest in first-hand accounts were nevertheless popular (and indeed remain so to this day), and Georgiana decided to try to raise a little ready cash by selling this fascinating manuscript.

After failing to capture the interest of the British Museum she instead ended up agreeing to allow it to be published and sold the rights to a London publisher, Richard Bentley, for a paltry £25. Bentley published it in August 1859 with the title *Journal of My Life during the French Revolution by Grace Dalrymple Elliott*. It is possible that Georgiana edited the journal before she let it fall into Bentley's hands and Bentley himself almost certainly added some embellishment, both in the preface to it and in the ending. The diarist Henry Greville (Georgiana's cousin via his Cavendish-Bentinck mother) thought £25 'an absurdly small sum, particularly when compared with that lately paid to Lady Morgan for some passages from her autobiography, viz. 6,000l., and which for the most part contain uninteresting gossip and fulsome praise of herself.'[2]

Georgiana's reason for editing the document would have been the polar opposite of Bentley's for enhancing it. Whereas he was happy to play on Grace's former notoriety to sell copies, Georgiana, with proper Victorian modesty and the antithesis of her infamous forebear, wanted to discreetly draw a veil on the worst of her beloved grandmother's indiscretions and instead concentrate on her bravery while she was trapped in France. Sadly, even digging up the skeletons in her family closet failed to have little impact on Georgiana's embarrassment of funds and just a matter of days after her half-brother Charley's death the newspapers the length and breadth of the country gleefully picked up on her unfortunate predicament:

> The Hon. Georgina [sic] Augusta Frederica Henrietta Cavendish Bentinck was before the Bankruptcy Court this morning. The bankrupt was described as 'spinster' of 5 Greek-street [Green Street], Grosvenor-Square, and to-day was appointed for the first meeting. The cause of bankruptcy is said to be the loss of a sum of money lent to the late Dowager Lady Rivers, and insufficiency of income to maintain the Hon. Miss Bentinck's position in life. The debts are nearly £1,700, Lady Clare being a creditor for £60, and the claims on the estate being made by a long list of West-end tradesmen.[3]

Lady Clare was the Honourable Elizabeth Julia Georgiana, Dowager Countess of Clare and the niece of Georgiana's former guardian the Marchioness of Cholmondeley.[4] The late Dowager Lady Rivers was formerly Miss Frances Rigby and it is not surprising that she should have failed to repay Georgiana for any loan she may have imprudently made as the Pitt-Rivers family was perennially short of cash. Frances Rigby and her late husband William Horace Pitt-Rivers (formerly Horace Beckford until he had inherited the title of the 2nd Baron Rivers from his maternal uncle), had been contemporaries of Georgiana's late mother before her marriage to Lord Charles Bentinck. Pitt-Rivers was notorious as a gambler and a spendthrift and he committed suicide in 1831 by jumping into the Serpentine in London's Hyde Park after suffering his final loss.

Lady Rivers' affairs had been in disarray for some time. In 1849 she had written to the 4th Duke of Portland requesting a loan to help out her son who was in financial difficulties and declaring she was 'miserable at her own indiscretion' in letting a bond that had led to the immediate pressing problem pass out of her hands. She later wrote 'my affairs have become so complicated that I have been obliged to give up the management of them.'[5] As she approached the duke, so too must Lady Rivers also have approached the more susceptible and gullible Georgiana and in turn Georgiana, when faced with difficulties, would have approached the duke with a similar begging letter. One has to feel for the successive 4th and 5th Dukes of Portland, kindheartedly and politely trying to accommodate the requests of the unfortunate ladies while no doubt thoroughly and disgruntledly tired of it all at the same time. When Georgiana's cousin Lady Harriet Bentinck made a codicil to her will in 1867 she pointedly left a £100 annuity to her on the express condition that it was only to be paid by her executors if Georgiana survived both Lady Harriet and the 2nd Marquess of Cholmondeley and if she was neither an outlaw nor an uncertified bankrupt![6]

A LADY BANKRUPT – At the London Bankruptcy Court last week, the first meeting in the case of Georgina [*sic*] Augusta Frederica Henrietta Cavendish Bentinck was held. The bankrupt is the niece of the Duke of Portland, and described herself in her petition as of 5 Green Street, Grosvenor Square, spinster. She attributes her difficulties to the loss of a sum of money lent to the late Dowager Lady Rivers, and insufficiency of income to maintain her position in life. The preliminary list shows debts to the extent of £1681, and the Dowager Countess of Clare is inserted as a creditor for £60. The claims upon the proceedings are of a very miscellaneous description, and numerous West-end tradesmen appear in the schedule. Amongst the creditors are jewellers, hairdressers, photographic artists, milliners, printsellers, confectioners, a ladies' hatter, an anatomical corset and belt-maker, etc.[7]

To Georgiana's horror the newspapers, sensing they had a story to run with, began to highlight her ancestry to their readers, a topic that Georgiana would much rather have allowed to disappear into the murky waters of the past. She could gain little but the knowledge that she was being gossiped about from being universally known as the illegitimate granddaughter of a former king at such an advanced stage of her life and she had never been in the limelight as her mother and grandmother had been before her. It was an unwelcome distinction and might mean the noble families she relied on for practical assistance would attempt to distance themselves from her in her disgrace.

However, she need not have worried for Georgiana's friends proved true to her in her hour of need. An emergency sum of £150 was set down for her in a cash account as a 'present from friends' (it was suggested in the London Bankruptcy Court that the sum was actually £1,500 but if it was, Georgiana preferred to keep the fact to herself). Mr Sargood, acting for one of the creditors, tried to find out who had contributed to the fund and the true extent of it but, beyond knowing there were 'certain noble names in the cash account and they spoke for themselves', he was to remain in the dark. Mr Lewis, appearing for Georgiana, protested that 'whenever a lady was connected with families in a high position it was sought to drag in other names for the purpose of putting on the screw.' Georgiana had already sold a large amount of her jewellery under the strictest secrecy and with the help of a male friend and so no further demands could be made on her to raise money by that means. She was, with the help of her friends, able to discharge herself from the bankruptcy order.[8]

Straight after this Georgiana dictated her last will and testament in a vain attempt to safeguard her remaining possessions in the event of her death. These possessions included a surprising amount of costly jewellery for someone who had so lately stood before the Bankruptcy Court and professed to have no further trinkets to sell (the jewellery she inherited from Lady Cholmondeley is not specifically mentioned in the will, so may account for the items that had been disposed of). The man who seemed to be most trusted was Hugh Horatio Seymour Esquire whom she appointed her executor, a man she had grown up with. His mother had been the daughter of the 1st Marquess and Marchioness of Cholmondeley but both his parents had died while he was still young. It was likely to have been Hugh Horatio Seymour who helped Georgiana to privately sell her jewels, or to hide them from prying eyes to keep them safe from her creditors.

Sir William Abdy had remained in the Hill Street mansion he had formerly shared with his errant wife, resolutely a staggeringly wealthy bachelor to the end of his days following their divorce. He died there on 15 April 1868 and in his will he left an exorbitant sum of money (almost £100,000) both to and in trust for a young single mother named Jane Goodbun and her illegitimate sons who were born in the 1850s. This lady was also known as Miss Talbot, a tall and beautiful actress who trod the boards from 1854 until succumbing to a long and serious illness from which she died while still a young woman in 1865. It is tempting to view Jane's boys as Abdy's illegitimate sons, sired when he was an old man in his 80s. In his younger days his former wife had suggested he was impotent but in his foolish old age he seems to have been dazzled (and perhaps duped) by a pretty young actress. It remains to be proven if her children were Abdy's.[9]

Caroline Louisa Bentinck remained a widow for five years following Charley's death before accepting the marriage proposal of a dashing and wealthy Scotsman, Harry Warren Scott of Balgay and Logie, a younger son of Lieutenant Sir William Scott of Ancrum in the Scottish Borders. He had formerly been a captain in the Lochee Rifle Company (a volunteer regiment) and was, at the time of his marriage, a Justice of the Peace. In 1852 Scott had matriculated at Merton College, Oxford University; one wonders if, while he was studying there, he heard the tales concerning Charley Cavendish Bentinck and his love for Sinnetta? Harry Warren Scott seems to have been a kind man, greatly esteemed and loved by many but first and foremost a private man who concerned himself with his family rather than seeking a public life. He had, it is true, attempted to stand for Parliament in the years before his marriage but, having failed in that ambition, Scott refused to stand again and subsequently paid scant regard to his Scottish estates. No children were born of his union with Caroline Louisa but he proved himself an excellent stepfather to her three young Cavendish-Bentinck daughters.

The couple had a London town house, 45 Grosvenor Place, and a country house on Ham Common known as Forbes House where they lived with an array of servants and a French governess for Charley's daughters. Two of the servants were from Bedfordshire and had remained with Caroline Louisa since the days of her first marriage. Henry Negus, a 24-year-old from Ridgmont was employed as a domestic servant within the household but was to become much more than that to the three Cavendish-Bentinck girls. To them he became a friend as well as a servant and a man they continued to trust throughout their lives. It was Henry Negus who, in 1900, helped Cinty to change the incorrect order of her father's forenames on his death certificate.[10]

Miss Georgiana Cavendish Bentinck, following her mortifying appearance in the Bankruptcy Court and the gossip columns of the newspapers, retired from public view and the 2nd Marquess of Cholmondeley allowed her the use of a small cottage near to his Cheshire estate of Cholmondeley Castle at

Malpas. Georgiana's cottage, known as Malpas Cottage, was set in a pictur-esque location on the banks of the River Dee and she lived there with just one or two servants and a lapdog for company. It was in this Cheshire cottage that she fell ill during the autumn of 1872 with a nervous complaint that rendered her right hand and arm temporarily useless. Confined to her bed, Georgiana was persuaded by her doctors to have her ailing limb 'strongly burnt with caustic' to try to arrest the progress of the disease but it had little effect other than to increase her pain and suffering. She needed nourishing food and drink so, as she had always been used to doing, she turned to her affluent relations for help, writing to the reclusive and eccentric but kindly 5th Duke of Portland, her first cousin once removed, asking if he would send her game and grapes. Addressing her letter to 'My Dear John' she ended it with an apology: 'Forgive my being so troublesome and boring you with my ills, and believe me your affectionate Georgy C. Bentinck.'

The duke sent a hamper of the game and grapes requested and so began a procession of similar boxes sent with some regularity into Cheshire from Wel-beck Abbey in Nottinghamshire, leaving Georgiana overwhelmed, grateful and well fed. She poured out her thanks in a profusion of letters for the game (mostly grouse but occasionally pheasant) and grapes, venturing after some months to hint for oysters and poultry instead, perhaps to alleviate the mon-otony of her menu. She added updates on her health, sometimes improving, sometimes relapsed, and talked about the weather and her small garden.[11]

Perhaps the duke was also sending hampers of game and fruit from Welbeck to the home of Lady Anne Bentinck in London? Now elderly, she was still irascible and her temper was as quick and as sharp as ever; she terri-fied many of the younger generation who were brought to see her. Lady Anne spent her last years living in retirement in her London town house, 31 Norfolk Street on the corner of Park Lane, with her eldest daughter for her companion and two female servants living in to look after them.

Maintaining the corkscrew curls of her youth underneath her prim mob cap and with a pet pug often to be found on her knee, Anne was nevertheless a somewhat daunting and scary presence to the young grandchildren and great-nieces and nephews who were brought to visit her. In the end, she became a superbly eccentric old lady, rising for breakfast at four o'clock in the afternoon and playing whist with her daughter and anyone else unwary enough to have been drawn into a game until dawn in a stifling and airless drawing room. She would not allow a window to be opened, no matter how hot the weather. Her old spirit seemed only to return when visited by the handsome men of the younger generation, when she would burst into laughter at their tales of scrapes and derring-do and press purses of sovereigns into their hands if they were short of money, perhaps reliving, through them, her own 'scandalous' youth.

It was at her Park Lane house that the formidable Lady Anne died on 19 March 1875, at the age of 87. Her burial took place in the Kensal Green cemetery where the little bodies of her grandsons by Charley and Sinnetta also lay; the grandsons she possibly knew nothing about at their birth and whom she almost certainly never set eyes upon. In attendance at her funeral was her son Arthur together with the Earl of Cavan (who had married her niece Caroline Augusta Littleton) and her nephew, the 2nd Baron Hatherton.[12]

Lady Anne Bentinck had died secure in the knowledge that Arthur, her youngest but only surviving son, was next in line to succeed his elderly, unmarried and childless cousin as the next Duke of Portland, the title that would have been Charley's had he lived long enough (the duke's younger brother had died without issue in 1870). However, like his elder brother Arthur was also destined to die too soon to fulfil this destiny. On 11 December 1877 while staying at Thomas's Hotel in Berkeley Square, a hotel the general and his wife used regularly when travelling to London from East Court, their home in Finchampstead near Wokingham, he passed away after a short but fatal illness. Arthur's 20-year-old son from his short-lived first marriage now stood a step away from the dukedom and only two years later William John Arthur Charles James Cavendish-Bentinck did indeed become the 6th Duke of Portland. True to the late 5th Duke's reclusive and eccentric reputation, he never met the young relative who would inherit his estates and title.[13]

In 1881, almost sixteen years after her father had died, Cecilia Nina Cavendish-Bentinck made a grand marriage to Claude Bowes-Lyon, Lord Glamis and the future Earl of Strathmore and Kinghorne. The family's estates included Glamis Castle in Scotland and St Paul's Walden Bury in Hertfordshire. A modest man, in later life Lord Glamis was often mistaken for a labourer as he contentedly toiled in his gardens; he was honest, kindly and unpretentious.

As he aged, Harry Warren Scott began to suffer from ill health and, because of this, he and his wife travelled to Italy to reside in an old Medici villa; they spent the greater part of the year there, passing only a couple of months during the summer at Forbes House on Ham Common. Their Italian villa was located on a hillside at Arcetri overlooking Florence and named Villa Capponi.[14] It was an enchanting place with tier upon tier of terraces and the villa walls were draped in roses and other highly-scented flowers, the noise from the city of Florence floated up and the bell of the Duomo, the Santa Maria del Fiore Cathedral, could be heard daily as it played the

Angelus. Charley's twin daughters, Cinty and Vava, travelled with their mother and stepfather and they too spent the majority of the year enjoying the sunnier climes of Italy, often visited by their sister Lady Glamis and her growing family.

In September 1883 Miss Georgiana Cavendish Bentinck, borne down by the trials and tribulations that had beset her old age, finally breathed her last. She died at her cottage on the banks of the River Dee aged 72. Perhaps her financial difficulties had finally tried the patience of the aristocratic acquaintances and family who continually supported her just a little too much, for she was not laid to rest in a family vault belonging to either the Cholmondeley or the Portland family but instead was buried in the more modest and unassuming surroundings of Overleigh Cemetery at Chester.

Predictably she left a tangled mess of debts and overdue bills behind her. Georgiana had optimistically made specific bequests to several people in her will; bequests both of her personal belongings and of money she assumed would arise from her estate after her death and all of which were well-intentioned rather than plausible. One of her creditors, John Guy, a chemist from Boughton, Chester, made a claim for the payment of his outstanding bill and was granted administration of Georgiana's estate, thereby negating all her bequests. A sale of her possessions was organized to raise the necessary money to repay her debts and it was, perhaps, the final insult to her status as Georgiana would have been horrified to know that her belongings were laid out for display and general purchase. One wonders if anyone was even aware of the historical significance attached to many of her portraits and jewels which had been gifts from and to some of the most well-known and notorious personalities of the eighteenth century and the Regency years?

If Georgiana had held such a sale during her lifetime she would have been able to pay off her creditors instantly, for the list of her possessions was staggering for a woman who had presented herself as being so needy. Miniatures of the Cavendish-Bentinck, Seymour and Cholmondeley families, diamond, pearl and emerald jewellery, antique silver, cut glass, expensive china, delicate lace, furs, books and oil paintings were all to be found catalogued in the auction; Georgiana might not have had much money in her bank account but she was certainly not short of valuable possessions.[15]

With her family nickname of 'Hippo' leading us to believe this perhaps related to her girth and that she was of large proportions (so unlike Grace Dalrymple Elliott, her tall and willowy courtesan of a grandmother of whom she was the only descendant), her prodigious appetite for the hampers of food freely despatched into Cheshire from Welbeck Abbey and her total inability to organize her finances and settle her debts, Georgiana Cavendish Bentinck would seem to have inherited all the worst traits of her dissolute reputed grandfather, King George IV.

Miss Anne Hyacinthe Cavendish Bentinck, meanwhile, the last remaining of the children of Lord Charles Bentinck and Anne Wellesley, was living a refined spinsterhood in the elegant confines of the house on the corner of Norfolk Street and Park Lane that she had previously shared with her mother. Like her late older half-sister Georgiana, she had devoted her life to being a companion but there the similarity between the two women ended, for Anne at least had the benefit of finally finding herself with independent means rather than still dependent upon the charity of friends and family. The two women were on visiting terms and in 1880 Anne wrote from Cannes to one of the younger members of the Wellesley family asking if their 'little ones were still near Chester?' and saying that when she went that way she would certainly go and visit them. Did she then go 'that way' towards Chester to visit her ailing half-sister?[16] In the early spring of 1888 Anne applied for a passport to travel to mainland Europe, as she had done so many times before in her life with her mother. This was to be Anne's last journey. She died shortly after landing in France at the Hôtel St Charles in Cannes and her body was brought home to be buried in the same grave as her mother in the cemetery at Kensal Green. Her closeness to her sister-in-law Caroline Louisa was evident in the fact that Harry Warren Scott proved Anne Hyacinthe's will. She left a personal estate worth over £48,000.[17]

Harry Warren Scott did not long outlive Anne Cavendish Bentinck and in the late summer of 1889 the Scott household was plunged into mourning when he died at Forbes House. Caroline Louisa, widowed for the second time, retreated to Italy with her two unmarried twin daughters for company. During this protracted stay overseas two visitors to the Villa Capponi were Lord Glamis' sister Mildred and her American husband, Augustus (Gus) Edward Jessup Jr, a wealthy Pennsylvanian and close to the DuPont family. Jessup, whose family had made their fortune from the paper mills they owned, had travelled to Europe to seek a titled bride to go with his fortune. Lady Mildred Marion Bowes-Lyon fell to his choice and the couple married in 1890 at Glamis Castle.

The Jessups travelled widely: Gus bought a twelfth-century castle in Switzerland (Schloss Lenzburg) and they spent a great deal of time in Italy, notably in Florence and Bordighera on the Italian Riviera where Mildred's musical talents were recognized and she composed several pieces of music including an opera, *Etelinda*. The Earl and Countess of Strathmore and Kinghorne, Mildred's father and Cecilia, Lady Glamis' parents-in-law, also lived for much of the year in Bordighera (their villa had been known as the Villa

Bischoffsheim but in 1896 the name was changed to the Villa Etelinda), making for a close-knit family group in Italy, all related by blood or by marriage. It seems inconceivable that the Jessups did not visit and spend time with Mrs Scott and her two Cavendish-Bentinck daughters in their pictur-esque Florentine villa, or that Mrs Scott and the Misses Cavendish-Bentinck did not visit the Strathmores and Jessups at Bordighera. However, the social merry-go-round took a tragic turn when Mildred died suddenly in 1897 at Saint-Raphaël on the Côte d'Azur in France, leaving Jessup to care for their two young sons.[18]

Not suited to life as a widower, Jessup did not have to cast his eye too far for a replacement bride and he soon married Hyacinthe Cavendish-Bentinck, making him a brother-in-law to Cecilia, Lady Glamis through both of his marriages. Sadly for Cinty, the union between the two was most definitely not a success and rapidly went downhill.

Cinty, in her late thirties, had given up all hope of marrying, let alone having children, before Gus's proposal but two daughters were born in quick succession: Mary Violet at Saint-Raphaël in the south of France early in 1901 and Clare Louise Olive in 1904.[19] Disastrously, the family finances began to fall into disarray and in 1911 the Swiss castle had to be sold, although Jessup managed to retain a handsome yearly income. Amid recriminations, the couple eventually separated and Cinty, who was frequently unwell, spent time living in Jersey. Gus Jessup moved to Italy where he installed his youngest daughter's Italian governess into his home as his mistress and the abandoned Cinty died, aged 52, in the summer of 1916 at her mother's home of Forbes House. She was buried in Ham cemetery.

Her older sister Cecilia was to have a much more successful life. In 1904 Charley's daughter became a countess when her husband succeeded to his father's titles and estates and Cecilia's youngest daughter was destined to eclipse even that.

Chapter Sixteen

Royal Descent

By all accounts Cecilia, Lady Strathmore was a talented pianist, a brilliant hostess and a wonderful mother to a large family of ten children. Her eldest daughter, who died aged only 11 of diphtheria at her grandmother's home, Forbes House, had been given Hyacinth as a middle name. Even in those staid late-Victorian years, the family continued to evoke the ghost of the exotic eighteenth-century French opera dancer who had so captivated the young Lord Mornington all those years ago.[1]

Lady Strathmore was known as a sensible and down-to-earth woman,

a large, stocky presence, with a square jaw and bright eyes, a great flywheel maintaining the momentum and balance of the household. Nothing could fluster her. Guests at Glamis remembered the tipsy footman, who seemed always to be falling about and pouring wine down people's backs but with whom Lady Strathmore coped quite unruffled.

She was also, as might be expected of the daughter of a clergyman, extremely religious:

The Strathmores were a pious family. Prayers were said every day in the little chapel at Glamis. The women would wear white caps made of thick crochet lace, fastened on to the head with hatpins. The cap was provided in the bedroom of each woman guest for her to wear every day, and on Sunday Lady Strathmore, with one such cap on her head, used to sit at the harmonium and accompany the little congregation of friends as they sang hymns. Upright, open and straightforward, the Bowes-Lyons lived by a simple, upper-class code, which made them at once fun-loving, considerate, unaffected – and totally self-confident.[2]

However, it is Cecilia's youngest daughter who is best remembered today: the Lady Elizabeth Angela Marguerite Bowes-Lyon born in 1900 while Queen Victoria was still on the throne and shortly before her father inherited the title of the 14th Earl of Strathmore and Kinghorne and her mother became his countess. Little Elizabeth often spent time in Italy holidaying at the villa owned by Caroline Louisa Scott, and no doubt listened to reminiscences about her long-dead grandfather at her grandmother's knee. The Villa Capponi had been sold and Mrs Scott had moved first to San Remo and then to Bordighera where she rented the Villa Bella Vista for a time before buying it and renaming it the Villa Poggio Ponente. It was this villa that Elizabeth Bowes-Lyon visited and when she did her Aunt Vava took the young girl to see the many art galleries and museums in the area. Elizabeth was later to recall:

> When we were children both my grandmothers lived in Italy in the winter, and I just loved Italian things. I had a very clever Cavendish-Bentinck aunt, who took us to the Uffizi in Florence. She only allowed us to look at one picture ... it was wonderful. Instead of poor little legs getting flabby with exhaustion, I remember looking at the Primavera. I can see it now. I suppose I was ten. I thought it was very clever of her really.[3]

The Scott household was a happy one and the two women, Mrs Scott and her daughter Vava, doted on their young relations who came to stay, both at Forbes House on Ham Common and at the Italian villa. Elizabeth later recalled the exciting train journeys to Florence with her younger brother and inseparable friend David; journeys that felt dangerously glamorous as the two young children were allowed to dine late at night amid the lights and bustle of foreign cities.

The advent of the Great War in 1914 necessitated a protracted residence in England and Caroline Louisa Scott together with her daughter Vava returned to Forbes House on Ham Common. Unable to travel abroad, they also took a house in the pretty seaside town of Dawlish in Devon where Mrs Scott died on 6 July 1918 in the closing months of the war.[4]

Vava Cavendish-Bentinck was left the Villa Poggio Ponente in Bordighera by her mother when she died but when in England she remained primarily based in Dawlish for the rest of her life, living in a house known as The Cottage, located at the end of Weech Road in the Empsons Hill area of the town. The family's trusty old servant Henry Negus moved to be near her and was employed as a chauffeur. Vava bought a nearby property known as Myrtle Cottage for Negus and his wife to live in. Later she had a cottage built on Badlake Hill (named Garden Cottage) for her housekeeper and companion, Miss Moseley. It would have been at the Dawlish house that Vava received news of her niece Elizabeth's engagement and forthcoming marriage.[5]

Strangely, with the gypsy connections already present in her ancestry, Lady Elizabeth Bowes-Lyon was reputed to have had her future told to her by a member of the Romany tribes and her glittering future revealed to her.

Around 1920, or a little earlier, Lady Elizabeth attended the races at Ascot with a friend, Rosita Forbes, the divorced wife of Colonel Ronald Foster Forbes and a decade Lady Elizabeth's senior. The pair had just lunched in the Bachelors' Club and were struggling through the mêlée outside towards the Royal Enclosure when a gypsy woman pushed in front of them and begged to be allowed to tell their fortunes. Mrs Forbes encouraged her friend and, entering into the holiday spirit of the crowds around her, she crossed the gypsy's palm with silver. The gypsy studied Lady Elizabeth's palm and her countenance changed and became serious. To the astonishment of Lady Elizabeth and to the amusement of Mrs Forbes, the gypsy foretold an out-landish prophecy: that one day Lady Elizabeth would take her place beside her future husband upon the throne of England.[6]

Bizarre as the gypsy prophecy must have sounded, on 8 July 1920 Prince Albert, the Duke of York and great-grandson to Queen Victoria (known informally as Bertie) met Lady Elizabeth Bowes-Lyon at a Royal Air Force Memorial Fund ball at the Ritz and was instantly smitten.[7] Elizabeth was undecided; she was full of fun, beautiful, confident and not short of admirers. Lady Mabell, Countess of Airlie, a close friend of Prince Albert's mother Queen Mary (she was the queen's lady-in-waiting) said that 'Lady Elizabeth was very unlike the cocktail-drinking chain-smoking girls who came to be regarded as typical of the 1920s.'[8]

The prince and Elizabeth were not exactly strangers to one another before the ball. They had known each other as children (at a children's party the 5-year-old Elizabeth gave Bertie, a shy 10-year-old, the cherries from atop her cake) and Elizabeth was friends with his sister, Princess Mary (she was one of the princess's bridesmaids at her marriage to Viscount Lascelles, later the 6th Earl of Harewood). However, it was not until the ball in 1920 that Bertie fell head-over-heels in love, although initially to no avail. Elizabeth refused the prince's first proposal but her mother knew that she was torn 'between her longing to make Bertie happy and her reluctance to take on the responsibilities which this marriage must bring.'[9]

The gossips of the day hinted that she was encouraged by her mother to hold out for a proposal from Bertie's older brother, the notorious but hand-some playboy Edward, Prince of Wales and a false report saying that Elizabeth was about to be engaged to the Prince of Wales appeared in the press in the first days of 1923.[10] A few days later Bertie proposed while the couple were walking in the wintry woodland near her father's home at St Paul's Walden Bury and Elizabeth accepted him. Her parents were invited to Sandringham to meet the king and queen and to spend the weekend there; both King

George V and Queen Mary were delighted with the match. The ensuing marriage, which took place later that year in the magnificent surroundings of Westminster Abbey, left Charley's granddaughter but two steps away from the throne.

Two daughters were born to the Duke and Duchess of York – the Princess Elizabeth in 1926 and Margaret four years later – and the marriage was a happy one. The duchess did not forget the relations who had been so kind to her in her childhood and youth and she took her two young daughters to visit her now elderly Aunt Vava at The Cottage in Dawlish. Vava died during the spring of 1932.[11]

The ailing and elderly King George V privately hoped that Bertie, although a younger son, would ascend to the throne as he held no high regard for his eldest son, the Prince of Wales. However, when the king died on 20 January 1936, it was the playboy Prince of Wales who took the throne. As the new Edward VIII was not married and had no heirs, Bertie and Elizabeth stood next in line. Throughout the year of 1936, as the storm clouds that would eventually lead to the outbreak of the Second World War began to gather over mainland Europe, the private life of the new king caused consternation and his insistence on marrying his mistress, an American divorcée named Wallis Simpson, eventually led to his abdication on 11 December. He had reigned for less than eleven months. Bertie was now the new king and Elizabeth his queen.[12]

Edward had never been officially crowned; preparations for a coronation were time-consuming and the ceremony had been set for 12 May 1937. Rather than waste the preparations already made, Bertie instead set his own coronation for the same day, choosing to be known as King George VI (his full name was Albert Frederick Arthur George). Charley Cavendish Bentinck's granddaughter was crowned alongside her husband, becoming Queen Consort of Great Britain, Ireland and the British Dominions, and also Empress of India. Back in 1821 Lord Charles Bentinck had played a prominent role at the coronation of his friend and employer, King George IV. Now, just over a century later, his great-granddaughter attended her own coronation. The Cavendish-Bentinck family had been closely linked to the British royal family for generations; now they were indelibly entwined.

Lady Strathmore lived to see her daughter become queen. Having survived her younger twin sisters (and four of her ten children), she died on 23 June 1938 after an illness of several weeks following a heart attack. The new Queen Elizabeth was devastated by her mother's death, as were the two young princesses who adored both of their Strathmore grandparents. The queen wrote to Prime Minister Neville Chamberlain after receiving the terrible news:

> I have been dreading this moment ever since I was a little child and now that it has come, one can hardly believe it. She was a true 'Rock of Defence' for us, her children, & Thank God, her influence and wonderful example will remain with us all our lives.
>
> She had a good perspective of life – everything was given its *true* importance. She had a young spirit, great courage and unending sympathy whenever or wherever it was needed, & such a heavenly sense of humour. We all used to laugh together and have such fun. You must forgive me for writing to you like this, but you have been such a kind friend and counsellor to us during the last year ...[13]

Although Charley never had the chance to see his eldest daughter grow up, he undoubtedly would have been immensely proud of her. We suspect Cecilia's character and personality mirrored those of the father she never really knew. In due course Charley Cavendish Bentinck's great-granddaughter became Queen Elizabeth II, a much-loved and respected monarch who has enjoyed a longer reign than any other British king or queen, and his granddaughter, the former Lady Elizabeth Bowes-Lyon, acquired the moniker by which she is still best known and fondly remembered, the Queen Mother. However, how different our modern history would have been, relating to the British royal family, if the gypsy girl who had married into a ducal family had not suffered such an early death.

In many ways Prince William, Duke of Cambridge reminds us of his direct ancestor, the Reverend William Charles Cavendish Bentinck. Both men quietly but resolutely insisted on ordering their private and personal lives to suit themselves. In marrying Catherine (Kate) Middleton, Prince William unconsciously mimicked Charley Cavendish Bentinck who also married the girl he fell head-over-heels in love with while a university student. Although the Middletons cannot be compared to the Lambournes, both families represented a more 'normal' life for the men who married into them, allowing them the chance to live more freely within the constrictions and conventions imposed upon them by their birth.

We would dearly have loved to give Charley Cavendish Bentinck and Sinnetta a happy ending but their story, sadly, cannot be changed. Perhaps their happy ending is that Charley's great-great-grandson, who resembles him in so many ways, is able to lead the happy and fulfilled life that fate denied to his gentle and free-spirited forebear?

Notes

1. Hyacinthe Gabrielle used Rolland and not Roland. It should be noted that, at her marriage, she also used Hiacinthe when putting her signature to the marriage certificate but on the same document she is also Hyacinthe. For ease we have chosen to use the latter variant of her forename.
2. *Survey of London, vol. 40, the Grosvenor Estate in Mayfair, Part 2 (The Buildings)*. Formerly numbered 20B, now it is 42 and 44 Hill Street. No. 42 was demolished in 1919 and rebuilt; both dwellings suffered bomb damage during the Second World War. Sir William Abdy was listed as the owner from 1810 to 1868.

Chapter 1: Lord Charles Bentinck and the Prince Regent

1. Lord Charles Bentinck's birthdate was 3 October 1780.
2. *A Regency Elopement*, Hugh Farmar.
3. This famous phrase is probably not strictly accurate. The Duke of Wellington returned one of Harriette's letters with the words 'write and be damned' written on the reverse, according to Harriette's friend Julia Johnstone (*Confessions of Julia Johnstone in Contradiction to the Fables of Harriette Wilson*, 1825). Elizabeth Longford in *Wellington* says he told Harriette's publisher, John Joseph Stockdale, to 'Publish and be damned!'
4. *Memoirs of Harriette Wilson, written by herself, volume v*, London, 1827. General John Fane, Lord Burghersh, married (in 1811) Lady Anne Abdy's cousin, Priscilla, daughter of William Wellesley-Pole. Ann Rawlinson later lived at 38 Manchester Street in Marylebone; Harriette Wilson gave this as her address and she can be found there from 1823 to 1828 on the land tax records. Mary Ann Eden Rawlinson (either Ann or her daughter) married François Joseph Snel at Marylebone on 25 September 1828 and a Wm Eden was a witness; an interesting combination of names given that little Ann's daughter had a Colonel Eden for a father. General William Eden of Ham, Surrey, left a bequest of £300 and an annuity of £150 (plus twelve Grand Junction Water shares) to Mary Ann Eden Rawlinson of Brussels in his will written on 4 February 1846.
5. Grace used a different spelling of her husband's surname after his divorce (Elliott), possibly to annoy him and to distance herself from him as much as she could. Grace's maternal aunt, Robinaiana Brown, was for many years the mistress of Charles Mordaunt, 4th Earl of Peterborough, with several children born out of wedlock. The earl already had a wife but upon her death in 1750 he hastily married Robinaiana who was again pregnant. Their son born after their union inherited the earldom, taking precedence over his older brothers. With this example before her, it is natural that Grace would have hoped for a marriage and to become Countess of Cholmondeley. See our previous book *An Infamous Mistress: The Life, Loves and Family of the Celebrated Grace Dalrymple Elliott* for more information.
6. It was while Georgiana was under the care of the Earl of Cholmondeley that she adopted Seymour as a surname. Lord Cholmondeley had an acknowledged illegitimate daughter,

Harriet, by Madame Saint-Albin (born in 1791). Priscilla Susan Bertie, the illegitimate daughter of his friend the 4th Duke of Ancaster and Kesteven (and the niece of his wife), was also brought up in the Cholmondeley nursery after the death of her father and the subsequent marriage of her mother.

7. Letter dated 15 July 1794. *Mrs Fitzherbert and George IV* by W.H. Wilkins.
8. Caroline of Brunswick and the Prince of Wales were first cousins; Caroline's mother was one of the sisters of King George III.
9. *Becoming Queen*, Kate Williams.
10. Letters that passed between the prince and Queen Charlotte in 1799 leave no doubt that both of them believed Georgiana to be the prince's daughter. See *An Infamous Mistress: The Life, Loves and Family of the Celebrated Grace Dalrymple Elliott* for more information.
11. Both the 3rd Duke of Portland, Lord Charles' father, and Grace Dalrymple Elliott, Georgiana's mother, settled £5,000 upon the couple.
12. The new Duke of Portland inherited an estate heavily burdened with debts and worked hard to clear them. A keen advocate of agricultural developments, he improved the land on his estate by introducing the latest farming techniques and was also particularly interested in yachting and horse-racing (a pastime favoured by all the Bentinck brothers).
13. The Prince of Wales' full name was George Augustus Frederick. Miss Seymour had been baptized as Georgiana Augusta Frederica and her daughter received the additional name of Henrietta, possibly as a nod to one of her godparents (the Duchess of Portland was named Henrietta). The first Lady Charles Bentinck died on 10 December 1813.
14. The gathering depicted took place on 24 June 1814 and was painted by Thomas Phillips RA. The National Trust Collections says of this piece: 'George O'Brien Wyndham, 3rd Earl of Egremont (1751–1837) is shown being presented by George, Prince Regent to the Tsar, Alexander I of Russia, in the Marble Hall at Petworth. The King of Prussia, Frederick William III, faces him, and other eminent dignitaries, royalty and the artist himself stand around. The paintings of Fox and Pitt hanging either side of the door are not at Petworth, and were probably introduced for symbolic reasons by the artist (there are, however, marble busts of both of them). The visit of the Allied Sovereigns to England in June 1814 was supposed to celebrate the Peace of Paris. The Tsar and Field Marshal von Blücher were the heroes of the hour, but the former's gauche behaviour, and his sister's meddling in the marriage plans of Princess Charlotte, made the hosts' patience wear rather thin before the visit had ended; whilst the Tsar was for his part dismayed by the Prince Regent's drunken behaviour.'
15. The court at Carlton House was held on 9 June 1814.

Chapter 2: The Wellesleys and the Duke of Wellington

1. Richard Colley Wellesley's middle name referenced his grandfather who had been born Richard Colley of an Anglo-Irish family. When he inherited the fortune and estates of a childless uncle he adopted his uncle's surname of Wesley that was later changed by his grandsons to Wellesley. Richard Wesley was created Baron Mornington in 1734. His son Garret Wesley was created Viscount Wellesley and the 1st Earl of Mornington in 1760. There were nine Wellesley children: Richard Colley, born 1760; Arthur Gerald, born 1761 (died young); William, born 1763 (who used the surname Wellesley-Pole after inheriting from his uncle and godfather William Pole of Ballyfin in Ireland in 1781); Francis Seymour (died young); Anne, born 1768; Arthur, born 1769; Gerald Valerian, born 1770; Mary Elizabeth, born 1772; and Henry, born 1773. Anne is often noted as the

only daughter and Mary, who died in 1794 aged just 22, is overlooked: there is little bio-
graphical information on Mary and in her book *Wellington: A Journey Through My Family*,
Jane Wellesley speculates that she may have had some mental or physical deformity.

2. *Sir Thomas Lawrence's Letter-bag*, edited by George Somes Layard; the portrait painter
Sir Thomas heard the anecdote from the Duke of Wellington's wife, Kitty, while she was
sitting to him for a drawing.

3. A report on a breakfast given by the Duchess of Devonshire to 'all the foreigners of distinction now in the country' described Hyacinthe Gabrielle as 'the only foreigner whose
figure and complexion approach nearest to those of an English Beauty.' *Morning Post*,
29 June 1802.

4. Hyacinthe's actress mother has usually been credited with the surname Varis; the more
common name in France is Varin and it is likely that the last letter has been confused and
misread.

5. The *Morning Herald*, 1 February 1786.

6. *The Eldest Brother*, Iris Butler. Hyacinthe Gabrielle Rolland's children by Wellesley were
born between 1787 and 1794. As a tour for Richard's health it was not of great benefit;
he was ill several times, finally contracting a severe fever that was probably malaria in
Rome on his journey back home.

7. *The Eldest Brother*, Iris Butler (citing the Dropmore Papers).

8. The two witnesses who signed the marriage register were the parish clerk Caleb Greville
and an S. Bernard. The *London Evening Standard*, writing almost a century after the event
(on 27 June 1871), claimed that Hyacinthe Gabrielle tricked Wellesley into marriage,
saying the couple had long been separated and Wellesley was induced to marry her as he
believed her on her deathbed and she could not receive the last sacrament if he did not do
so. After the marriage he went to Eton for a week to be out of the way and to await news of
her death, only to find that his new wife had made a miraculous recovery as soon as he had
left her house. It has echoes of the Prince of Wales' trickery of Mrs Fitzgerald to persuade
her to marry him and is an ill-written piece that has dates and the names of their children
recorded incorrectly.

9. Add. Ms. 37315, Richard Wellesley, 2nd Earl of Mornington; Marquess Wellesley: Family
correspondence: 1800–1842, British Library.

10. The office held the title of Governor General of Bengal; in 1833 it was renamed Governor
General of India.

11. *The Eldest Brother*, Iris Butler (citing the Carver papers).

12. On 1 January Edward John Johnston imparted the news of his mother's death at Heavitree
near Exeter in Devon to the Marquess Wellesley; Johnston had been with her when she
died (*The Eldest Son*, Iris Butler). On 8 January, at Heavitree, Elizabeth Johnston aged 61
was buried; surely the same woman. In the baptism registers for St Pancras Church two
interesting entries are to be found: William Edwards Henry born 26 May 1794 and
baptized 9 July 1795; and Edward John born 25 August 1795 and baptized 30 December
1796; both listed as the sons of William and Eliza/Elizabeth Johnstone.

13. In *White Mughals*, William Dalrymple hints that gossip claimed Richard and Lady Anne
Barnard had an affair during his stay at the Cape. Lady Anne was a charming and fascinating woman, married to a man twenty years her junior, but Richard took care to describe
her as 'very plain and 45 years old' in a letter home to his jealous wife (*The Eldest Brother*,
Iris Butler).

14. *The Cape Diaries of Lady Anne Barnard*, 1799–1800, vol.1. By 'cut neat' Lady Anne is referring to the women who travelled to India 'husband-hunting', suggesting they would have no cause to feel themselves superior to Hyacinthe Gabrielle. Lady Anne later wrote in her diary that, should Lady Mornington travel to India and become the governess of the country, she would have no hesitation in visiting her or being civil towards her.

15. John Severn, in *Architects of Empire: The Duke of Wellington and His Brothers*, says the letters between Richard and Hyacinthe Gabrielle reveal them as being devoted to one another, adding that through Hyacinthe 'one is led to a very human, almost normal man in Richard Wellesley. This private correspondence reveals emotional sensibility, sexual tension, self-doubt, a vision of the future, jealousy, and anger. Absent is the pomposity that historians associate with Mornington's personality and his career.'

16. *The Eldest Brother*, Iris Butler. 'Handsome Jack' St Leger was a roistering crony of the Prince of Wales.

17. Arthur Wellesley was appointed Colonel of the 33rd Regiment of Foot in 1796, a commission paid for by Richard Colley Wellesley.

18. It was at this time that the brothers changed the spelling of their surname from Wesley to Wellesley.

19. *Wellington: A Journey Through My Family*, Jane Wellesley.

20. An *accoucheur* was essentially a midwife. The man so employed by the marquess was William (later Sir William) Knighton, a society doctor who was to serve as private secretary to King George IV.

21. In *The Eldest Brother*, Iris Butler gives further details on Miss Leshley, or Miss Leslie/Lesley as she is usually styled in biographies on the Wellesley brothers. A Miss Leslie was named in Richard's will written in 1797 before he sailed for India and he wanted his wife to bring her out as a lady-in-waiting, should she make the journey herself (in 1799 Hyacinthe Gabrielle wrote to her husband to say that Miss Leslie had died of a consumption at Hampton Court). This was a different Miss Leslie, however, as Mary Ann Leshley was too young (she was born in 1788 and baptized at Chichester as the daughter of George and Mary Leshley), but she was living with the marquess in Ramsgate in 1809. Miss Leshley was also known as Sally Douglas (*Morning Chronicle*, 'Mirror of Fashion', 23 April 1808) and subsequently married a Spanish gentleman named Antonio Caballero. She died in 1877 at Tunbridge Wells in Kent, an extremely wealthy widow aged 89.

Chapter 3: Unfortunate Marriages and Alliances

1. *The Eldest Brother*, Iris Butler (citing the Carver papers). Letter dated 19 February 1810.

2. *Wellington at War, 1794–1815: A Selection of his Wartime Letters*, Anthony Brett-James.

3. Arthur Wellesley was raised to the peerage in 1809 as Viscount Wellesley in thanks for his actions at the Battle of Talavera. The name Wellington was chosen by his brother William but fully approved of by Arthur (although Kitty did not like it at all). It referenced the Somerset town of Wells near to Welleslie, the ancient home of the Wesley/Wellesley family.

4. After her marriage Kitty told a friend she had made three resolutions when she was a girl: she would not marry a soldier, or an Irishman, or have a long engagement. As she wryly noted, she had broken all three, the duke being both a soldier and an Irishman and their engagement lasting twelve years (*Under Five Reigns*, Lady Dorothy Nevill). The duke's descendant Jane Wellesley in *Wellington: A Journey Through My Family* wonders whether his decision to wed Kitty was not totally due to acting honourably but, either

subconsciously or consciously, it was motivated by a wish to take some revenge for the humiliation of having his earlier proposal rejected. Or perhaps Arthur, the great military strategist, was just naïve when it came to affairs of the heart. Arthur Richard Wellesley, later the 2nd Duke of Wellington, was born in 1807 and his brother Charles in 1808. Edward (Ned) Pakenham was sent to North America in 1814 as the commander of the British Forces and was killed during the Battle of New Orleans. Hercules Pakenham eventually became the lieutenant general of the 43rd Light Infantry and died in 1850.

5. *The Eldest Brother*, Iris Butler (citing the Carver papers).

6. *Architects of Empire: The Duke of Wellington and his Brothers*, John Severn.

7. The marriage between Henry Wellesley and Georgiana Charlotte Augusta Cecil took place on 27 February 1816 at the chapel in Hatfield House. Georgiana Cecil and Henry Wellesley were related via their respective mothers. Georgiana was the granddaughter of Trevor Hill, 1st Viscount Hillsborough, and Henry the grandson of Arthur Hill-Trevor, the 1st Viscount Dungannon; the two viscounts were brothers, both the sons of Michael Hill and his wife, Anne Trevor.

8. The grand mansion at Grosvenor Square had formerly been the residence of Lady Tynley-Long whose daughter Catherine was to make a disastrous marriage to William Wellesley-Pole, son of Marquess Wellesley's brother of the same name, a year later.

9. *The Eldest Brother*, Iris Butler (citing the Carver papers). Iris Butler notes that Hyacinthe Mary took only the finest qualities from her two parents and combined them into a person of exceptional merit; it could perhaps be argued that her sister Anne took only the worst. Also Add. Ms. 37315, ff.8, Richard Wellesley, 2nd Earl of Mornington; Marquess Wellesley: Family correspondence: 1800–1842, British Library.

10. *Wild Mary: The Life of Mary Wesley*, Patrick Marnham.

11. Anne Wellesley was born on 29 February 1788. Her birthdate is given in the record of her baptism at St George's, Hanover Square, on 16 March of that year. Her marriage to Sir William Abdy was on 3 July 1806.

12. Add. Ms. 37315, Richard Wellesley, 2nd Earl of Mornington; Marquess Wellesley: Family correspondence: 1800–1842, British Library.

13. *A Regency Elopement*, Hugh Farmar.

14. Napoléon Bonaparte surrendered to Captain Frederick Lewis Maitland on board the *Bellerophon* on the morning of 15 July 1815; sailing to England the ship anchored off Brixham in Devon on 24 July awaiting further orders before sailing around the headland to Plymouth two days later. There Bonaparte was transferred to HMS *Northumberland* and taken into exile on St Helena, never having set foot on British soil.

15. *A Regency Elopement*, Hugh Farmar.

16. Ibid.

Chapter 4: Elopement in High Life

1. *Oxford University and City Herald*, 1 June 1816. The elopement took place on 5 September 1815.

2. At the ensuing divorce proceedings, the Dowager Lady Abdy claimed that the letters were discovered in a locked portfolio at Hill Street on the day following Anne's elopement with both Sir William and his mother present; this contradicts Hugh Farmar's narrative in *A Regency Elopement* which has the Dowager Lady Abdy and her daughter taking possession of these letters before Sir William's return from the country.

3. Lord Charles Bentinck used Messrs Snow & Co. as his banking house.

4. *Morning Chronicle*, 13 September 1815.
5. *Morning Chronicle*, 15 September 1815.
6. *Bury and Norwich Post*, 11 October 1815.
7. *The Eldest Brother*, Iris Butler (citing the Carver papers).
8. *A Regency Elopement*, Hugh Farmar.
9. Rosina Burrell married Robert Parnther on 13 August 1810 at the church of St Mary, situated in St Marylebone, London. Her two sons were Robert, born 1812, and Charles Henry born a year later. Hugh Farmar, who had seen letters from both Lady Wellesley and Rosina Parnther, wryly observed that both Rosina's handwriting and her French were better than Hyacinthe Gabrielle's.
10. *A Regency Elopement*, Hugh Farmar.
11. Thomas Noel Hill, 2nd Baron Berwick, had proposed marriage to her but, after thinking about his offer for three months, Hyacinthe refused him (*The Eldest Brother*, Iris Butler). In 1812 Lord Berwick married Harriette Wilson's younger sister, Sophia.
12. The marriage, which took place on 21 December 1812, was conducted by the Archbishop of Canterbury and the register signed by the bride's father Marquess Wellesley, her brother Richard Wellesley and Littleton's father Morton Walhouse. The Littletons' children were Hyacinthe-Anne born 1813 and Emily in 1814, followed by Edward Richard born 1815 and Caroline Anne in 1817, both after their aunt's elopement.
13. Letter written from Bath and dated 20 September 1815. *The Piozzi Letters: 1811–1816*, Hester Lynch Piozzi.
14. *A Regency Elopement*, Hugh Farmar.
15. Ibid.
16. Ibid.
17. Lady Frances Wedderburn-Webster was the daughter, by his second marriage, of Arthur Annesley, 1st Earl of Mountnorris who, many years before and when known as Viscount Valentia, had been the cause of Grace Dalrymple Elliott's downfall and subsequent divorce when he was discovered with her in a London bagnio.
18. *A Regency Elopement*, Hugh Farmar.
19. Ibid.
20. Ibid.
21. Ibid.

Chapter 5: Criminal Conversation and Doctors' Commons

1. Ibid.
2. Harriette Wilson did later use Henry Brougham's 'flaming love letters' to her as a bargaining tool with the result that, when he was Lord Chancellor, he paid her the sum of £40 a year for her silence (*London Review of Books*, vol. 25, no. 20, 23 October 2003 – 'A Useful £40' by John Wardroper in response to an article by Rosemary Hill in issue no. 18).
3. The allowance was fixed on 7 June 1816 and printed in the *Scots Magazine*, September 1816.
4. *A Regency Elopement*, Hugh Farmar. Presumably it was either Hyacinthe Littleton or her brother Richard who had written to the duke appealing for help.
5. The year of 1816 is often referred to as 'the year without a summer'. A volcanic eruption in the East Indies disrupted weather patterns worldwide and in Europe the months of June to September were notably cold across England. The date of the marriage licence was 22 July 1816 and the marriage took place on 23 July 1816. It was witnessed by two men:

John Clarke (who witnessed many marriages at the church and was probably connected with it in some capacity), and Edward Clarke.

6. Anne Hyacinthe Cavendish-Bentinck was born on 1 September 1816.

7. The two gentlemen were listed among the arrivals at Payn's York Hotel in Dover on 25 August 1816 bound for Brussels, printed in the *Morning Post*, 27 August 1816. The Honourable Mr King was probably one of the two surviving sons of Peter King, 6th Baron King: either the eldest son Peter who was later to become the 7th Baron King or the Honourable George King.

8. The Duke of Cambridge was expected to leave England in the first week of September on his return to Hanover where he was the military governor. *Royal Cornwall Gazette*, 24 August 1816.

9. *A Regency Elopement*, Hugh Farmar.

10. Ibid. The date of Lady Wellesley's death was 7 October 1816.

11. PROB 11/1588/61, The National Archives (hereafter TNA). Lady Anne's siblings agreed between themselves to abide by the will and ignore the codicil as it referred to Anne (indeed, they hoped to keep it entirely from her view), and so she shared with her sister the marchioness's wardrobe including laces, silks and Indian shawls.

12. *A Regency Elopement*, Hugh Farmar.

Chapter 6: The Birth of the Next Generation

1. Nottingham University Manuscripts and Special Collections, the Portland (Welbeck) Collection. Pl F8/9/8/1.

2. *A Regency Elopement*, Hugh Farmar.

3. Ibid.

4. *Morning Chronicle*, 10 November 1817 reports the birth taking place on 8 November and other newspapers report the event at the same time, although most omit the actual date of birth. When Charles was baptized some months later on 14 May 1818 at Brompton along with his elder sister, his birth date was noted in the register as 8 September 1817. His sister's birth date was 1 September 1816 and it would appear that the careless clerk has duplicated the month by accident. However, in the Carver papers at Southampton University is a letter from Lord Charles Bentinck to his brother-in-law Richard Wellesley, informing him that Anne was 'brought to bed this morning of a boy', and dated 6 November 1817 (Carver MSS 63/87). Charley's name is sometimes recorded as William Charles Frederick Cavendish Bentinck, but Frederick is not included in his baptismal name.

5. The Duke of Kent and Princess Victoire of Saxe-Coburg-Saalfeld married on 29 May 1818 in her homeland and then again, in a joint wedding with his brother, the Duke of Clarence and his bride Princess Adelaide of Saxe-Meiningen at Kew Palace on 11 July 1818.

6. Arthur Cavendish Bentinck was born on 9 May 1819 (*Morning Chronicle*, 11 May 1819) and Emily less than a year later on 14 April 1820 (*The Annual Register of World Events*, 1820). For reference to the Duke of Wellington standing as godfather to little Arthur, see *A Regency Elopement*, Hugh Farmar.

7. *A Regency Elopement*, Hugh Farmar.

8. The likeness between Edward John Johnston and the Marquess Wellesley can be seen in a large portrait of Johnston by the Scottish artist Andrew Robertson which is in a private collection, and in a marble bust by the sculptor Sir Francis Leggatt Chantrey created in 1819 and now in Birmingham Art Gallery.

9. *The Eldest Brother*, Iris Butler. The duke had called on Hyacinthe Littleton to ask her to persuade her sister to attend and had followed that up with a personal letter to his niece. Lady Anne replied to say she would attend in the evening. The dinner party took place on 27 July 1819.

10. King George IV planned to abandon Carlton House for Buckingham House after it had been remodelled into a palace by the architect John Nash. In fact it was never finished in his lifetime and the first monarch to live in Buckingham Palace was Queen Victoria.

11. King George III died on 29 January and was buried on 16 February 1820 in St George's Chapel in Windsor. His son Prince Edward, Duke of Kent and Strathearn was buried there four days before his father. The coronation of King George IV took place on 19 July 1821. When Lord Charles Bentinck lived at Eaton Place, it was described as being in Pimlico; it is now more often placed in neighbouring Belgravia.

12. The ruby ring was actually a large sapphire with an overlaying cross made of rubies; it is sometimes referred to as 'The Wedding Ring of England'. Bluemantle Pursuivant of Arms in Ordinary is a position held by a junior officer of the College of Arms in London; in 1821 one William Woods held the office.

13. Many years later Edward Littleton, Baron Hatherton, used the name Charley for his nephew when writing to his wife, revealing this as the name by which he was familiarly known to his closest family and friends. To help distinguish him from his father we have chosen to use Charley when referring to William Charles Cavendish Bentinck.

14. Peter Drummond-Burrell's mother was Lady Priscilla Bertie, the sister of Georgiana Charlotte, Marchioness of Cholmondeley and one of the guardians named for little Georgiana Cavendish Bentinck. The marchioness and her sister were hereditary co-heiresses of the office that had been held by their father but, as women, could only nominate someone to hold the office.

15. *The Court of St James's*, Christopher Hibbert.

16. *The Mistresses of King George IV*, M.J. Levy. Harriet Fane married, as his second wife, the diplomat and politician Charles Arbuthnot.

17. *Bell's Weekly Messenger*, 23 July 1821 and *Morning Post*, 25 July 1821.

18. *The Mistresses of King George IV*, M.J. Levy.

19. See our previous book, *An Infamous Mistress: The Life, Loves and Family of the Celebrated Grace Dalrymple Elliott* for more information.

20. In 1832 John Elger, a builder, remodelled 1 North Row and its next-door neighbour, 19 Norfolk Street, into one substantial dwelling. It was originally renumbered as 25 Park Lane then, in 1872, as no. 39 but from 1934 has been known as 138 Park Lane.

Chapter 7: Trials and Tribulations

1. *Bell's Life in London and Sporting Chronicle*, 28 July 1822.

2. The kilt had been prohibited as everyday wear by the Dress Act (repealed in 1782) after the 1745 rising, although it was used for army uniforms. Sir Walter Scott issued instructions that any gentleman not in uniform must wear 'the ancient Highland costume'. Sir David Wilkie later painted the king in the garb he had worn on the trip but flattered him by slimming him down, lengthening the kilt and leaving off the pink tights.

3. Grace Dalrymple Elliott was bequeathed a sum of £5,000 in the will of 'Old Q', otherwise William Douglas, the 4th Duke of Queensberry (1725–1810), a notorious old rake who also revelled in the sobriquet of the 'Old Goat of Piccadilly' (he lived next door to the Cholmondeleys for some years). The will was contested and dragged through the courts

for many years, becoming known as the Queensberry Cause. Grace, quite rightly as it turned out, despaired of ever seeing her inheritance but she stipulated in her will that if the money did materialize it was to go to her granddaughter. Neither Grace nor Georgiana ever saw a penny. See our previous book, *An Infamous Mistress: The Life, Loves and Family of the Celebrated Grace Dalrymple Elliott* for more detail.

4. They married on 29 October 1825. Marianne's first husband had been Robert Patterson (1781–1822), a merchant and son of a wealthy Irish emigrant to America. Patterson's sister Elizabeth (Betsy) had been married to Napoléon Bonaparte's younger brother Jérôme Bonaparte and bore him a son but Napoléon annulled the marriage and barred her from entering France. Marianne suffered from asthma and it was for the sake of her health that she had travelled to Europe.

5. *The Diaries of the First Lord Hatherton* (extracts from the personal diary, between the years 1817–1862), edited by Ken Lees.

6. Edward John Johnston married Cornelia Martha Powell Schuyler in 1824 and had at least two daughters, Cornelia Eliza Mary Wellesley Johnston (1828–1872) who married George Cobb Ledger at Taunton in 1847 (she used the name St Leger in later life), and Elizabeth Charlotte Wellesley Johnston (born in 1830 and living in Paris in 1877) who married a Frenchman named Plus in Boulogne-sur-Mer in 1857. Cornelia Martha Powell Schuyler was the daughter of Courtland/Cortlandt Schuyler (from a prominent Dutch family with connections to New York and New Jersey) and his wife Martha. She was born in Bombay, India, in 1803 where her father was serving with the 84th Regiment of Foot. Courtland Schuyler was later the British Envoy to Goa in Western India. Edward John Johnston can be found in the 1861 census living with his son-in-law George Cobb Ledger at Berry Farm House in Clayhangers Wood End, Tiverton, Devon (RG 9; Piece: 1482; Folio: 61; Page: 3) and it is from this document that his date and place of birth are taken. He died in 1877 in Paris. Henry Fitzroy, the husband of Lady Anne Wellesley, was connected via his mother Anne Warren, daughter and co-heir of Peter Warren of the Royal Navy, to the Schuyler and Van Cortlandt families and so was clearly related to Cornelia Martha Powell Schuyler.

7. K.D. Reynolds, author of Harriette Wilson's entry in the *Oxford Dictionary of National Biography*, thinks Harriette Wilson is unlikely to be the author, despite her name appearing as such. *Paris Lions and London Tigers* was published on 19 September 1825. On 15 September 1825 a letter from a shopkeeper named Hobby concerning an outstanding bill owed by the recently-deceased Grace Dalrymple Elliott was sent to Lady Cholmondeley and it mentioned that Hobby had approached Lord C. Bentinck in Paris regarding the matter (Houghton Hall Archives).

8. Sir Henry Halford (born Henry Vaughan) had been physician in ordinary to the royal household for many years. Dr Pelham Warren was the son of George III's physician, Richard Warren.

9. The *London Courier and Evening Gazette* of 7 October 1828 reported Lady C. Bentinck's arrival at Bath. She was back in London by Sunday, 12 October when the altercation with the cook took place and Lady Anne appeared before the magistrates on 15 October 1828 (*Morning Chronicle*, 16 October 1828).

10. *The Times*, 16 October 1828. The newspapers would have a reporter working within the building; just a few years after Lady Anne's appearance, Charles Dickens was employed there by the *Morning Chronicle* newspaper.

11. The Macnamara family had originally won Llangoed Castle in a game of cards. There is a question mark over the address at which the robbery occurred. Lady Charles Bentinck is listed as the occupier of the North Row house for some years following her husband's death (up to 1831); however, some sources, notably the Old Bailey transcript, say the house that was let to Mr Macnamara by Lady Charles was located on George Street, Hanover Square. Possibly she stayed in Hanover Square for the duration of the trial while her own house was occupied and the addresses have been confused.

12. *The Eldest Son*, Iris Butler (citing the Carver papers). Richard Wellesley's wife was Jane Eliza Chambers; they married in 1821.

13. New Road was renamed in 1857 and now comprises Pentonville, Marylebone and Euston Road.

14. Lady Anne's artistic abilities have not previously been mentioned; we would dearly love to know who else she painted. London Street is now known as Maple Street. Dr Hill died at Boulogne-sur-Mer in October 1825 of an apoplectic fit as he was embarking onto a steam boat destined for England.

Chapter 8: Belgian Revolution

1. *Becoming Queen*, Kate Williams. Frederick, Duke of York, second of the royal brothers, had died childless in 1827.

2. *The Life and Times of William IV*, Anne Somerset. The diarist Charles Cavendish Fulke Greville who recorded the duke's thoughts was the cousin of Lord Charles Bentinck's children.

3. Rowland Hill, 1st Viscount Hill, commissioned Captain Siborne to construct this model; Siborne was in Brussels to carry out research for his project, which was not completed until 1838. George Harley Drummond had several children with his mistress the actress, dancer and singer Nanette Johnstone née Parker between 1814 and 1819 (she was formerly the wife of the Drury Lane comedian Henry Erskine Johnstone, but had abandoned him for the Covent Garden theatre manager Henry Harris before taking up with Drummond), but at his death in 1855 he named another woman, Sarah Emma Bulkeley née Donovan, the wife of James Nathaniel Fielding Bulkeley of the Royal Navy and of the Reform Club in Pall Mall. His wife, whom he had married in 1801 when aged only 17, was Margaret Munro, daughter of a Glasgow merchant, a *hallucate* (hare-brained) lady according to John Ramsay of Ochtertyre (*Letters of John Ramsay of Ochtertyre, 1799–1812*, John Ramsay, Scottish History Society, 1967).

4. This episode mirrors an adventure of Lord Charles Bentinck's first mother-in-law, the intrepid Grace Dalrymple Elliott who, many years earlier, found herself in one of the houses facing the Parc de Bruxelles during action in the opening stages of the French Revolution. Mrs Elliott had charitably passed food from her windows to the exhausted French troops camped overnight in the park, even though she considered them her enemy.

5. The *Morning Post* of 6 October 1830 reported George Harley Drummond's return to Piccadilly from Brussels.

6. Leopold was crowned on 21 July 1831. He previously turned down an offer of the Greek throne due to instability in the country. In 1832 he married again, to Louise-Marie of Orléans, daughter of Louis Philippe I, King of France and granddaughter of Louis Philippe, Duke of Orléans who was guillotined during the French Revolution. Louis Philippe I of France had refused the Belgian crown that had been offered to his son Louis, Duke of Nemours.

7. Richard Wellesley died on 1 March 1831 and Gerald Wellesley on 22 July 1833. Gerald's will revealed his children, Agnes Maria (born on 6 May 1825), Charles Alfred (born on 19 January 1827) and Frances Jane (born on 23 December 1827) and he left annuities for each of them, specifying that the children were to be placed in the care of Mrs Maria Vaughan (late Lermit) and her sister Jane Baker. He also left money to Richard's children, to the Reverend Henry Wellesley and his sisters Anne and Hyacinthe. PROB 11/1820/ 462, TNA.

Chapter 9: The Summertown Gypsy

1. Although he consorted with gypsies, James Lambourne's ancestry indicates that he was not one himself. His family (perhaps even his father) is reputed to have supplied the original persona upon whom Sir Walter Scott based his character of Michael Lambourne in *Kenilworth: A Romance*, written in 1821 and based on the secret marriage between Lord Robert Dudley, 1st Earl of Leicester and favourite of Queen Elizabeth I, and Amy Robsart. Cumnor Place, demolished in 1810, saw the death of Amy Robsart, the wife of Lord Robert Dudley, in 1560.
2. The marriage was witnessed by Joseph and Susannah Buckland (Buckland is a known gypsy surname); Susannah was originally, like Sinnetta, a Smith and had married Joseph in Buckinghamshire in 1814. It is probable that Sinnetta and Susannah were sisters. Sinnetta and James's may have been a hasty marriage, for in 1816 the Warwick races were held over 3 and 4 September.
3. Caravans were used to transport animals to markets and shows and from 1816 (with the addition of springs and a padded interior) they were used for racehorses. Perhaps the Lambournes' homely caravan was adapted from one that James had previously used to transport his equine stock to the racecourses for sale?
4. Sinnetta Lambourne was baptized on 12 October 1817 at Cumnor, then in Berkshire but now in Oxfordshire due to boundary changes.
5. A few families were 'long-travellers' but they were the minority. The traditional view is that the gypsies would roam far and wide but in fact they generally confined themselves to a small area; one in which they knew they could ply their trades and find work, knew the areas in which to camp and to overwinter and where they would not encroach onto other family circuits. Shifts in the geographical area of their annual circuits tended to be made gradually over many years.
6. The family does not appear on the 1821 census for Cumnor listed in the Vicar's Book in the vestry of the church, so possibly did carry on their travels in the warmer months for a transitional period. The Diamond Hall had ceased trading as an inn in the 1790s and had stood empty for some time; by 1832 when John Badcock wrote his history of the village four tenements stood in its stead. The signwriter was named Costar and James Lambourne paid 4s 6d for the painted board.
7. *Making of a Regency Village: Origin, History and Description of Summertown in 1832 by John Badcock*. William Cullimore was born on 12 July 1809 and confirmed on the same day as the young Sinnetta Lambourne. *Oxford University and City Herald*, 4 March 1826.
8. *Berkshire Notes and Queries*, vol. 1, part 3, 1891, reprinted in 'Sineta [sic] Lambourne and Sineta Smith' by E.O. Windstedt in the *Journal of the Gypsy Lore Society*, series 3, vol. 23, 1944.
9. PROB 11/1942/415, TNA. Oxfordshire has two villages named Wootton; the one in which James Lambourne owned property is situated approximately a mile and a half to the

south of Cumnor, near to Boars Hill. Two years later one of the two elder Lambourne boys had an accident in St Giles when the horse he was riding fell, breaking the boy's thigh. *Oxford University and City Herald*, 6 August 1836.

10. *Jackson's Oxford Journal*, 7 May 1836.

11. John Light's age is taken from his transportation records; he gave his birthplace as Bristol. His trial was on 13 July 1836, he was taken from Oxford gaol to the Leviathan hulk at Portsmouth on 26 July and sailed on the *Eden* (27 August) to Tasmania (Van Diemen's Land), arriving on 22 December 1836. He married and raised a family in Australia, dying there in 1889.

Chapter 10: Passed from Pillar to Post

1. A *History of Harrow School, 1324–1991* by Christopher Tyerman. Charles Thomas Longley (1794–1868) was appointed as headmaster in April 1829 and remained in that position until 1836 when he was appointed Bishop of Ripon. Twenty years later he became Bishop of Durham and following that the Archbishop of York.

2. A *Regency Elopement*, Hugh Farmar. Letter written in May 1832.

3. Ibid.

4. In addition to the money held in trust for her, George James, 1st Marquess of Cholmondeley, left a generous bequest of £1,000 to young Georgiana in his will. PROB 11/1727/98, TNA.

5. The party took place on 30 December 1832. The 2nd Marquess of Cholmondeley married twice: his first wife, Caroline Campbell, died in 1815 only three years after their wedding, and he married again, in 1830, to Lady Susan Caroline Somerset, daughter of the 6th Duke of Beaufort. Both marriages were childless.

6. *The Eldest Brother*, Iris Butler. Charlotte Anne Mackenzie Vandyck was born c.1818 and baptized at Hammersmith as the daughter of Adrian Van Dyke Esquire of Amsterdam; she was then baptized a second time at Burwash in Sussex on 10 December 1823 as Charlotte Ann Mackenzie, the daughter of Adrian and Anne Van Dyke, aged 5½. The Reverend William Mackenzie of Burwash had married the widowed Anne Van Dyck at Lambeth on 30 November 1822 (he was also a widower) and had added his surname into his stepdaughter's name at her second baptism.

7. Letter dated 10 May 1835 and written from Dunsfold. *Surrey Archaeological Collections*, vol. XXXII, 1919. The marriage took place on 12 June 1835.

8. *The Diaries of the First Lord Hatherton* (extracts from the personal diary, between the years 1817–1862), edited by Ken Lees.

9. Letter dated 27 September 1835 and written from Harrow (Shropshire Archives, Shackerley Collection, 1781/6/45).

Chapter 11: Love amid the Dreaming Spires

1. Oxford University contemporary room rent books record that Charley rented a room on the Front Quad at Merton College from January 1838 at a cost of £2 per annum. The Front Quad, considered to be Oxford's oldest quad, was originally the back gardens of three houses acquired by Walter de Merton in the 1260s.

2. 'Gypsey Experiences', *Illustrated London News*, vol. 19, 1851, written by Tom Taylor under the pseudonym 'A Roumany Rei' and reprinted in *In Gipsy Tents* by Francis Hindes Groome. Taylor was identified as the author by Watts-Dunton in *Old Familiar Faces*.

3. Letter from the Duke of Wellington to his son, the Marquess Douro, undated and as quoted in *Wellington: A Journey Through My Family* by Jane Wellesley. Both of Arthur's

sons had attended Oxford but left under a cloud and without degrees, turning instead to Cambridge where they were more successful.

4. Besides the gold heart, the bequests were a sapphire brooch and earrings together with a turquoise and pearl cross brooch and earrings all given to Lady Cholmondeley by the first Lady Charles Bentinck, blue china ornaments once belonging to Georgiana's mother, and a yellow topaz necklace, bracelet and earrings, a diamond amulet, an enamel strawberry set, a broad pearl ring with turquoises in the centre, two blue Sèvres butter boats and a lace veil. Among Lady Cholmondeley's bequests to other people were a mother-of-pearl tablet case and pencil with drawings by Miss Bentinck (which was given to Lady Tarleton, widow of Sir Banastre Tarleton and niece to the Marchioness of Cholmondeley), and two blue china vases that had belonged to Georgiana's mother and were bequeathed to Miss Elizabeth Blackwell. PROB 11/1897/368, TNA.

5. Bridal veils were increasingly being worn in the nineteenth century but a bonnet was a much more practical option. Charley and Sinnetta's wedding was extremely private and suited to the economy of their means; it is therefore unlikely that Sinnetta wore anything other than her 'Sunday best'.

6. *Queen Victoria's Journals* (online).

7. The information that James Lambourne gave his permission for his daughter to marry, recorded on the marriage licence, was given under oath by Charley. Both James Lambourne and his wife Sinnetta 'made their mark' on various documents, indicating that they were unable to sign their own names.

8. Did Lord Hatherton know something of his nephew Charley's intentions with regard to Sinnetta? Letter dated 6 September 1839, twenty days before Charley's marriage. Records of the Littleton Family of Teddesley and Hatherton, Barons Hatherton, Staffordshire Archives.

9. Letter dated 16 October 1839. Records of the Littleton Family of Teddesley and Hatherton, Barons Hatherton, Staffordshire Archives.

10. This took place on 14 May 1840. Queen Victoria's journal for the day recorded: 'Lunched early & at 2 went to St James's Palace for a Drawing room, at which none of the Family were present. It lasted till nearly ½ p[ast] 3. We came home before 4. – I felt dreadfully tired and rested for some time.'

11. The little Cavendish Bentinck boy died on 13 July 1840 and was buried five days later. Kensal Green cemetery was relatively new, having been founded in 1833. It was inspired by the Père-Lachaise cemetery in Paris where, coincidentally, Grace Dalrymple Elliott (the mother of Lord Charles Bentinck's first wife) is buried.

12. The Bethnal Green Library now stands on the site of the old asylum and, to this day, the land surrounding it is known locally as 'Barmy Park'.

13. 1841 census HO107; Piece 20; Folio: 8; Page: 9 and Piece 771; Folio: 1; Page: 22. Nancy Lambourne married Isaac Drewitt (or Drewett) in 1823. Annoyingly, the entries for the 1841 census relating to Paddington have not survived, making it impossible to see who was living at 20 Pickering Terrace at the time of the census and probably hiding Charley and his mother-in-law Sinnetta Lambourne from us.

14. This second son was baptized at St James's in Paddington on 25 August 1841. He died on 3 March 1842.

15. *Berkshire Notes and Queries*, vol. 1, part 3, 1891, reprinted in 'Sineta [sic] Lambourne and Sineta Smith' by E.O. Windstedt in the *Journal of the Gypsy Lore Society*, series 3, vol. 23, 1944.

16. *The Eldest Brother*, Iris Butler (citing the Carver papers).
17. Records of the Littleton Family of Teddesley and Hatherton, Barons Hatherton, Staffordshire Archives.
18. The archivist for Oxford University noted that Charley's four years at Merton should have been sufficient for him to complete his Bachelor of Arts but evidently his domestic distractions hindered him. The Reverend Henry Wellesley was appointed the principal of New Inn Hall a few years after his nephew had attended there; his term of office was 1847 to 1866.

Chapter 12: Ducal Discoveries
1. Records of the Littleton Family of Teddesley and Hatherton, Barons Hatherton, Staffordshire Archives.
2. Ibid.
3. Nottinghamshire University Manuscripts and Special Collections, Pl F8/11/1/1. The fund had accumulated to £9,622 16s 3d in the 3 per cent stock by 1845.
4. Records of the Littleton Family of Teddesley and Hatherton, Barons Hatherton, Staffordshire Archives.
5. Charlotte died on 25 September 1845.
6. *Morning Chronicle*, 20 October 1845 (the *Newcastle Courant* reported the same news earlier on 10 October) and *Morning Chronicle*, 24 October 1845.
7. Nottingham University Manuscripts and Special Collections, the Portland (Welbeck) Collection.
8. *Morning Post*, 11 November 1845.
9. The Reverend William Harry Edward Cavendish-Bentinck was archdeacon at the church of St John the Evangelist in Westminster. He was the grandson of the 2nd Duke of Portland; perhaps he felt a familial connection to Charley and was disposed to help him gain a position in the church? Or maybe, for all his refusal to grant Bothal, the 4th Duke was not above pulling strings to improve his nephew's lot?
10. *The Diaries of the First Lord Hatherton* (extracts from the personal diary, between the years 1817–1862), edited by Ken Lees.
11. The Reverend John Hodgson was appointed to Lidlington in 1835 and remained vicar of the parish until his death in 1863.
12. J.T. Brooks' diary mentions Charley and Sinnetta for the first time on 21 July 1847 'to pay visits, to Ampthill … the Bentincks'. John Eagles, an attorney and solicitor, and his wife Frances lived on Dunstable Street in Ampthill. The Reverend George Maule and his wife lived on Church Street. The dinner party at which the goldfinches were exhibited and the Dawsons' evening party both took place in February 1848. The rector of Flitwick was the Reverend William Alfred Dawson and his wife was Flora née Foster of Brickhill House in Bedfordshire. Diary of J.T. Brooks of Flitwick, Bedfordshire Archives, LL17/282 and Diary of Mary Ann Brooks of Flitwick, Bedfordshire Archives, LL19/2.
13. The manor of Ampthill had been owned by Henry Fox, 3rd Lord Holland who, in 1797, had married Elizabeth Vassall, the divorced wife of Sir Godfrey Webster (it was her daughter-in-law whom Charley visited at Battle Abbey in Sussex as a youngster). When Lord Holland died in 1840 his widow was left Holland House and Ampthill but she was in debt and persuaded her son to agree to them being sold. The Duke of Bedford bought them in 1842, adding them to his holdings in the area. Bedfordshire Archives, R.H. Russell (Holland) of Ampthill.

14. A handstile is possibly a clapper or tumble stile whereby the crossbars are hinged and weighted. The user presses down and steps over, releasing the crossbars to return to their original position once on the other side. *Northampton Mercury*, 21 June 1845.

15. *The Diaries of the First Lord Hatherton* (extracts from the personal diary, between the years 1817–1862), edited by Ken Lees.

16. In 1861 on the census return under 'Rank, Profession, or Occupation' Sinnetta Lambourne listed 'House Property' indicating that her income came from rents on property she owned, presumably the same property that had formerly been owned by her husband and inherited by her at his death (RG 9; Piece: 110; Folio: 121; Page: 13). Following her appearance in the Insolvent Debtors Court, Sinnetta's name was reported as Sineta Lambour. She listed her former addresses for the court: 11 Skinner Street, Somers Town (not to be confused with Summertown in Oxfordshire), 6 Winchester Road, New Road, and occasionally of Sunbury in Middlesex (*London Gazette*, 6 March 1849).

17. Information in *Survey of London: Volume 40, the Grosvenor Estate in Mayfair, Part 2 (The Buildings)* says: 'A charity book of the 1830s kept in the vestry of St. George's, Hanover Square, shows that many inhabitants of Grosvenor Mews were recipients of relief, and in 1858, when the prevalence of disease in the neighbourhood led to the prosecution of a house-owner for allowing part of his premises to be dangerous to the public health, it was revealed his house "contained fifty or sixty persons".'

18. The inkstand was supplied by Mr Bull, a silversmith at Bedford. *Cambridge Independent Press*, 18 August 1849.

19. The Reverend Charles Cavendish Bentinck was appointed to the living of Husborne Crawley on 3 November 1849 and to the living of Ridgmont on 23 November 1849. The population of the village of Husborne Crawley was about at its peak in Charley's day; it had risen from 543 in 1801 to 680 in 1831, then began to fall as people moved away to seek work. The 1851 census, the nearest to Charley's time there, recorded the population of the village as 614 inhabitants. In the latest census taken in 2011 the population was only 237 people.

20. *Northampton Mercury*, 6 September 1845.

21. Their first home in Ampthill is now 41 Church Street.

22. The late Andrew Underwood, historian of Ampthill, lived in a portion of this mansion after it had been converted into two properties. No. 37 became The Wingfield Club and no. 39 Foulislea Cottage (the latter had possibly once been the coach house to the mansion). The name Foulislea, used in Victorian times, commemorated the Reverend Sir Henry Foulis who was the uncle and guardian of the orphaned children of the Wingfield family.

23. The Duchess of Bedford was also the niece, via her mother, of the notorious Lady Seymour Dorothy Worsley who had scandalized eighteenth-century society with her elopement from her husband and the subsequent Crim. Con. trial. Lady Worsley was a close friend of Grace Dalrymple Elliott, Lord Charles Bentinck's first mother-in-law.

Chapter 13: The Love Story ends in Tragedy

1. Sinnetta's death certificate erroneously gave her age as 28 and newspaper reports on her death said she was 29. Her death was registered by Hannah Sadler, either a nurse or maid who was with her at the end.

2. Records of the Littleton Family of Teddesley and Hatherton, Barons Hatherton, Staffordshire Archives.

3. If there ever was a fourth child, to date no trace has been found and if such a child did exist then it too must have died tragically young. A much later report (in the *Bedfordshire Times and Independent* newspaper of 22 October 1943) ascribed the death of this fourth child to a fall and suggested that this final calamity broke Sinnetta's heart and led to her death.

4. The *Gentleman's Magazine*, Volume 187, April 1850.

5. The late Andrew Underwood taught in the village pre-1966 and recalled the traditional legacy of the name Sinnetta that was bestowed on several of his pupils.

6. A fanciful newspaper article on Sinnetta, written nearly a century after her death, claimed her 'grave clothes were of pure silk and in the Romany colours, with kerchief and neck-wear befitting her rank and as a princess among her own people.' *Bedfordshire Times and Independent*, 22 October 1943. J.T. Brooks, in his diary, recorded meeting Henry Wellesley and Lord Hatherton at Ampthill the day before the funeral and also mentioned his attendance at the service on the following day.

7. Bedfordshire Archives, 1925 Valuation books, DV1/C54/84.

8. *The Diaries of the First Lord Hatherton* (extracts from the personal diary, between the years 1817–1862), edited by Ken Lees, and Records of the Littleton Family of Teddesley and Hatherton, Barons Hatherton, Staffordshire Archives.

9. Tom Taylor, newspaperman, playwright and comic writer, was known as something of an expert on the gypsies and on gypsy culture. Taylor attended Cambridge University at the time Charley was at Oxford, but he is mentioned as later being an Oxford don.

10. Augusta Ada, Countess of Lovelace, died towards the end of the following year of uterine cancer. 1851 census HO107; Piece: 1755; Folio: 111; Page: 27, Piece: 1646; Folio: 15; Page: 23, Piece: 2122; Folio: 216; Page: 11 and Piece: 2418; Folio: 583; Page: 18.

11. Hugh Farmar wryly noted in *A Regency Elopement* that the funeral carriage found a permanent parking-place in the crypt of St Paul's and was unlikely to be dislodged, even by an atomic bomb or the most radical of deans. It was, however, moved to Stratfield Saye in 1981.

12. *The Diary of a Bedfordshire Squire* (John Thomas Brooks of Flitwick 1794–1858), Bedford-shire Historical Record Society. Henry Robert Edward Wellesley (born in 1838) attended Eton between 1852 and 1854.

13. As was the tradition with the Cavendish-Bentinck men, although the new duke had William as a first name he used his second, John, instead. While the dukedom could not pass to the 4th Duke of Portland's daughters, his estate in Marylebone descended to his daughter Lady Lucy, the widow of Charles Augustus Ellis, 6th Baron Howard de Walden for her lifetime and then to her sisters who were childless. After their deaths it would pass to Lucy's grandson (by seniority) and so, much as Princess Charlotte's death in 1817 had sparked a scramble for the sons of George III to marry and beget an heir, so too did this bequest. The Ellis boys quickly married with the eldest, Frederick, winning the race by virtue of his seniority, despite the fact that his younger brother, the Reverend William Ellis of Bothal (the living once destined for Charley) had managed to sire a son first. *My Grandfather, A Modern Medievalist: The Life of the 8th Lord Howard de Walden* by Thomas Seymour.

14. The date of the marriage was 18 February 1857. The Dutch branch of the Bentinck family traced its lineage back to Hans William Bentinck, the 1st Earl of Portland who was a page of honour to Prince William of Orange (later King William III alongside his wife Mary, daughter of King James II) and served in his army in the seventeenth century. In 1877 the

Yorkshire Post said of Arthur that he was a 'portly and handsome man, with something so peculiar in his build that, I have been told, a stranger seeing him on some public occasion, once put the question, "Who is that Dutch gentleman?" I need not remind you of the Dutch origin of the house of Bentinck, which, however, has ceased to be traceable in the appearance of most of its modern representatives.'

Chapter 14: A New Beginning

1. *Morning Post*, 2 November 1859.
2. Caroline Louisa Burnaby was baptized on 5 December 1832 at Hungarton in Leicestershire.
3. *Memoirs of Lady Ottoline Morrell: A Study in Friendship, 1873–1915*, edited by Robert Gathorne-Hardy. Lady Ottoline Violet Anne Cavendish-Bentinck (1873–1938) was the daughter of Charley's brother Arthur and his second wife, Augusta Browne. She married Philip Morrell MP in 1902 but they had an 'open marriage'. She took a succession of lovers and was nicknamed 'Lady Utterly Immoral'.
4. The levee took place on 24 April 1860. Queen Victoria was in mourning for her brother-in-law, Ernst Christian Carl IV, Prince of Hohenlohe-Langenburg (husband of her older half-sister Princess Feodora of Leiningen) and was described as wearing, on the occasion, 'a train of black corded silk, trimmed with a ruche, and rosettes of black crape; the petticoat to correspond. On her head she wore a black jet circlet as a head-dress.' *Morning Post*, 25 April 1860.
5. Ridgmont parish baptism register. The old parish church at Ridgmont is now a roofless ruin.
6. The date of the wedding was 10 June 1862.
7. Nottingham University Manuscripts and Special Collections, the Portland (Welbeck) Collection.
8. *Further Letters of Mrs Gaskell*, John Chapple and Alan Shelston.
9. Caroline Anne Davenport was the daughter of Richard Hurt of Wirksworth, Derbyshire. She survived Lord Hatherton, dying in 1897. Their marriage took place on 11 February 1852.
10. *Bath Chronicle*, 31 August and 21 September 1865, and *Morning Post*, 13 September 1865. The child was born on 8 September 1865 at Eaton Place. It is something of a parallel to the short-lived fourth child that Charley is in some sources reputed to have had with Sinnetta, of whom no trace can be found. Perhaps in part the confusion has arisen by later writers confusing the child born in 1865 with a child of Sinnetta's?
11. For Charley's will see the Principal Registry, probate date 12 September 1865.
12. Bedfordshire Archives, SF15/15.

Chapter 15: Victorian Values and Sensibilities

1. The temporary incumbent was the Reverend Edward Lawson of neighbouring Longhirst. The Reverend Henry Hopwood married again in 1853 to Frances, younger daughter of Alexander Radclyffe Sidebottom of Lincoln's Inn.
2. *Leaves from the Diary of Henry Greville*, third series. Lady Morgan was Sydney, Lady Morgan née Owenson, c.1781–1859. While the first part of Grace Dalrymple Elliott's journal is accurate except for discrepancies in names and dates due to the fact that she wrote it some years after the event, the latter part contains many proven falsehoods. With the original now lost, it is impossible to say for certain if the inaccurate information stems from Grace's pen or from Richard Bentley's over-enthusiastic presentation of it in an

attempt to generate more interest and increase sales. In our previous book, *An Infamous Mistress: The Life, Loves and Family of the Celebrated Grace Dalrymple Elliott*, we endeavour to separate the fact from the fiction in Grace's *Journal of my Life*.

3. The *Pall Mall Gazette*, 31 August 1865.

4. Lady Clare was the daughter of Peter Burrell, 1st Baron Gwydyr and Lady Priscilla Barbara Elizabeth Bertie, Baroness Willoughby de Eresby, who was the Marchioness of Cholmondeley's sister. Lady Clare's husband, John FitzGibbon, the 2nd Earl of Clare, had died in 1851. Both the Marchioness of Cholmondeley and the Baroness Willoughby de Eresby had been named as guardians of the young Georgiana Cavendish-Bentinck.

5. Nottingham University Manuscripts and Special Collections, the Portland (Welbeck) Collection: Pw H 997/1-2 (25 July 1849) and Pl F6/8/10/4-20 (30 August 1849 to 5 July 1860).

6. Lady Margaret Harriet Bentinck (1798–1882). Nottingham University Manuscripts and Special Collections, the Portland (Welbeck) Collection, Pl F9/6/1/4.

7. The *Caledonian Mercury*, 4 September 1865.

8. *Manchester Times*, 20 January 1866.

9. Abdy left £5,000 to Jane Goodbun, £10,000 to her son William Henry (born 1850), £5,000 to Percy (born 1853), and £6,000 to Henry (born 1856), plus bequests totalling £70,000 to be held in trust for their benefit. Another son, Archibald, was born in 1858 (died 1863) and a further son, James Louis Goodbun, was born in 1863; these last two were not mentioned in Abdy's will. Jane Goodbun died aged 38 in 1865, three years before Sir William but was still named in his will. *Chelmsford Chronicle*, 29 May 1858.

10. 1871 census RG10; Piece: 862; Folio: 57; Page: 3. Hyacinthe Mary (Cinty) Cavendish-Bentinck and Henry Negus submitted a Statutory Declaration to correct the order of Charley's forenames and this was actioned by R.M. White, Deputy Superintendent Registrar, on 4 April 1900.

11. Nottingham University Manuscripts and Special Collections, the Portland (Welbeck) Collection, Pw K 456–480.

12. In the 1871 census Lady Anne and her daughter also have a boarder living with them in their house: George [Augustus] Nicholson, a 24-year-old photographer's assistant from London. 1871 census RG10; Piece: 95; Folio: 70; Page: 11.

13. In 1893 the 6th Duke of Portland also became the 2nd Baron Bolsover of Bolsover Castle in Derbyshire, a title that had been created in 1880 and first held, as Baroness Bolsover, by his stepmother Augusta Cavendish-Bentinck until her death.

14. It was named after the Capponi family who owned the villa from the sixteenth century. Ferdinando Carlo Capponi, in the eighteenth century, created the gardens for which the villa is still well-known today. The Villa Capponi was bought by Caroline Louisa's mother-in-law, Lady Elizabeth Scott, in 1882 and remained in the family until 1908 when Caroline Louisa sold it.

15. Georgiana Augusta Frederica Henrietta Cavendish Bentinck died on 12 September and was buried on 19 September 1883. For Georgiana's will see the Principal Registry, probate date 24 January 1884.

16. *The Eldest Brother*, Iris Butler (citing the Carver papers). The letter continues: 'I rather like boys to be little D___ when young, they always grow up to be the steadiest men.'

17. Anne Cavendish-Bentinck died on 7 June 1888.

18. *Etelinda* was written by Mildred to her husband's libretto. A semi-serious melodrama, it is set in Scotland. The composer's name was not initially announced but on the second

performance, with its success assured, Mildred appeared on stage at the end to accept the acknowledgement of the audience.

19. Mary Violet was born on 28 March 1901 and Clare Louise Olive on 9 May 1904 at Hampstead, London.

Chapter 16: Royal Descent

1. Violet Hyacinth Bowes-Lyon was buried alongside Harry Warren Scott at Ham Cemetery on 21 October 1893.
2. *George VI*, Denis Judd.
3. *Counting One's Blessings: The Selected Letters of Queen Elizabeth The Queen Mother*, edited by William Shawcross. The Primavera (also known as the Allegory of Spring) is a fifteenth-century panel painting by Sandro Botticelli. In 1909, while on a visit to her grandmother in Bordighera, Lady Elizabeth Bowes-Lyon bought a pair of antique angels for three lire. She kept them for the rest of her life, later placing them on the corner of her bedhead at Clarence House.
4. At the outbreak of the First World War, Princess Marie of Croÿ (1875–1968), the daughter of Prince Alfred Emmanuel de Croÿ-Solre and both a nurse and member of the French and Belgian Resistance during the war, was staying with her friend Violet Anne Cavendish-Bentinck and her mother, Mrs Scott. Princess Marie recalled that 'about the 29th of July [1914], a telegram from a well-informed friend told me, "If you are going home, go at once". Notwithstanding the protestations of my friends, who would not even contemplate the possibility of war, until they got a great shock on receiving from the military authorities orders for sending their dearly-loved horses for census taking, I started on the 1st of August, and although at that time the "man in the street" in England had not yet begun to realize the seriousness of the situation, the trains were crowded with Germans leaving for home, and by the time we got to Calais the least observant could see that grave events were imminent.' *War Memories* by Princess Marie de Croÿ.
5. Violet Anne Cavendish-Bentinck leased The Cottage on 28 June 1916 for a term of fourteen years with the option of purchasing the property for £4,500. On 18 January 1918 she purchased the property for the sum of £3,950 in consideration of the rent that had already been paid. The Cottage is now known as Weech House. William Shawcross, in his book *Queen Elizabeth the Queen Mother: The Official Biography*, states that the Villa Poggio Ponente was left by Mrs Scott at her death to one of Lady Strathmore's sisters; Hyacinth Jessup had died two years before her mother so it must have been Violet who gained the villa. Myrtle Cottage was bought in 1919 and Garden Cottage was built in 1928.
6. The *Queenslander* (Brisbane, Australia), 18 February 1937. The gypsy also foretold Mrs Ronald Forbes' future, predicting that she would travel widely. Either the encounter with the gypsy at Ascot was earlier than 1920 or the gypsy knew something of who the two unsuspecting women were, for Rosita Forbes (born Joan Rosita Torr at Riseholme Hall in Lincolnshire) had already begun her career as a travel writer by that date, publishing her first book in 1919 describing a journey around the world with a female friend that ended in North Africa. She was to achieve worldwide recognition as a traveller and writer.
7. Elizabeth had been presented to the king and queen on 5 July 1920 at Holyrood Palace in Edinburgh, before travelling back to London. *The Times*, 6 July 1920. The meeting between Elizabeth and Prince Albert is sometimes given as May 1920 at a ball given by Lord and Lady Farquhar; however, William Shawcross, in *Queen Elizabeth the Queen Mother: the Official Biography*, places it at the RAF ball, quoting a letter that Elizabeth

wrote following it to her friend Beryl Poignand: 'I danced with Prince Albert who I hadn't known before, he is quite a nice youth.' Elizabeth appears to have forgotten the meeting in their childhood when she gave him the cherries from her cake.

8. *Thatched with gold: the memoirs of Mabell, Countess of Airlie*, London, 1964. Lady Mabell Airlie admitted, with total understatement, to 'a little discreet meddling' in the courtship between Bertie and Elizabeth. Bertie replied to her: 'It seems marvellous to me to know that my darling Elizabeth will one day be my wife. I owe so much to you and can only bless you for all you did.' *Edinburgh News*, 1923–1936: 'A royal match', 1 April 2002.

9. *Elizabeth: A Biography of Her Majesty the Queen*, Sarah Bradford.

10. Wallis Simpson later claimed to believe this to have been the case. The *Daily News* published the story of the rumoured engagement between Lady Elizabeth Bowes-Lyon and the Prince of Wales on 5 January 1923.

11. Princess Elizabeth Alexandra Mary of York was born at 17 Bruton Street, Mayfair, the London town house belonging to her maternal grandparents, the Earl and Countess of Strathmore. Violet Anne Cavendish-Bentinck died on 15 May 1932.

12. As king, Edward was also the head of the Church of England; legally he could marry Wallis Simpson but it would be in direct contradiction to the tenets of the Church of England which did not allow remarriage of divorcées and Edward's ministers were against the marriage. The Queen Mother famously hated Wallis Simpson, referring to her as 'that woman'.

13. *Elizabeth: A Biography of Her Majesty the Queen*, Sarah Bradford.

Bibliography

Primary Sources

Allen, Lake, *The History of Portsmouth* (London, 1817)

Anonymous, *A Brief Account of the Coronation of His Majesty, George IV, July 19, 1821* (London, 1821)

Arnold, Matthew, *Letters of Matthew Arnold 1848–1888, collected and arranged by George W.E. Russell*, vol. 1 (Scholarly Press, 1968)

Badcock, John, *Making of a Regency Village: Origin, History and Description of Summertown in 1832* (St Michael's Publications, 1983)

Baker, T.F.T., Bolton, Diane K. and Croot, Patricia E.C., 'Paddington: Westbourne Green' and 'Paddington: Bayswater' in *A History of the County of Middlesex: Volume 9, Hampstead, Paddington* (ed., C.R. Elrington) (London, 1989)

Barnard, Lady Anne, *The Cape Diaries of Lady Anne Barnard, 1799–1800*, vol. 1 (Van Riebeeck Society, Cape Town, 1999)

Blackmantle, Bernard (pseudonym), *The English Spy, an original work characteristic, satirical, and humorous. Comprising scenes and sketches in every rank of society, being portraits drawn from the life* (London, 1825)

Boyle, Eliza & sons, *Boyle's Fashionable Court and Country Guide, and town visiting directory, corrected for April, 1824* (London, 1824)

Bradford, Sarah, *Elizabeth: A Biography of Her Majesty the Queen* (Penguin, 2002)

Brett-James, Antony, *Wellington at War, 1794–1815: A Selection of his Letters* (Macmillan & Co. Ltd, 1960)

Brown, Lally, *The Countess, Napoleon and St Helena* (2014)

Butler, Iris, *The Eldest Brother: the Marquess Wellesley 1760–1842* (Hodder & Stoughton, 1973)

Chapple, John and Shelston, Alan, *Further Letters of Mrs Gaskell* (Manchester University Press, 2004)

Corbett, Edward, *An Old Coachman's Chatter with some Practical Remarks on Driving* (Richard Bentley & Son, 1890)

Courthorpe, William, Esq. (ed.), *Debrett's Baronetage of England* (London, 1835)

Croÿ, Princess Marie de, *War Memories* (London, 1932)

Dalrymple, William, *White Mughals: Love and Betrayal in Eighteenth-Century India* (Harper-Collins, 2002)

Dauglish, M.G. (ed.), *The Harrow School Register, 1801–1901*, second edition (Longmans, Green & Co., 1901)

Farmar, Hugh, *A Regency Elopement* (Michael Joseph, 1969)

Foster, Joseph, *Alumni Oxonienses: The Members of the University of Oxford, 1715–1886*, later series, A–D (Oxford & London, 1883)

Fraser, Flora, *The Unruly Queen: The Life of Queen Caroline* (Macmillan, 1996)

Gathorne-Hardy, Robert (ed.), *Memoirs of Lady Ottoline Morrell: A Study in Friendship, 1873–1915* (Alfred A. Knopf, 1964)

Glover, Gareth, *The Waterloo Archive: Volume III: British Sources* (Frontline Books, 2011)

Groome, Francis Hindes, *In Gipsy Tents* (Edinburgh, 1880)

Hibbert, Christopher, *The Court of St James's: The Monarch at Work from Victoria to Elizabeth II* (Quill, 1983)

Holmes, Richard, *Wellington: The Iron Duke* (HarperCollins, 2002)

Johnstone, Julia, *Confessions of Julia Johnstone in Contradiction to the Fables of Harriette Wilson* (London, 1825)

Judd, Denis, *George VI* (I.B. Tauris, 2012)

Kassler, Michael, *The Music Trade in Georgian England* (Ashgate Publishing, 2011)

Kelly, Ian, *Beau Brummell, the Ultimate Dandy* (Hodder & Stoughton, 2005)

Layard, George Somes (ed.), *Sir Thomas Lawrence's Letter-bag* (London, 1906)

Lees, Ken (ed.), *The Diaries of the First Lord Hatherton (Extracts from the personal diary*, between the years 1817–1862) (The Cromwell Press, 2003)

Levy, M.J., *The Mistresses of King George IV* (Peter Owen, 1996)

Lodge, Edmund, *The Peerage of the British Empire as at present existing* (London, 1839)

Lodge, John, *The Peerage of Ireland: Or, a Genealogical History of the Present Nobility of that Kingdom*, volume iii (Dublin, 1789)

London County Council, *Survey of London: Volume 40, the Grosvenor Estate in Mayfair, Part 2 (The Buildings)* (London, 1980)

London County Council, *Survey of London: Volume 41, Brompton* (London, 1983)

Longford, Elizabeth, *Wellington* (Abacus, 2012)

Major, Joanne and Murden, Sarah, *An Infamous Mistress: The Life, Loves and Family of the Celebrated Grace Dalrymple Elliott* (Pen & Sword, 2016)

Marnham, Patrick, *Wild Mary: The Life of Mary Wesley* (Vintage, 2007)

Morgan, Richard (ed.), *The Diary of a Bedfordshire Squire (John Thomas Brooks of Flitwick 1794–1858)* (Bedfordshire Historical Record Society, 1987)

Nevill, Lady Dorothy, *Under Five Reigns* (New York, 1910)

Ogilvy, Mabell Frances Elizabeth, Countess of Airlie, *Thatched with gold: the memoirs of Mabell, Countess of Airlie* (Hutchinson of London, 1964)

Old Etonian Association, *The Eton Register, part ii, 1853–1859* (Spottiswoode & Co., 1905)

Oxford Historical Society, *Collecteana: Fourth Series*, The Committee of the Society (ed.) (Oxford, 1905)

Piozzi, Hester Lynch, *The Piozzi Letters: 1811–1816* (University of Delaware Press, 1999)

Severn, John, *Architects of Empire: The Duke of Wellington and his Brothers* (University of Oklahoma Press, 2007)

Seymour, Thomas, *My Grandfather, A Modern Medievalist: The Life of the 8th Lord Howard de Walden* (National Trust, 2012)

Shawcross, William (ed.), *Counting One's Blessings: The Selected Letters of Queen Elizabeth the Queen Mother* (Pan Macmillan, 2013)

Shawcross, William, *Queen Elizabeth the Queen Mother: The Official Biography* (Pan Macmillan, 2009)

Sheppard, F.H.W. (ed.), 'Bourdon Street and Grosvenor Hill Area' in *Survey of London: Volume 40, the Grosvenor Estate in Mayfair, Part 2 (The Buildings)* (London, 1980)

Smith, E.A., *George IV* (Yale University Press, 1999)

Smith, Margaret, *The Letters of Charlotte Brontë: Volume III: 1852–1855* (Clarendon Press, 2004)

Somerset, Anne, *The Life and Times of William IV* (Weidenfeld & Nicolson, 1993)

Stafford, Countess of (ed.), *Leaves from the Diary of Henry Greville, third series* (Smith, Elder & Co., 1904)

Tennent, J. Emerson, *Belgium*, vol. ii (London, 1841)

Thorne, R. (ed.), *The History of Parliament: The House of Commons 1790–1820* (Boydell & Brewer, 1986)

Tyerman, Christopher, *A History of Harrow School, 1324–1991* (Oxford University Press, 2000)

Vickers, Hugo, *Elizabeth, The Queen Mother* (Random House, 2005)

Wake, Jehanne, *Sisters of Fortune: The First American Heiresses to take England by Storm* (Vintage Books, 2011)

Watts-Dunton, *Theodore, Old Familiar Faces* (London, 1916)

Wellesley, Jane, *Wellington: A Journey Through My Family* (Weidenfeld & Nicolson, 2008)

Wellesley, Richard Colley, *The Wellesley Papers: The Life and Correspondence of Richard Colley Wellesley, Marquess Wellesley 1760–1842*, vols i and ii (London, 1914)

Wilkins, W.H., *Mrs Fitzherbert and George IV* (London, 1905)

Williams, Kate, *Becoming Queen* (Arrow Books, 2009)

Wilson, Frances, *The Courtesan's Revenge: Harriette Wilson, the Woman Who Blackmailed the King* (Faber & Faber, 2003)

Wilson, Harriette, *The Memoirs of Harriette Wilson, written by herself*, vol. I (London, 1909)

Wilson, Harriette, *The Memoirs of Harriette Wilson, written by herself*, vol. V (London, 1827)

Wilson, Harriette, *Paris Lions and London Tigers* (London, 1825)

Witte, E.L.S., *Political History of Belgium from 1830 onwards* (Brussels, 2009)

Archival Sources

Bedfordshire Archives

Houghton Hall

Nottingham University Manuscripts Collection, Portland Papers

Shropshire Archives, Shackerley Collection

Southampton University, Carver MSS

Staffordshire Archives, Records of the Littleton Family of Teddesley and Hatherton, Barons Hatherton

Magazines and Periodicals

Bedfordshire Magazine, Volumes 10–11, 1966

Cook, Peter, *Scholarship and integrity: Matthew Arnold's 'The Scholar-Gipsy' and Anita Desai's 'Scholar and Gypsy'*, critical essay printed in Alif. Journal of Comparative Poetics, January 2009 (via www.freelibrary.com)

Dawlish Local History Group Newsletter, September 2012

England's Triumph: being an Account of the Rejoicings, &c., which have lately taken place in London and Elsewhere including the Restoration of Louis XVIII, the Proclamation of Peace and the visit of the Emperor of Russia, and the King of Prussia, &c, London, 1814

Hill, R. (2003), *I am the thing itself*. [Review of the books Harriette Wilson's Memoirs and The Courtesan's Revenge: Harriette Wilson, the Woman who Blackmailed the King.] London Review of Books, 25 (18), 19–20. Retrieved from http://www.lrb.co.uk/v25/n18/rosemary-hill/i-am-the-thing-itself

Gentleman's Magazine, Volume 187, April 1850

London Review of Books, volume 25, no. 18, 25 September 2003

London Review of Books, volume 25, no. 20, 23 October 2003

Minn, H., *A Manuscript History of Summertown, Oxoniensia: A refereed journal dealing with the Archaeology, History and Architecture of Oxford and Oxfordshire*, volumes XI–XII (1946–47) (http://oxoniensia.org/volumes/1946-7/minn.pdf)

New Sporting Magazine, volume 14, June 1838

The Annual Register of World Events: A Review of the Year, Vol. 62, Pt 1, 1820, edited by Edmund Burke

The Architectural Review: A Magazine of Architecture & Decoration, vol. L., July–December 1921, Westminster, 1921

The Edinburgh Annual Register for 1814, vol. 7, parts i and ii, Edinburgh, 1814

The Journal of the Gypsy Lore Society, series 3, volume 23, 1944

Surrey Archæological Collections, relating to the History and Antiquities of the County, vol. XXXII, Surrey Archæological Society, London, 1919

Online Sources

Bedfordshire Borough Council, Community and Living, Archives and records service, Community archives (www.bedford.gov.uk)

Bodleian Library external source on the parish of Cumnor (http://www.bodley.ox.ac.uk/external/cumnor)

British Listed Buildings (www.britishlistedbuildings.co.uk)

Croxton Village Information (www.croxton.reallyfast.info/ChurchHistory.html)

Dawlish Local History Group (www.dawlishhistory.org.uk)

Matthews, Jodie, 'Reading the Victorian Gypsy', PhD thesis, Cardiff University, 2008

Middleton, Dorothy, 'Forbes, (Joan) Rosita (1890–1967)', rev. Oxford Dictionary of National Biography, Oxford University Press, 2004; online edn, Jan 2011

National Trust Collections (www.nationaltrustcollections.org.uk)

Nottingham University Manuscripts and Special Collections, Portland of Welbeck Abbey

Old Bailey Proceedings Online (www.oldbaileyonline.org, version 7.2, 14 August 2015), July 1829 (18290716)

Pigot's 1830 Directory: Oxfordshire (www.oxfordhistory.org.uk)

Queen Victoria's Journals (www.queenvictoriasjournals.org)

Reynolds, K.D., 'Wilson, Harriette (1786–1845)', Oxford Dictionary of National Biography, Oxford University Press, 2004; online edn, Sept 2010

St Paul's Knightsbridge (www.spkbinfo.org)

The Esoteric Curiosa (theesotericcuriosa.blogspot.co.uk/2010/03/wicked-uncle-gus-augustus-edward-jessup.html)

The Harley Gallery, The Portland Collection (www.harleygallery.co.uk/portland-collection)

Newspapers and Other Publications

As referenced in the text and endnotes.

Index